The Overfunctioning Woman's Handbook

Uncommon Sense to Deal with Impossible Jobs and Impossible People

by Rosalyn Rivkin, M.S.W. and Sally Park Rubin

an Oinfroin Media, LLC imprint

The Overfunctioning Woman's Handbook

www.oinfroin.com/overfunctioningwoman
www.overfunctioningwoman.com

Oinfroin Media, LLC
7046 Homewood Drive
Oakland, CA. 94611

Cover Concept: Sally Park Rubin
Cover and Book Design: Ed Rubin
Cover Photo: Heidi Alletzhauser www.heidiphotos.com
Back Cover Portrait of Sally: Dan Griffin

Printed on 100% recycled paper ♻
Printed in the United States of America

ISBN-13: 978-0-9796807-0-0
ISBN-10: 0-9796807-0-0

Publisher's Cataloging-in-Publication
(Provided by Quality Books, Inc.)

Rivkin, Rosalyn.
      The overfunctioning woman's handbook : uncommon sense
      to deal with impossible jobs and impossible people / by
      Rosalyn Rivkin and Sally Park Rubin.
        p. cm.
      Includes index.
      ISBN-13: 978-0-979-6807-0-0
      ISBN-10: 0-979-6807-0-0

      1. Overachievement. 2. Women--Psychology.
      3. Quality of life. 4. Self-actualization (Psychology)
      I. Rubin, Sally Park. II. Title.

BF637.O94R58 2008   158.1
                QBI07-600273

Reading <u>The Overfunctioning Woman's Handbook</u> was like looking into a mirror. I saw myself in every page and, as a result, a potential shift within my own consciousness was ignited. The handbook is a sure recipe for learning and change.

~ Shakti Butler, Ph.D., Social justice filmmaker and speaker: *The Way Home and Mirrors of Privilege, Making Whiteness Visible*

I related to so much in this unique book that a men's edition would be appropriate; in fact, there's every reason for men to read <u>The Overfunctioning Woman's Handbook</u> to gain insights not only for themselves but about the distaff side of the family. Exemplary and encouraging, this book delivers a welcome message: Be who you really are, and offers the authors' inside look how to get there in a diverse, readable and entertaining way.

~ Chris Forsyth, author: *The Great Cricket Hijack, The Governor-General, Pitched Battles, Can Australia Survive World War III?*

TABLE OF CONTENTS

Key for Symbols:
  ✂ = Chickpoints
  ✋ = Warnings
  ⌂ = Parent Alert!
  △ = Treacherous Triangle

FORWARD
A Voice from Inside the Triangle

Yes, I am one of those women who is invariably trying to squeeze ten pounds into a five-pound bag. I am a single mother, a corporate executive, homeowner, landlord, community volunteer, and caregiver for my irascible, immobile but still hardy 81-year-old mother. I care about myself, so I spend time at the gym. I care about my child, so I spend time with his teachers, at his hockey games, going here, going there. For the two of us as a family, quality time is a car ride, and our meal of choice is purchased at the burrito truck near 5th and Lake.

Sound familiar?

I squirreled away a few hours between my son's violin lessons, my staff meetings, and our doctors' appointments (not to mention while I was waiting for the plumber) to read and relish *The Overfunctioning Woman's Handbook*, a book about me.

Part anecdote, part analysis, part self-help, part humor, *The Overfunctioning Woman's Handbook* had me from the start and held me to the finish. As a resolute overfunctioner, I used to make myself finish every book that I started. Around last year, I thought better of that rule and cut myself a break. Now, if I find myself part way into something that isn't relevant, meaningful, or fun, I put it aside without remorse, and I spend only a couple of minutes swatting away those inevitable feelings of failure—was it really the book? Or is it really me? That's not important here, however, since I was never once tempted to set *The Handbook* aside. This book is—from first page to last—relevant, meaningful, and fun.

The Overfunctioning Woman's Handbook surfaces issues that successful and resourceful women all across this land are grappling with—what we as women do, feel compelled to do, feel bad if we don't do, and then feel even worse when we *do* do. It is unsettling to read tales that are similar to your own worst moments, but, at the same time, it is reassuring. We are not alone in our behaviors and assumptions. Nor are we without a way out, as the book guides us through. Others have been here before, and they moved beyond false needs and unhealthy compulsions. Therefore, we can too.

I had long known, for example, that I preferred the wrong men. But *The Handbook* helped me to see why my latest boyfriend, while different from his predecessors and in many ways more suitable, was a variation on a theme that represented more work than joy, more effort than respite.

And, for as long as I can remember, before I leave the house for work in the morning, run errands on Saturday, or get on a plane for a business trip, I have felt a compulsion to wash every dish in the kitchen. Since reading *The Handbook*, I'm almost ready to let those dirty dishes go.

This book is not just about how to prioritize tasks, shed deadwood, or run one's life more efficiently, it's about how to recognize and navigate a life course that allows you to use your time to affirm your sensibilities and give them a high priority on your list of things to do. It also teaches us how to stop sabotaging our efforts to change overfunctioning. This is key to <u>not</u> falling prey to the usual disappointments or feelings of failure. Face it head on: Why *are* we trying to stuff ten pounds into that five-pound bag?

So, if you can, if you will, slow down and have a cup of tea. Find a comfortable chair, or spend the day in bed. Wrap yourself tenderly in your favorite blanket. Grab a bowl full of your snack of choice— mine is chocolate truffles, yours might be potato chips, carrot sticks or ripe raspberries. Reward yourself for all that you are, do, and can be by tucking away with this book about yourself, ourselves. You may wonder. You may weep. But you are sure to enjoy the journey of *The Overfunctioning Woman's Handbook*. You will be, by the end, even more of yourself once you have arrived at the destination.

Enjoy!

Alexandra Roddy
Senior Vice President, Marketing (financial services business)

VOICES OF THE AUTHORS

THE VOICE OF ROSALYN RIVKIN

When we recognize a need for things to be different in our lives, what does it take to actually begin changing and make the changes stick? Why do we frequently fall short of the mark we've set for ourselves and end up frustrated? The answer to these questions often lies in the fact that *a gap exists between our capacity to understand what is wrong and our ability to implement actions to deal effectively with what is wrong.* In addition, many of us, no matter how sensible we are, sometimes don't see how we sabotage both good advice and our own best interests. This makes no logical sense, but we do it all the time.

The ruts in which we get stuck—and struggle, attempting to get out—are, happily, less of a mystery than we think. Because the "quick fix" is so highly valued these days, we tend to overlook the *internal* psychological components necessary for securing the *outer* changes. For instance, enthusiastically coaxing women forward, as many well-meaning books, articles, and people do, may be friendly and supportive but proves insufficient. In fact, a "backlash" effect often occurs. We are left feeling worse because we failed to make the desired transformation. But truly, this is through no fault of our own; the approach itself is flawed. It's like telling a woman with a broken arm that she ought to strengthen that arm by lifting weights. A good idea, we agree, but clearly unrealistic because it is premature. Therefore, it will fail. First, someone needs to help that woman put her arm in a cast. This will heal the bone (the basic structure). Afterwards, the recommended weight-training will make the healed arm stronger. *Likewise, when the root psychological structure is ignored, no real progress can occur.*

It would surely save a lot of anguish and reinventing of the wheel to understand the underlying psychological structure and to strengthen its various facets. It is not too complex to discuss, and I do not believe it needs to be a closely guarded secret.

Working as a therapist for many years, I am in the "change" business. I help my clients to define their discontent and troubles and to set new goals. Then, we proceed together to resolve the problems and achieve the goals. Mine is a wonderful and often exhilarating career.

For many years, I have been involved with a colorful parade of individuals (and their families) and organizations (which operate in ways remarkably similar to families). During this time, I have made many useful observations about how people get stuck and how they change. This has led me to a goal of my own—to share my ideas with a larger group than just my own clients.

As we go along, *The Handbook* will let you in on the some of the basics that psychologists know. The good news is that the concepts presented here, fundamental for change, are quite accessible. You don't need to be a professional to master these, and they're both practical and useful in plotting a solid and satisfying life course. And since that vital understanding/action gap has not been addressed sufficiently, we'll discuss that too.

What's being offered here is a logical and practical system to assess where you are in your life—what makes good sense about it and what doesn't—and to learn methods for proceeding from where you are to where you want to be. For example, what are the basic rules by which all relationships operate? Are you able to recognize different character types (especially the emotionally taxing or toxic ones)? If you have some dicey individuals in your environment, how should you deal with them? These matters will be explained along with other universal themes in interpersonal dynamics, and you will see how to create more satisfying relationships. While reading this book, you will gradually develop the inner security and courage to unchoose people and situations that don't work for you and to choose those that will likely bring your most cherished priorities and goals into reach.

We'll talk about real self-esteem and finding an inner sense of who you are, not about perfection (that seductive lure) or self-promotion which requires external validation. We will clarify facts about feelings—especially the ones with bad reputations, like anger and anxiety. Rather than focusing on how to get rid of these unwelcome emotions, you will discover what they are really all about, why they are indispensable, and how to get them to work *for*, not *against*, you. We'll explore the advantages of living with anxiety instead of dancing around it and of framing anger as a positive emotion for communication and empowerment, not a liability to be avoided. We'll look at how to recognize the difference between anger and rage and to distinguish *declining to do* from *passivity*. We'll consider intuition—the good type and the bad. And we'll compare self-respect and self-protection with selfishness and self-degradation. Finally, you may become convinced that asking for help (and not seeing this as defeat) is better than always doing everything yourself. This is *uncommon sense.*

While this book will provide you with a great deal of information and many tools that can make your life better, it is not intended to be a substitute for psychotherapy. Psychotherapy with its one-on-one, nuanced focus, is a unique and powerful process for personal and family growth. Anyone who seeks it out will find it invaluable. If at any time while using *The Handbook*, you find yourself hitting a barrier, that would be a good moment to consider getting some therapy.

One of my clients recently described his journey to uncommon sense as a trip during which he gradually traveled from inside a box out onto a beach. Perhaps, you too will feel this way or some other special way.

As you come to surprising realizations and gather new skills, you can cast your net more widely (or less, your choice) according to your own design. You will also take wiser risks. As your actions and reactions (and those of others) become clearer, you won't be easily ambushed by life's events. Instead, you will be able to guide a steady course in the realms that matter most—partnering and parenting, working, laughing, and finding solace.

Now, to establish this solid base of emotional safety, savvy, and adventure in your life, I invite you to join Sally and me in the pages of this book.

RR

THE VOICE OF SALLY PARK RUBIN

Over a decade ago, Rosalyn and I were having a cup of tea in my kitchen. Her daughters—then girls—were attending their dance class next door, and my son and his little pal, Hannah, were toddling around the house. We talked about the problems women were facing in the hey day of the dot-com boom. So many women, we thought, seemed to feel overworked, overwhelmed, and doomed with no way out. Not only was it tough to feel good about oneself in a culture that expected so much, but we could see an increase in the burden women carried by expecting so much of themselves. The problem seemed to involve what we have come to call "overfunctioning." Even some of our most esteemed public role models appeared to preach a kind of anxious perfectionism—they still do— an ideal that so many people feel the need to attain but can't reach. Even when we make ourselves look better and have our sound-bytes honed, when we honestly check in with ourselves, we may not really *feel* better. With the advent of economic downsizing and outsourcing, "overfunctioning," if anything, has gotten worse.

How did I get here? So far, I've been a flight attendant, artist, animator, producer, business owner, writer, martial artist, mother, wife, homeschool teacher, chicken farmer, gardener, knitter, homemaker, and a yoga/meditation practitioner. Good golly, I have not followed that perfect career track, have I? Hmmm… How *ever* have I gotten by?

I would characterize myself as having come from the overfunctioning mold. I know the territory backwards and forwards. Most women do. Say the word OVERFUNCTIONING and women either gasp, "Yup! That's me!" or they, literally, let out a breath—a sigh of resignation, it seems—or is it relief at being seen, "gotten," understood. The problem so many of us face, at last, has a name! The word itself touches the core of what we, as women, do, and what we have become. We see it. We feel it. It may not leave a good taste in our mouths to be labeled such, but, in fact, it sounds spot on. (And, frankly, men seem to be joining the party in droves. But, for a moment, we won't concern ourselves with them. Okay?) Overfunctioning, yes, it *is* familiar territory.

Picture me, Sally, working on my laptop plugged into the cigarette lighter in my car while sitting in the parking lot of my son's school, waiting for him to tear out of math class so that I can drive him to Hip

Hop. I've got my headset on, catching up with messages on my cell phone. My files are seated in portable containers piled in the backseat, along with the clothes I've been intending to drop off at Goodwill® for the last three months. The can of paint I bought a few weeks ago has yet to make it into the house. Some lost homework is crumpled beneath a fragrant new rose bush I intend to plant in the garden, still sitting in my car. There's a fifty-pound sack of chicken food in the trunk, blankets, emergency supplies, and a small cooler filled with delicious snacks (high-protein, of course) to keep us going throughout today's orbit of activities.

I have my face in the latest book. I email or call my congresswoman almost weekly. I write essays for public radio. I make lists in my sleep, brush my teeth while talking on the phone (my aunt just hates that!), cook dinner while correcting homework. I'm the mom at the bake sale with the guilty smile who's spirited in the box-recipe brownies. (They really are "delicious, just like homemade," as the manufacturer claims.) The time-saving freedom of packaged foods brings me to my knees. I let my fingers do the shopping on the Internet whenever possible. I treat myself to the eight minute chair massages at the mall when I can afford them. (You know, those little time-saving "module" versions of relaxation that are almost relaxing.) The spa visit recommended by all the ladies' magazines—that self-pampering MUST DO—that I really can't find the time or money TO DO—, I don't do even though it's been penciled into my To Do List forever.

Throughout history, we've seen various trends come and go for how a women should be. But they all boil down to this: We continue to feel pressure to do more and more to keep apace.

Rosalyn and I thought and talked about and began writing *The Overfunctioning Woman's Handbook* as an antidote to the "cures" that were being touted for women's "troubles"—particularly how to manage the various pressures related to home and work. It was my intention to write a tongue-in-cheek book based on real psychological patterns. That was the beginning of our teaming up on this project. But, as Rosalyn continued to speak about things from a psychological standpoint, I realized that the approach I had in mind did not honor the depth and width of this terrible problem. Through our many discussions related to this writing, I gained new insights into overfunctioning as both a personal and cultural ditch into which women blindly fall.

Many books have come out in the last ten years. They've presented solutions ranging from aromatherapy to running one's home like a CEO. Many of the suggestions had merit. With the exception of meditation (and, perhaps, some specific relaxation techniques), however, none offered methods that led to the kind of *internal change* based on building a *capacity to observe* one's life differently. Our perspective seems more needed than ever.

It was then and *still is* my intention to inspire a new conversation for women recognizing our uniqueness as women—not to continue measuring ourselves by male standards, but to invent our own bar for success. This will help us to recognize and respond to our own most heart-felt yearnings, to seek resolutions for the obvious mess we're in, and to find and feel deeper gratification for our lives.

You would not believe the number of editors who wouldn't touch this topic: "There's no way around this! We're indoctrinated, and we can't get out of it. Period!" One even said she couldn't face reading the manuscript because it "hit too close to home!" Consequently, she took it home, put it in her bathroom, then her bedroom, and finally brought it back to work, only to lose it under a pile of other manuscripts. (This is anxiety based on overfunctioning.) And she could have changed— if she had read it. I've changed by writing this book, and I assure you that you can recognize and do something about overfunctioning, too.

I invite you to join with Rosalyn and me in generating that new conversation for and with women, one that is life- and health-affirming, one that supports us in being true to ourselves, authentic, with all our lousy moods, our "off" days, our "on" days, our bouts of self-doubt, our imperfections, and our idiosyncrasies and one that attends to our most heart-felt desires.

Do I still overfunction? Not nearly as much as I used to, but sure…. Sometimes, I race around and things don't get done properly. I can easily resort to the breakneck pace of my past. (Old habits do die hard.) How do I feel about it? Unapologetic. I'm not perfect and that feels okay—great, in fact! (Now, that's a liberating concept!) Who am I in the matter of this book? Look, I am the quintessential, complex, overburdened, trying to figure it all out, modern-day woman. I'm one of you and I offer you my hand.

SPR

INTRODUCTION
Begin where you are

Even though women in our culture now roam confidently in the whole of the wide world, many of us still feel a charge to carry emotional visions and attachments for home and family. Whether single or married, without children or mother of many, whether employed or not, it is a surprise to some of us and obvious to others that we all feel a pull to create something called Home.

This deep sense of dual commitments is the essential underpinning of the problem we have named Overfunctioning (OF). The responsibilities of homemaking and child-rearing, with their abiding pleasures, have been handed down through the generations from mother to daughter. While many of us may be content (if we're lucky enough) to have someone else do the vacuuming, dusting, and managing of the comings and goings of the household, we're not happy unless we have our hand in to stir up something special.

In an heroic attempt to keep life going and "quality of life"— an elusive standard that makes us cringe—most of us orchestrate things in an anxious, chronic state of overdoing, while attempting to control all the variables seamlessly. This is Overfunctioning in action. Many people talk about the problem these days, but no one has solved it. By now, discussing what to do has become—guess what? —just another item for the To Do list.

Look at Dehlia and Maxine, two successful professional women with two different styles of homemaking. The first casts a blanket of warmth and coziness around those in her midst. This eludes the second, despite all the energy and cleverness she has put into creating a picture-perfect house. Maxine looks to Dehlia for:

That Winning Recipe

Dehlia's teenage daughter, Erin, rushes in from school with her friend Jon in tow. The two teens aimlessly throw down their packs by the back door and head for the kitchen in Dehlia's rambling old house. This homey room is not in good repair. Colorful materials from her own and her children's many projects cover the cluttered desk. Artifacts, which her three kids have unearthed from ponds, beaches, and the backyard, are piled in intriguing heaps on every available surface. Several walls are decorated with the children's paintings. Dehlia's kitchen is, in short, a museum of charming chaos.

Maxine, Jon's mother, is a magazine restaurant critic. She and Jon's father both work full-time even though they are wealthy. Maxine is an excellent cook herself, but their refrigerator is surprisingly understocked and the house rather spartan. So, Jon prefers to spend time in Dehlia's kitchen. Dehlia is a writer and illustrator. She enjoys her work, and she delights in her home. A good old-fashioned cook, of a late afternoon, her kitchen fills with wonderful warm smells. After school, the kids always ask for toast with jam or cinnamon. They sit around the table eating and chatting with Dehlia as she bustles about.

Dehlia's family eventually moved upstate, and the kids didn't see each other much. But one weekend, the two families got together. Jonathan said dreamily to Dehlia, "Do you remember all those days that we just hung out in your kitchen and ate toast? I miss that! I can smell and taste it even now." Whereupon, his mother said to him, "I didn't know you did that, honey!" Turning to Dehlia, Maxine then asked, "What *kind* of bread did you use?" Dehlia replied, "I don't know. Whatever I had."

Fulfilling family relationships, whether or not children are part of the mix, are made up of personal emotional bonds. These bonds are created by doing things together (sometimes at a meandering pace), having the house seem cozy physically, and sharing or passing on a passion or two or three. We're talking, not merely about the how-to's, but about the special little rituals, gestures, and moments from which a sense of connection emerges. This weaves the blanket that wraps everybody up with a sense of "all is right with the world" and "we're okay."

It's easy to see why Jonathan yearned for the toast and why it really didn't matter what kind of bread Dehlia used to make it. *"It's not about the bread,"* we want to shout or whisper to poor Maxine. We treasure those small acts of love. They are laced with the wisdom of togetherness. That's all. These days, we're in serious danger of losing touch with this.

And most of us feel that danger.

Because we seldom have time to handle so many things in a satisfying way, we're in a terrible bind. Items are scheduled back to back in tightly organized, time-sensitive, rigid little modules so we can fit everything in. Meanwhile, we hold ourselves to high standards and expectations of performance. Creating a home, accepting a variety of worldly challenges, having children perhaps, maintaining some form of a career or serving as the main breadwinners, staying in good physical shape, even having fun and relaxing, all of it is crammed into our To Do Lists. "Doing it all"—according to the standards to which we subscribe—necessitates ever more overfunctioning. But this is unsustainable.

Even when we seem to be succeeding for a while, we are so pressured and on edge that, on balance, the sum of all that we do never feels quite right. Further, despite overfunctioning, or perhaps because of it, our self-esteem (which ought to be at an all-time high with so many achievements to our credit) actually skids along on thin ice. Living in this top-speed blur can continue unnoticed, unabated, for years… until something big (and often bad) happens to us. Only this causes a pause long enough for the shadow cast by our precarious "lifestyle" to become obvious. The worst part is that, even as we recognize what is happening and don't like it, it is almost impossible to see any way to slow it down or turn it around.

A FRESH NEW APPROACH STARTS HERE

The definitions for the Overfunctioning Woman and High-Functioning Woman are fundamentally different. The High-Functioning Woman is indeed also busy and productive, but she picks and chooses what she will and will not do. The Overfunctioning Woman, by contrast, must do it all. Only in this way can she demonstrate both her competence and basic worth to herself and others.

The Overfunctioning Woman is caught in a Treacherous Triangle and does not know how to get out. The three points on the Treacherous Triangle form an interdependent relationship of 1) overfunctioning, 2) poorly constructed or flagging self-esteem, and 3) a susceptibility to attend to the needs of others.

Strangely, the Overfunctioning Woman seems to make the grip of the Treacherous Triangle on her life tighter by seeking relationships with those who have "it's all about me" personalities. She tends to fly like a moth to the flame towards these Impossible People. This is particularly perilous because they are so demanding and she is *internally driven* to make everything work. The Overfunctioning Woman *needs* to make situations, relationships, activities "right"—no matter what the △ cost in energy, time, and her self. With regard to Impossible People (Point #3), whether a boss, co-worker, partner, relative, or even someone with whom she thinks she'd like to be friends, she often finds herself trying harder and harder (Point #1) while feeling worse and worse. Insidiously, this chips away at her easily shaken self-esteem (Point #2). As you can see, it does not matter at which point on the TT a woman starts. She (and you) inevitably connects to the other two points.

Again and again, overfunctioning generates the TT. Over time, the TT creates conflicting states of mind, high fatigue, overwhelming anxiety or detachment from emotions, high-maintenance and poor-quality relationships, avoidance of painful issues, and erosion of good judgment. All too often, this combines to create a sense of alienation and a variety of physical symptoms. The burden of overfunctioning generates an ever-escalating cycle.

Is there a way out? Yes. *The Overfunctioning Woman's Handbook* offers reliable strategies for change. To start our healthy escape, the first step is to acknowledge that overfunctioning takes away from us more than it gives back, ultimately leaving us disenchanted and exhausted rather than satisfied.

We now will present a clear, detailed vision of Overfunctioning (so you can't miss it even if you try). We'll show you how to recognize the internal directives that fuel and sustain it, and how to develop and mobilize uncommon sense—an unusual set of tools—to make major alterations. Uncommon sense is a blend of emotional wisdom with self-reflection and grounded rational thought. It makes possible the accomplishment of many important things: accessing and using basic human emotions like anger and anxiety for constructive ends; recognizing and controlling the impact of impossible people; saying NO without guilt; appreciating and honoring personal idiosyncrasies; parenting with effectiveness and joy; slowing time down. Developing and following this counterpath of uncommon sense will begin to turn your life around.

So, come along with us and break out of the Treacherous Triangle. After all, it doesn't matter how well or how stylishly you go down the wrong road.

"the readiness is all."
(Hamlet, Act V, Sc. ii*)*

CAUGHT IN THE IMPOSSIBLE

I
OVERFUNCTIONING
"I'll Just Do It Myself"

WOMAN WANTED (any age may apply): You cheerfully do what there is to be done, what significant others (boss and management included, of course) say they want, while trying to anticipate the physical and emotional needs of all (no matter what) to get jobs completed. You act as a domestic manager, overseeing everything (schedules, important events, holidays, recitals, dental/doctor appointments, clothes and food shopping, gift buying, and surprises). You add special touches to the home—fresh flowers here, a closet rearranged there. A fine cook and hostess, you also always look your best. You're interesting, clever, and witty, but also non-threatening and low maintenance.

You are in charge of the family social life. You keep the extended family members in touch. You send thank-you notes or feel guilty if you don't. You care for elders on both sides of the family. You get involved with the children's schooling, monitoring, and chauffeuring, and handle teen issues such as sex, drugs, and alcohol. You help with the college applications, fundraisers, bake sales. You read the latest how-to books on parenting, family health, and financial planning. You are always available for that heart-to-heart with your child, partner, parents, or in-laws. You are committed to the needs of the environment—saving the whales, the air, the trees, and wild rivers. You improve the lot of the less fortunate.

You have dreams. You make them come true. Creative and innovative, you always have a special project at hand. You serve as a great role-model, not overwrought, unreasonable, or controlling. You do not let anyone down. You are self-sufficient, good company, cheerful, fun, sexy, and an articulate conversationalist. You are able to relax! You play sports. You are strong, courageous, and fit, but also soft, feminine, lovely, pretty, and sweet—not to mention supportive and a good listener. **Please respond ASAP.**

WOMEN GET THE MESSAGE

For decades now, women have gotten the message: *If we want control over our own lives, show that all limits are falsely imposed.* So, that's what we did: the Overfunctioning Woman was born. Her mission is to do it all and do it all well. There are few or no areas in her life in which she feels comfortable not being competent.

Inevitably, there's a problem. As time goes on, the momentum of overfunctioning takes over, and the Overfunctioning Woman begins to experience a sense of being swept away by all she has set out to do. She falls short in some way personally meaningful to her. Eventually, she loses the sense that she's doing a very good job at anything.

Entering a downslide into disenchantment, she goes from feeling exhilarated, hopeful, proud, and competent to experiencing vague uneasiness, doubts, tiredness, and irritability. She may slide gradually, imperceptibly. Or she may slide rudely, suddenly, into full-scale self-doubt, exhaustion, or numbness; she experiences a sense of things somehow being *off*. This is what overfunctioning does to us.

Overfunctioning women are everywhere. We are married, single, gay, straight. We have children; we have no children. We come from all economic strata of life, from diverse ethnic and racial heritages. We exist in a number of variations—Awesome Superwoman, Survivor, Traditional Homemaker, and everything in between.

THE HISTORICAL CONTEXT

For the greater part of human history, men have been in charge. They were masters who could give and take away unchecked. Yet, they had a paradoxical relationship with us. Wrapped too tightly not only in corsets, but also in household chores and tied down with babies, we were alternately put on a pedestal and put down. We were taken for granted but were also depended upon absolutely.

Things have changed a lot, right? Well, right and wrong. A new ideal exists, but, to a great extent, paradoxical attitudes towards and expectations of women haven't altered much. And, women are complicit in this stuckness. Briefly examining how the Overfunctioning Woman evolved sheds light on why we persist both to perform and perfect the job and to recommend it to others.

✂ We've taken on new responsibilities without fixing the old foundation.

Today, though we have a stronger sense of self and power, that traditional pattern of deference to men has not been completely eliminated. Because of this long history, we've arrived in the work arena lugging our baggage. We have a tenuous sense of self-worth and an orientation to look outwards for approval. Even as we've tried to rid ourselves of men's dominance, we have continued to accept their evaluations and their sense of entitlement to evaluate and judge us. As long as this remains true, gender equality will elude us.

What women have accomplished has been groundbreaking. But, unfortunately, many of us have willingly overextended ourselves to prove to men (and ourselves) that we're solid. Better than solid, we're phenomenal! Rather than facing how our historical hook to men is the cement in the foundation of our self-esteem, we've tried to hide the issue with our efficiency, absolute determination, and willingness to take total responsibility for anything and everything. And we've called this stance "Freedom." It isn't freedom. It's Overfunctioning.

As a way of trying to ease the confusion and pain created by this paradox, we have been embracing overfunctioning ever more fervently as the solution, trying to perfect it so we'll finally get it right and feel good. It may temporarily elevate self-esteem, but, in the long run, because overfunctioning stimulates more of itself, it produces feelings of failure sooner or later. And this produces more overfunctioning to try to compensate for those feelings! Unless we act differently, the cycle will be never-ending.

✂ Overfunctioning is an untenable job with defeat built in. What started out as a way to elevate self-esteem has become something that further reduces it.

OFF TRACK

Here are a few Overfunctioning Women you probably already know: your friends, acquaintances, siblings, and perhaps yourself.

Awesome Jaclyn still basks in the first stage of unequivocal celebration. Yet, the building blocks of her life stack up to a house of cards. She has not yet begun to feel it, but she is teetering on the edge. Jaclyn is:

⌂ The Over-Organized Woman

Traveling cross-country with her baby, after having missed their first flight, she emerges from the jet bridge. Impeccably put together, she appears completely unruffled. Hanging from her left shoulder are her purse, a giant baby bag, and a video camera. Hooked under her right elbow, her seven-month-old son is in a portable baby seat. Via her cell phone (right hand, right ear), Jaclyn is handling a "little problem" at her company back in her home city. Without slowing her pace, she leans forward to kiss me on the cheek. At baggage claim, we pick up her additional luggage for the visit—a sportswear-sized bag filled with *cloth* diapers, baby clothes, and toys. A portable crib. (I have one. She didn't ask.) This is the beginning of a relaxing weekend in California "bundled with" a mandatory business conference during which I, a seasoned mother and her trusted friend, will care for her baby. As she dances off to her meeting the next day, Jaclyn presents me with detailed instruction sheets for her little Harry. "Sally, don't forget to recalculate the time difference between coasts," she adds.

> **BABY'S SCHEDULE (abridged)**
> **7-8 AM WAKE UP:** Gets 4 oz. warm breast milk or formula. (He will not always finish.)
>
> **8 AM BREAKFAST:** Rice cereal and 1 serving fruit (usually applesauce/prunes) (Rice cereal = 2 oz. cereal mixed with 2 oz. formula to make a pudding texture.)
>
> **8-10 AM After breakfast, Playtime!** He is usually ready for a nap 2 hours after wake up. So, if he woke up at 7:30, he can be put to bed @ 9:30 or so--when he gets fussy. Offer a bottle with 2-3 oz. formula. He usually goes to sleep

after 5-10 minutes of goofing around or occasional whimpering. If he really starts to cry, pick him up, comfort him. His naps can be as short as 1/4 hour or as long as 2 hours. If he is really unhappy--don't bother with the nap....

12:30 PM LUNCH

1-3 PM After lunch, Playtime! Change clothes. Give vitamins. He really likes the jolly jumper for exercise--after 1/4 hour of that he is usually ready for another nap around 2-3 PM. Again, offer a bottle with 4 oz. formula.... This is also a good time to take him for a walk for 1/2 to 1 hour. He often falls asleep during the walk.

This schedule continued until 8 PM, with full detail....

7 PM BATHTIME (bath lasts about 10 minutes)
He bathes lying on terry "sling." Washing takes about 5 minutes. (Use small washcloth.) Sit him up to wash his back and play with toys. Make sure you hold him all the time!!! Be careful! He's really slippery particularly when you lift him out (underarms). Wrap him well in towel, making sure to dry all nooks and crannies.

7:30 PM STORY TIME while rocking.

7:45 PM BEDTIME SNACK: 5-6 oz. breast milk (or warm soy formula)
Rock him while you feed him. Lights should be off with door mostly closed. Make sure you burp him before he gets too sleepy. Pull door closed once you leave room. MONITOR HIS SLEEPING WITH PORTABLE MONITOR...[1]

Wow! On the one hand, organized, thorough, responsible...on the other hand, there is something so tight about it. Too tight...it seems almost desperate, as if she trusts no one in the world but herself: the bath, scheduled in precisely, the exact-by-the-clock times for "spontaneous play," the specific placement of the door when the baby is put down to sleep. It's hard to know if this is an example of brilliant time-management (control), or whether Jaclyn is on the brink of losing control, trying to hold it together by micro-managing from afar. 7 a.m. till 8 p.m. 11 hours... Even with the perfect schedule in place, no matter how dazzling and efficient his caregiver may be, this is a long time for a mother and her baby to be apart.

But Jaclyn is that ideal new woman—Superwoman. Though a bit frayed, she is on top of her game. For now, she is holding onto things so intently that she doesn't sense anything precarious. It is admirable; it is alarming. Maybe it's you.

Or you may fit more into the Survivor Group, those who are simply dealing with getting through each day. Tracy falls short of Jaclyn in every way. She already both looks and feels undone. Some of us identify with her. We all feel for her. Tracy's monologue speaks volumes about how it is. The gilt on the lily is fading and her guilt is rising. Tracy is:

⌂ The Disorganized Woman

"I rush out of the office at 5:30 sharp every day to pick up my son. One day, I had to buy him new sandals—his toes had been sticking out of the front for weeks. I'd been promising to take him for days. What else is new? I thought I should feed him before going out to the mall. So, home we went for a snack and God Bless America! I found a note reminding me of a meeting with his teacher that night at 7:30. It's not that I didn't know about this meeting a week ago. It's just that, well, you know, that was a week ago. So we had to change our plans about going for shoes, right? Thank God for Kentucky Fried Chicken™! I grabbed it from the fridge. As we're on our way out the door, I notice that Buddie's pants are wet. 'Buddie,' I say, 'Did you just spill something on your pants or are you wet all the way through?' He was wet all the way through. Shit! So, okay. He's five. He wants to change his clothes himself. So I let him. It takes, of course, forever.

I eat chips. He's disappointed about the shoes again. So am I. We go to the meeting, which goes better than I expected. On the way home, I remember I've forgotten cereal for the morning—breakfast will be a disaster! 'Buddie,' I say, 'I've never done this before, but Mommy just doesn't have time to take you inside. I'm going to lock you in the car. I want you to get down in front of the backseat and stay there until I get back.' I jump out of the car, lock it, and run into the mini-mart. The lady behind the counter says, 'No yawning!' I look at her and say, 'I've had the day from hell. I'm going to yawn if I want to.' I realize she was just trying to be friendly. Too late. Thank God Buddie is still in the car when I get back. He falls asleep on the way home. I carry him in and put him to bed. I get into bed myself but lie awake thinking, 'Oh, shit! I forgot to do this. Oh, shit! I forgot to do that. My entire morning will be consumed with dealing with it all.' That's bad enough, but then I start considering what I can't get back—a cozy little dinner with my son, and a relaxing, sweet evening reading stories, having a snuggle, whatever. I'm in a cycle I just can't seem to control."

Tracy, unlike Jaclyn, knows something is wrong. She is frantic and upset. She feels she's failing. She's convinced that she's missing out on the important things no matter how hard she tries. Though she would put herself down in comparison to Jaclyn, in fact, Tracy is the more aware of the two. She has identified her disenchantment. Still, she isn't sure how, or if, she can change her life. Though clearly different, there is a significant similarity between these two women. *Their expectations of themselves exceed their capacity.* It is impossible for them to perform well in all the areas to which they (whether by choice or default) are committed.

Women who are overfunctioning in the traditional housewife role feel equally pressed and overloaded. Trying to create the ideal home environment, which will not only be beautiful but also support the family to do well in the outside world, Carolynn is not measuring up to her own standards. But she doesn't have time to come up with a solution. She tries telling herself that everything's okay, yet she's not convinced. She's hard on herself, apologizing to everyone constantly. Proud in patches, but it's not sustaining her. She, like Tracy, is aware of her disenchantment. But, Carolynn laments:

⌂ "What Can I Do?"

"The house is never clean. I walk through it and it's like 'Oh, well.' But, it's really not okay with me. I just bear it because 'what can I do?' I'm running around with the kids' schedules all the time. They range in age from six to sixteen. They—especially my teenagers—are over-scheduled and this gnaws at me. Where's the balance? How concerned do I need to be at this age about their getting ahead? How are they going to get their homework done after their sports practices and dance classes and tutoring? At 10 p.m.? They'll be exhausted. My natural tendency is to be a dreamer and visionary. I'm not one of those organized mothers. I'm really sorry about this. I get distracted at least once every minute by one of my kids. For over two weeks, one of the couches in the living room has been completely covered with clean laundry that needs to be folded. I vacuumed one third of the house one day. Hey! Another third another day....

"How do I feel about this? I'm hard on myself. I want to walk through the house and feel that it's beautiful, radiant, and clean. I want it to be special, not chaotic. I'm so sorry about this. Paperwork? It's ten inches deep. It's grinding me down. I won't even open things. Just throw them out, I tell myself, but I need to get better at this too. I feel like I'm in a sitcom. The parakeets. The dog. One day, there was a stray rooster that got into our yard. (Where the heck did he come from? We live in the city!) We had to rescue it and find the owner— another distraction. I want to fit in my art and other things that mean something to me personally. I want my kids to see me being creative. I'm *so* sorry about this. Sometimes I wake up in the middle of the night thinking, 'Oh! no! I had a traffic ticket! Is it past the deadline? I know it's in the pile, but where?' I don't know if I have a story about my life for you. I'm going to have to think about it. I'm sorry."

Those of us who have no responsibilities for children fare no bet-ter than those who do because the responsibilities we do have are still endless. In addition, overfunctioning is a job from which you cannot retire. Even after the kids are out of the house and have taken the dog with them, you're still at it.

TO THE POINT

What is your Job Description? Are you able to articulate your overfunctioning story? Do you see that no matter which style of Overfunctioner you represent—the Awesome Ones, the Survivors, the Traditional Homemakers, or some combination—it's all Mission Impossible?

The job of the overfunctioning woman has serious defects. Yet, it gains more acceptance and a more tenacious hold on us. We continue to apply for the job and try to live up to its demands.

PRESCRIPTION:

The first steps towards breaking out: 1) see that it's not you who is "off"; it's the Job(s) and the choices that are impossible and 2) begin dismantling external evaluations and start to make your own, based on different internal criteria. We can hold ourselves to a standard that is written by woman and includes:

— the sum of the unique qualities that we bring to life's table,

— a capacity for a complete spectrum of feelings (such as empathy, intensity, subtlety, kindness, nurturance, happiness, sadness, fear, anger, uncertainty, certainty, nervousness, assertiveness, sentimentality),

— a respect for our sense about what is right developed from our blend of the rational and the emotional,

— the vibrancy of our spirits,

— and living in a rhythm that allows time for savoring.

With this fresh perspective and the set of psychological insights that will be discussed in this book, you can take action to change your overfunctioning life.

Your Turn! HOLDING THE BAG EXERCISE
(optional to do, but read it through)

Topic: Status quo and the state of the Overfunctioning Woman

Purpose: To gain awareness of where you are and how it feels

A) First realize that all of us are left holding the bag. If you are confused on this point, reread the "Job Description" on page one. Once you acknowledge that reality, notice what kind of bag you lug around. Diaper? Laptop computer? Shopping? Overnight bag? Cosmetics bag? Rolling carry-on airplane bag? Cocktail party bag? Exercise gym bag? "Kiddies" birthday party bag? Backpack? Fanny pack? Paper or plastic? Environmentally correct cloth grocery shopping bag? Garbage bag? Or the fantastic combo bag that does it all for you?

B) Stand up slowly (close your eyes if you feel comfortable) and feel yourself holding the bag. Are you loaded down? Where does it hurt? Shoulders? Neck? Back? Head? Stomach? Which part of your body is taking it the hardest? Be aware that you not only have a tea or coffee of choice, political party of choice, etc., but you also have a body part or organ of choice...you know, the one that always goes wrong when things get dicey. Can you identify which one this is for you? If not, pay attention over the next few days or weeks, and see if you can figure it out. As you've no doubt already observed, there are the headache people, stomachache people, can't sleep...can't get up...sore throat...back's out...people, among others. This information is valuable because when that particular part goes "off," it is sending the warning that you are going off. To avoid chronic trouble, you can learn to take especially good care of this body part which is loyally serving as a sensitive barometer for you.

C) Now, back to the bag: If you had to put its psychological weight in pounds, how heavy would you say your bag is? Can you see well into it or is it too heaped up by now? Is it like an archeological dig? Perhaps it's more like a bottomless pit, dark and deep.

D) Concentrate on what's in your bag(s). Use whatever excavation techniques are necessary and look at every different individual thing. Then, in your imagination, try to fit the contents onto a large banquet-size dining room table (seating twelve). Will it all fit? Is there any room left for you to sit down?

No wonder you're weary and your enthusiasm is waning. Overfunctioning does not feel good.

2
THE SELF-ESTEEM FACTOR
The Pressure To Be Perfect

Alterations Needed
by Sofia Haas (age 15)

Two girls asked my sister if her breasts were too big. Their words were jagged, and my sister cried because she knew they were labeling her for alterations. They want her to be pleated, hemmed, cut up, mended. But that only works with dresses. Those girls are all twisted inside out, afraid of anything that isn't a fallacy propped up by insecurities. So they think my sister should trade herself for plastic scars for style?... to make herself into a breathing lie? I hope my sister told them that she wasn't on the rack for sale, and that she doesn't like butchers who use people to test their tools. If beauty is such pain, we should all quit and start something new. Society's clothes should be made to fit us real women, homemade. Not the other way 'round. But it's too late. So many girls have already been sold. They have grown gaunt, skinny, and sad...empty of smiles. Now, they've invited my sister to join in.

READING BETWEEN THE LINES

Even as we roll our eyes at the endless body images touted on every street corner of the land, the relentless daily bombardment still affects us, abrading self-esteem. No matter how confident you may be, the pull is there to be "more" (or "less" in certain areas, like weight) than you already are. And, it has a mind-numbing effect. The message? You're not okay. Nothing destroys self-esteem more than the crippling, creeping concern that you really might not be measuring up.

When you overfunction, you are striving to perform to an insatiable ideal. Whether consciously or not, you are compensating for the "sad fact" of your inferiority. When examined from this perspective, the mechanics that connect overfunctioning to self-esteem are obvious: the undermining belief of not being enough leads to overfunctioning.

Yet, locked onto the hamster wheel of overfunctioning guarantees that you will always fall short of achieving the goals projected upon you (or which you project on yourself). With the willingness to take on impossible tasks, overfunctioning pushes self-esteem down and perpetuates looking outside yourself for validation.

Because the body is so essential to all aspects of performance, attention cast upon it proves difficult to ignore. A lot has been written about this subject, but we would like to punctuate an important point: The common, modern consensus is that the body is malleable and able to be easily manipulated, controlled, improved, or perfected. Alas, it is a "project" (Overfunctioners love projects!) that should and *must* be worked on in the usual overfunctioning style.

We wrap ourselves around body issues, attending to "the project" in a variety of ways. Questions center around not whether to do anything, but what kinds of transformation should be attempted and how? Self-esteem, then, hinges on how good a job we do on this front. We have a high-powered armory at our disposal—an unending proliferation of products, machines, and services (brilliant experts of every sort to guide us), and, of course, the knife. The knife is versatile, clever, even mathematical. It adds and subtracts skin and bone. It stuffs and sews. When did we get so gullible? Or so desperate?

Rosalyn worked as ship's mental health counselor for Semester-at-Sea (think: college on an ocean liner) on two occasions. She noticed that the fashion—for breasts, that is—was different on each voyage.

◻ Boobs

On Semester-at-Sea 1998, the small-boobed girls reigned supreme, lying out in slab-like display on the deck. By 2004, the big boobs ruled the kingdom of desirability on the ship.

While taking a stroll on the deck one day, a naïve older passenger was overheard: "I've never seen so many identical perfect figures!" "Oh, didn't you know?" one of the lovely students matter-of-factly piped in, "It's breast implants or breast reductions, depending on what you need. I got mine as a twenty-first birthday gift from my dad."

Huh? Is this what "Parental Guidance" has come to?

Building an identity should be a highly personal matter, an exciting, enjoyable challenge that involves the mind, spirit, and body. Overfunctioning leads us astray in all dimensions. And, as it relates to bodies, overfunctioning can be downright dangerous. Experiences that are otherwise empowering and character-building (like exercise and a healthy diet) can turn daunting, compulsive, superficial, and ugly when you apply a standard of perfection that is, for most, impossible to achieve.

Sadly, more and more true these days, in the absence of self-esteem built up from inside, strengthened by an emotionally rich, nurturing childhood, we are left vulnerable to society's images of womanhood and femininity. As our identities are shaped by ongoing negotiations with the social world around us, our sense of self continually shifts between the values and traditions we carry within—those derived from our family, ethnic group, and community—and the transient standards of the surrounding milieu. This pressure continually puts us on a downward slope of uncertainty and self-recrimination.

Younger women are the hardest on themselves, constantly pushing to meet ever more unrealistic criteria. They feel they can succeed where their predecessors have failed. As a result, they are becoming the most determined promoters of overfunctioning and other myths of perfection-doing.

This is a tragic consequence of the magazine—and TV, infomercials, Internet advertising...—advice aimed towards women. These endless messages focus on our pernicious shortfalls or that elusive standard of perfection. The "You are not enough" external subtext taps $\triangle$ into the "I am not enough" (Point 2 on the TT) internal conversation. By contrast, men's magazines have traditionally talked about what works for men—strength, virility, age, money. Lately, however, these too have been pointing out men's short-comings. The pressure is on with (no surprise) similar consequences. For example, the rate of anorexia in college-age men is significantly on the rise.[2]

When we don't achieve perfect happiness through our body makeovers, we experience a double-failure. In this way, weak self-esteem, which has made us prey to the pressures of overfunctioning in the first place, leaves us sitting ducks (feeling like ugly ducklings)

for ever lower self-esteem. It's a vicious cycle. And we know it.
We really do know it. But we don't act like we know it, and we're
not standing up on our soapboxes, fighting back, saying we're mad as
you-know-what and we're not going to take it anymore!

⌂ WHAT PRODUCES SELF-ESTEEM?

How, then, do we stop the downward slide? What *really* produces
high self-esteem in people? It starts at home. Remember home? That's
where the earliest, most abiding emotional connections (or lack thereof)
occur. It is these connections, deep and well made that vaccinate us
against the media's barrage. They also keep us safe from profound pain
and doubt about ourselves and from frantic, repetitive acts of perfec-
tion-seeking.

Home is where one is, we hope, paid attention to, acknowledged,
and given uninterrupted time. Home is that place where magic is made
out of the real cloth of love. It creates a safe, welcoming haven from and
a safe, supportive launching pad into the world.

> ✂ What we carry forth into the world, we bring there from
> Home.

The operative words are safe, welcoming, and supportive. Welcome
is derived from "well" and "come." Support literally means "to carry."
Home is the place where emotional intimacy is most likely going to
happen (if it happens at all). Why, as a culture, are we not doing well
building that firm ground of self-esteem for ourselves and for our
children?

For a variety of reasons (either economically based and, therefore,
out of our immediate control or based on a culturally accepted form
of narcissism, which we will cover later), we have lost the knack for
providing love at its nurturing best. Instead, love gets confused with
a strange combination of constant overindulgence and pressure to
perform well at many things—a kind of perfectionism masquerading
as love. This is what we have bought into. Do we ask why and at what
emotional cost? No. We confuse and press our children so heavily that

we guarantee them a charter membership in Club Overfunctioning.

Ashley's mother quit her post in a marketing firm to raise her children. However, instead of relaxing and enjoying it, she made herself the CEO of the family and put all that career savvy into creating perfect children with a perfectly planned future. Ten-year-old Ashley is:

The Modern Child —as told by a neighbor

"Ashley is the new girl in the neighborhood. It is such a thrill that a ten year old has moved in because there never have been any girls my daughter's age close by. Ashley is a lively and sweet child. It all seems so perfect, but it isn't. Ashley rarely has time for us because she is scheduled from morning until night with school and after-school programs. Her parents seem happy that my daughter is living nearby. 'It's just great! It's just right!' they say. 'Exactly what we've dreamed of for Ashley!' And they think they mean it. But it doesn't play out because Ashley is on the Kiddy Fast Track. At age ten, her life is already tied-up and bound by her To Do List and I-can't-be-here-because-I-have-to-be-there list. One day, I asked Ashley what she daydreams about becoming when she grows up. 'Oh,' she replied matter-of-factly, 'I never daydream! I don't have time for that.'"

Now, we're going to rant a bit, bearing in mind this question: When did the hearth become merely a logistics hub? Clues are evident in the following modern home:

The Empty Full Nest

Knock, knock—who's there? Why, this is an odd place! Teeming with sound and action, but each inhabitant is busily alone. At other times, a complete silence pervades, not a footstep, not a person. From about 7 a.m. or earlier until about 6 p.m. or later, no one is here, except perhaps a pet or teen with no after-school activity that day.

Daytime sounds: appliances—refrigerator, furnace, telephone, answering machine. No ticking clocks. This house is filled with high-tech digital things, computers to bathroom scales, TVs, music gadgets, and toys. One room or more resembles an office: cell phones, answering machines, faxes, scanners, printers, copiers, Personal Digital Assistants in-house room-to-room intercoms for family communication.

And there's a "home fitness system!"

And parking space.

It's easy to see that home has become: a conference, entertainment, transportation, and planning center, a workplace with sleeping quarters, consumer space, personal workout annex, and parking lot.

Our eyes pan the rooms. We notice many things in impressive packages, the Complete Nutritious Meal Kit, vitamins for each particular age and gender, CD-ROM educational kits (Read-Faster-Sooner, Write-Faster-Sooner, Go-to-the-Parthenon-Virtual-Reality-While-Never-Leaving-the-Comfort-of-Your-Home Travel Excursion), endless toy kits—beading, construction, jacks (used to be just a cheap, tiny game sold in corner stores; that did not include a nine-page instruction book of variations with pictures). "Picture-Making" (used to be called Drawing) materials are boxed in neatly stacked modules on the shelf.

Moving in for a random sample: "The Rag-Rug Making Kit," packaged at $14.95 plus tax. It contains, of course, the nine-page instruction book (with developmental, educational, and creative value assurances and liability statement), one tiny plastic rug hook, and many pre-torn strips of rags. We pause. Can we pull off this fabric-ripping project? All these instructions make us doubt our ability. Maybe it's harder than we thought? What the heck in here is worth all this money? It can't possibly be the plastic hook! Maybe we should put it off. But, then we think, hmmm…we don't have time to search out and tear rags, so maybe it *is* a good deal.

Is your self-confidence eroding yet?

When at home: adults are moving swiftly within, conversations rapid-fire. The focus: scheduling, planning. Dinner (if there is one together) is characterized by a review of today's logistics and preparation for tomorrow's tactical issues. Phones interrupt. Is it the land line or the cell phone? Whose is it? Where is it? It's those marketers! Even if they don't land us this round, we've been interrupted yet again and distracted from our already tenuously jury-rigged Quality Family Time module.

A knock at the door. Now what? It's doubtful that it's the neighbor or a friend coming to chat, borrow some milk, or share some pie. What pie? Who's got time to bake pie? Who can eat pie? (The calories! The fat! The sugar content!) Whatever it's about, it's going to take up time and energy we don't have to give. Sigh. But… it could be a good cause…

> ✋ Living in an extension of the workplace, we, as employees or employers, have come to believe that, for seven days a week, we don't have the right to put the workday to bed before we go to bed.

Little Robbie, after nine hours in day care and a trip to the market on the way home, falls asleep just as we are starting to read that special book to him (highly recommended by…who was it?). It's frustrating. THAT quality time module didn't work…AGAIN. How about the fitness or entertainment modules? A game of ping pong anyone? Not likely. With 2.32 TVs per dwelling, members of the household often wander off solo, watching their own programs or *fitting in* that workout on their portable-easily-stowed-hide-away-under-the-bed gyms. And then there are the earphones. Those little "ear buds" have replaced conversation.

Spontaneity? Not in the schedule. Bedtime? Now, if you can sleep. Of course, there are always those little "nighttime remedies."

The modern homemaker? She moves too fast for us to keep her in our view-finder. Hang on! Oh, there she is! Pan in for that close-up. Hmmm…seems she's sagging. Her inner experience is that she has no chance to think, no sense of clarity. What skills, information, passion, and enthusiasm she possesses she doesn't have enough time or energy to share with her children or others nearest and dearest. So many experts! So many choices! The crown deeming her Queen of the Homely Arts has probably slipped behind the couch and is covered with dust balls, surely; maybe it's lost altogether, along with that triumphant sense of self.

✌ Encumbered with many helpful devices, the multitasking modern homemaker is logistically challenged.

Carolynn, reappearing from Chapter One, confesses: "I'm sitting in the private chamber of my car, waiting for one of the kids to get out of some class, wondering when things took this turn. I've lost touch with the quiet things, my vision of what feels right to do for my family, myself. I have no real sense of home anymore as I envision it. As a parent, I'm always providing, you know, researching the best options and facilitating everything. Making it all look seamless to them, of course. But, I'm not interacting that much. More and more, I have begun to divest myself of my power. When I do try to assert myself (with the soccer coach, the dance instructor, the classroom teacher, or administrator), I am often either brushed off or stonewalled. If I offer my opinion or some information about my child, I appear to be stepping on their toes. I imagine these folks are just trying to protect the little bailiwick of authority they still have left. Still, I feel intimidated at times."

So, how does all this help raise self-esteem? The answer: It doesn't. So many of us search outwardly for what could make things, at least, seem...seem what? Better? Okay. Cheer up! Relief *is* on the way! A quick fix is hawked from every corner.

Special occasion? No problem! In the domestic consumer space we call Home, everything can be "handled"...totally orchestrated children's pre-fab birthday parties in kit form including place, games, props, and pop-in tape of "spontaneous" singing of "Happy Birthday." (We think you can still sing it in private without fear of copyright infringement.) ...weddings (ifwecanfititintoourschedule.org) ...again, delegated and designed as modules for us by PROFESSIONAL coordinators!

Even Christmas. By the way, this holiday *must do*, from *The San Francisco Chronicle* engagingly instructs us how to pose a festive front for family and friends—"the whole package from $1,000"—and that doesn't even include the gifts themselves. There is an "idea book" that offers three different looks: "A Family Tree [is] a warm, fuzzy design" ...

"A Country Christmas [has] a casual look...bows and gingerbread men" ... "A Formal Affair [offers] a more refined, classic look." "Homeowners," one decorator comments in the article, "are finally realizing that red and green are not the only Christmas colors. ... People on a tight budget need not despair...you can do a lot with a can of spray paint, and don't scrimp on the ribbon."[3] Well, thank goodness for all that! Whew!

The breathless list of ways in which we've lost our brains, not to mention the communal essence of such occasions, appear to be endless. For example, something as natural as rain—having a baby—has been co-opted by the consumer framing department as: The Birth Experience. And there are "Right" and "Wrong" ways to do it!

What a consumer event it is! First, the props: The baby carriage options, depending on your environment—urban, suburban, or country—range from $49.99 to $2995. A Google™ search will give you about two million baby carriage hits, with accessory options that include baby carriage suckers for the guests at the baby shower and nifty little items like shopping cart covers, so baby won't get any nasty germs. Don't forget the jog stroller for dad! This is more exhausting than shopping for a car! And you can't ride in it to see if you like the feel. Speaking of cars, the car seat, (the best-seller priced at $269.95) starting with the newborn size—upgrading to that 60-pound legal limit. And you'll need accessories to keep your child safe from the sun and hot buckles...actually a deal when you consider the future healthcare costs from exposure to the sun. Hey, this is really starting to add up! The book *Baby Bargain Secrets* asserts that "With the average cost of a baby topping $6,000 for the first year alone, you need creative solutions and innovative ideas to navigate the consumer maze that confronts all parents-to-be."[4] There are the crib brands, the diaper bags, thermometer options, high chairs, the environmentally correct diapers options, intelligence-enhancing baby toys....

As if being pregnant doesn't make you tired enough! There's the cast and crew decisions for the birth event itself: Doula? Midwife? Doctor? Will you video-tape the big event? Who's got *that* 'job'? Ugh! Then, there's the staging: Home? Hospital? Cab on the way?

The medical liability options are endless: Has the doctor thoroughly informed you about your child's vaccinations? Does he actually *offer* you choices on this To Do item? What standard for safety is at work in protecting a newborn—yes, a "newborn"—from sexually transmitted diseases? With 48 doses of 14 vaccines to get into school, you can be sure that your child will be "safe" and you won't miss those three extra days you can't afford to take off from work. And then there are the genetic tests (only some of these are mandated by law; perhaps more should be because they really *do* save lives and there is no potential down-side to them) available to rule out several potentially dangerous inherited conditions that, if detected early enough, can be successfully treated? Don't forget the optional DNA test for certifiable identification.

And the slats on the crib have to be the appropriate width apart. And the door-locks, the toilet-locks, pill caps, the wall plugs. These really are great inventions, but one has to wonder: Is anyone keeping an eye on the child? Oh! We forgot the special gate so that mommy can work out on the home exercise equipment and toddler won't accidentally get a limb amputated. With a fortress of consumer protection options like this, you can be sure that if something happens to the unsuspecting newborn consumer, it's covered in some non-liability clause somewhere.

And, when you can't be rocking the little darling in your designed-by-engineers rocking chair, baby can get a whiff of mommy from the bonding blanket. How do they work? Well, first mom sticks these mini-absorbent pads in her bra to soak up a little breast leakage (which no one mentions before you get pregnant!). Then, the now appropriately "scented" pads are lovingly tucked into specially designed pockets in the bonding blanket so the baby can smell mom when she's at work. As if this little item on the To Do List is essential to building a sense of well-being in a child. Sigh, again!

Whatever else you do, don't forget to get the application in for your unborn child to attend the right preschool. You can't start on that college track too soon! (Hey, don't knock it. The waiting lists are long.) Of course, it's not the end of the world if little Aiden doesn't get into the Bentley of preschools, is it? Nothing to lose sleep over, right? Right?

Meet Anna Jen. AJ is caught up in overfunctioning. Outwardly, she *is* the epitome of success. She pulls things off so very well. She insists on attending to all the little details for her daughter's birthday party because she truly wants to do them. It's admirable. But she does not feel good. This was the first red flag (which, of course, she ignored and pushed away) that something was fundamentally "off" in her life. She tells her story best:

OFF TRACK   ⌂
The Beginning of The End
"It actually started with a deal that needed to be pitched in Honolulu. I was swamped preparing for the presentation, and my daughter's fifth birthday was coming up at the end of the same week. My husband suggested that I delegate the birthday preparations to hired helpers. That solved it for him. This 'option' so offended my sense of motherhood that I couldn't even consider it though it was sensible, of course, and, logically, the path of least resistance. But it mattered to me that the preparations be personal. Who else would really know the nuances, the special little touches? And, of course, I wasn't going to dare suggest to my boss that we put the meeting off by a day so I could prepare for my daughter's birthday too. No, I just forged ahead alone with both the party plans and the deal preparation, staying up late several nights to make sure everything got done.

"At the last minute, the business deadline got moved up a day which meant that I now would not be able to make it to the party unless I flew to Honolulu on the Red-eye, pitched the deal, and came back the same day. That's what I did. Everyone was impressed, including me. Nevertheless, I found the whole process very disturbing. I had pulled it off, but I felt oddly let down and resentful at...I didn't even know towards whom or what. When I got to the party, I was pumped up enough not to feel tired, but I was too filled with mixed emotions to relish in how thrilled my daughter was."

Though Anna Jen didn't have much time for those feelings, discontent began to rear its ugly head in spite of her efforts to ignore it. Though, at the time, it didn't feel like progress, this disturbing experience turned out to be a *positive* turning point, her first step out of overfunctioning.

So, what really does produce self-esteem in women? And joy?

✂ Psychologically speaking, self-esteem is the result of warmth, connectedness, love. It is about paying careful attention consistently, uni-tasking often, listening, remembering and asking questions about what you've heard—always. It is about tuning in, not tuning out.

All this is hard to do when you're busy and strapped for time. And there are no short-cuts for it. Now that the hearth has become a hub, isolation, frustration, and emotional hunger prevail. How did we end up with the activity card so full and the heart so empty?

TO THE POINT

We've accepted the hype without blinking because we have so little time to consider things. We're so worn out and inhibited that we are not sure we have anything high-quality left to offer. The CAN DO approach, teetering on the precipice of a NO CAN DO reality, inevitably leaves us with shaky self-esteem. Pass the Prozac® please!

Your Turn! YOUR ALICE-SIZE

Topic: Placating and self-esteem

Purpose: To gain understanding of your fluctuating self-esteem and self-confidence; to get personal control over your internal "size"

Here is an interesting experiment about shrinking and expanding yourself (like Alice in Wonderland), and determining who's steering your *internal* ship.

A) At any time of day and in any situation, you can discretely and quickly check your Alice-size. Are you so tiny that no one can see you at all? Are you a small Alice for whom a spilled glass of water is a river that will carry you through a keyhole? Are you a child-size Alice with childish ideas and childish expectations? Are you a grown-up Alice, old enough to vote and with ideas of how to cast your vote? Are you a gigantic Alice who can lift and push over large objects and people but can also crush them? At first, choose several events in a 24-hour period and check in with yourself how you measure up.

B) Notice which cues (from whom) and which stimuli cause you to change your size quickly and back and forth all day long, particularly when certain people are around or certain kinds of events are happening.

C) Reflect on how often your size shifts in a 24-hour period. Does it happen over 2 or 3 times? Which size feels the most comfortable or natural? Tiny, meek, shaky Alice? Large, bordering on tyrannical Alice? Does this discovery make you happy or uneasy? What adjustments would you like to make in your Alice-size? What size do you want <u>you</u> to be? Who would support you in this? Who might try to discourage you?

D) Notice that as your Alice size becomes bigger, others, who have formerly loomed large, appear to level out.

3
IMPOSSIBLE PEOPLE
"It's All About Me" People!

Echo and Narcissus

Okay, here's the pitch: Narcissus, see, he's this guy who's like the local catch. At least, that's how he is perceived. All the girls want him. Echo, well, she's a little complex. When we first come onto the scene, she's talking a mile a minute with Hera, the wife of Zeus, king of the gods. Seems Echo's covering something up and Hera senses it, suspecting that her husband has been dallying around with Echo. Hera doesn't know for sure, but she sure doesn't like being taken for a fool. And she doesn't like this Echo. Period. So, she puts a curse on her, takes away her gift of gab. All Echo can do from this point on is repeat whatever is said to her.

But Pan doesn't mind. Pan, he's a poet and a flute player. He's good, sincere, pure of heart. He tries to win Echo's heart with his artistry. But, it's too easy, see. Echo needs intrigue, complexity. No matter what Pan does, Echo just won't give this nice guy the time of day. She's stuck on Narcissus, the cool guy.

But Narcissus is stuck on himself. He really doesn't give Echo any attention. Instead, he sits beside a reflecting pool and gazes at his own face, constantly telling the "stranger" in the water how beautiful he is. When he says, "I love you!" to his own reflection, Echo, standing loyally by, poor dear, repeats, "I love you."

You'd think that the tale ends when Narcissus dies and Echo, ever waiting, fades away there by the pool. But something miraculous happens. A little cluster of flowers grows up on that very spot. To this day, we call them Narcissus. And Echo? She can still be heard senselessly repeating the words called out by whomever passes by.

And she calls to us through the ages, to gain wisdom from the meaning of her sad, sad tale. Let's review the Treacherous Triangle:

Point One is *overfunctioning* and Point Two is *poor self-esteem*. We've seen how they are interconnected. As illustrated in this story, Point Three on the Treacherous Triangle (TT) is *susceptibility to (attend to the needs of) Impossible People* (IP). Consider poor Echo in terms of the TT. She tried and tried harder (overfunctioning) and slavishly hung in there with Narcissus (low self-esteem and overfunctioning); because she was so focused on his wishes and whims (overfunctioning), she failed to take care of herself (low self-esteem). Though the artistic Pan offered her his sincere affection, she did not give him the time of day. Even after Narcissus died, Echo remained under his spell, never finding or regaining her own voice. (Choosing IP.) Does this sound like any women you know?

Are there people in your life to whom you continually defer at your own expense? Do you echo them?

…even when you know they are high-maintenance and frequently distort what's going on? Many of us have a hard time either noticing this is happening or keeping track of it because it plays into our traditional female expectation of not being taken seriously, of not being heard, of needing to overfunction to (maybe) be noticed, and of repeatedly trying to prove ourselves.

TO THE POINT

In the overfunctioning mode, we give equal weight and attention to everything. We tend to accept all challenges, often without taking the time to size them up clearly and scrutinize them well. And we never give up. This mind-set puts us at high risk for tolerating IP's with impossible demands. After all, we overfunctioners are always accomplishing the impossible, so why not this, too? …whatever or whomever it is.

We're so busy handling this, handling that, from small logistical issues to big decisions with our families or at work. In the midst of these many interactions, we may find there are some people with whom inter-action is simply not possible. Our comments may automatically be belittled, distorted, or totally ignored. …like Echo's were by Narcissus. It's easy to get tripped up just to keep things moving forward.

Meet Heather and her father. Traditionally Heather has been in a passive, placating, overfunctioning trance in relation to her dad since childhood. Now that she's thirty-five, what, if anything, has changed? What hasn't changed? Heather is making plans to:

Visit Grandpa

"When I was making summer arrangements for my family to visit my dad, I called first to find out which weekends would work for him. Then my husband, Dave, and I literally spent hours arranging the itinerary to fit both Dad's availability and our job schedules. When I called back to confirm, Dad told me that he'd made other plans for those particular days, and we'd have to come a different weekend. Why didn't he call me when he knew his needs had changed? I thought this but, of course, didn't say it aloud. I didn't want to be disrespectful, but I was upset. Adjusting our travel dates cost an extra $450!

"When we appeared on the late June afternoon of his choosing, our son, Aaron, age three, complained of a stomachache at dinner. Dad suggested that since Aaron might be sick, we should probably find a hotel because he didn't want to get sick. I suggested that the long flight and the airline food were the likely culprits. There was no response to my comment. I felt awkward; we were being put out after our long travel day; it was late, dark, and it wasn't negotiable. This was familiar territory for me with Dad and, right on cue, I heard myself say, 'Gee, I'm sorry, Dad,' Then, up we got, carrying the sleeping Aaron, and left to find a local hotel (…an additional expense, I might add).

"In the morning, Aaron felt fine and I called Dad. He had already made other plans because, he said, he thought Aaron was going to be sick. However, he hadn't called us back to check this out, nor to check and see how his only grandson was doing. Aaron was a little confused that we weren't going back to Grandpa's house. We scurried around, finding other things to do. Finally, we hooked up with some old friends from college. Aaron never did get sick. I called my dad several times more. We were just fit in for drinks once and a quick bite at restaurants a couple of times. We did not spend any substantial time with him.

"Several months later, Dad complained about our not having visited him 'because you wanted to spend your vacation with your friends.'

He seemed to feel genuinely hurt and left out. Instantly, I felt guilty. (What had I done to make Dad feel so bad?) I also felt a familiar sensation in my head—kind of a fuzzy headache, a feeling of being twisted into a knot. At these times, I exhaustively question myself and replay events, looking for what I might have missed.

"I am beginning to understand the signs though. I have been programmed since I was a kid to automatically accept that Dad *must* be right. After all, he's Dad. I was taught not to question this, only to question my own actions and try to make them perfect. Thus, my wimpy behavior on the trip. I realize now that this has got to change. So that in itself is progress. But I am still searching for the words to say to him, knowing that he will find a way to twist them around. It's not because my words and thoughts are wrong or imperfect. Finally, I can see that. I don't have to try harder. I will continue to look for a way to change how I interact with him whether he approves or not. (What did I just say? Of course, he won't approve or understand. Oh, gosh! There's my child's heart ever-hoping, ever-wishing he would be different.)"

Because overfunctioners are particularly vulnerable to going the extra mile to succeed at everything and please others, we're, by definition, unwilling or very reluctant to quit trying. Since we don't know when or how to give up, we tolerate damaging and outrageous behaviors such as substandard communication. We try harder and feel guiltier. Because this is such a common and serious problem, we have to explore it in detail.

🖐 Overfunctioners routinely get entangled with people with whom genuine dialogue and mutual exchange is neither occurring in present time nor possible at any time.

Observe the following fairly minor exchange. A friend calls, interrupting you. You tell her that you cannot talk right now. She's offended. You counter-offer to talk later. It's not a rejection. You are just prioritizing in this moment. You'll call back. You've called back before. After all, you're friends. You are willing to talk later; you've just explained this, just not this instant, on demand. What she hears is, "You don't care about me. I don't count." Who is making the situation difficult? You or her? Do you see that you have an Impossible Person on the line?

Then, there's the friend who invites you to read a passage from your book with her literary group at a bookstore in her locale. You're thrilled. You agree to go. Ever overfunctioning, you've misplaced the directions and google the store name (as you remember it) and location just before running out the door. When you get there, you find you've arrived at the wrong location. The store is boarded up. A sign says it has moved to another location a few miles from there. You go there—no store. You call up your friend—the one who invited you—for clarification as to where you're supposed to show up and she screams over the phone, "This is NOT my problem!" Well! So much for asking for directions.

These people are drawn to us because we'll work so hard in their behalf and put up with so much. We often stay in these relationships for long periods of time without asking the common sense questions we would in any basic evaluation—of a job candidate, for instance. This makes us easy prey to associations with people who fit certain roles demanded by the stories that run us: the cold, critical mother; the self-absorbed, demanding father (like Heather's); the manipulative, helpless, crisis-ridden sibling, the "hot and cold" friend.

To quickly extricate yourself from these overfunctioning quagmires, both big and small, you need to be able to recognize when communication isn't just stalled, but is simply <u>not</u> <u>happening</u> at all. You will feel as if you have not been heard. Likely, you'll also experience frustration or a sense of suffocation. Have confidence in your assessment. Then, you won't waste any more time and energy trying to engage in dialogue on an equal footing with an Impossible Person. You will be convinced that such dialogue won't occur. It's very difficult to believe it. But gradually you will.

✂ Good communicators can be defined as: those who, when you speak to them, allow your words, like pearls of water to seep in. They listen and receive, just as you listen and receive (hear) them.

We are not necessarily talking here about agreement. Honest discussion definitely includes disagreement at times. This can be temporarily discouraging, but it never makes you feel crazy and desperate the way that <u>not</u> <u>being</u> <u>heard</u> does. Dialogue falling below a certain level of mutual understanding makes you feel tiny, helpless, frustrated, stifled, achy/headachy, squeezed out—even, in some instances, as if you don't exist at all. (Revisit the Alice Exercise in Chapter Two.) This was Heather's dynamic with her father. She tried harder and over-accommodated, and he just waltzed along unfazed, re-articulating reality as it suited him.

No wonder Heather gets a loud message that what she wants doesn't count. Her father, by his behavior, is communicating callous, self-centered disrespect towards his daughter and her family though he doesn't see it that way at all! We call this kind of dialogue "firewalled" because nothing seeps in (to Heather's father, that is). For Heather, his response to her inevitably triggers discomfort, self-doubt, and more overfunctioning. It's toxic to her. It does seep in. And it stays in and it festers.

> ✂ Allowing yourself to be treated as if you don't exist is hazardous to your health.

As you begin to take stock of this phenomenon, you will probably notice that there are a large number of people who have a difficult time engaging in genuine conversation. Impenetrable, they often repeat themselves in a mechanical fashion no matter to what lengths you go to be heard and understood. They also tend to distort facts and events. The function of their words is not to exchange ideas and feelings with you, but to shield themselves (to feel safe) to ward you off, to gain power and control in the moment, and to constantly and single-mindedly get their needs met. They will always resist letting in new concepts about themselves or the events at hand. Don't be fooled by an arrogant façade, a stance that characteristically masks fear.

The following story concerns an earnest overfunctioner (Raelyne) who could not meet on common ground with her own sister (Colindy).

Colindy could never let in what Raelyne was trying to say without feeling threatened. So, she put a spin on it. Raelyne had convinced herself years before that the only "solution" in dealing with her sister lay in more and better overfunctioning combined with placating and constant reassurance. Raelyne! Raelyne! How:

Does Your Garden Grow?

"My younger sister (Colindy) and I had been volunteering in the garden at the Zen Center for years. As far as the center manager was concerned, I was in charge, but Colindy decided that she wanted to share the position. I was happy to do that because it's a huge job and, after all, she's my sister. I liked the idea of doing it together. But there was tension from the start. I initiated several discussions to sort out our job descriptions, expectations, and desires. The conversations started and ended with Colindy getting defensive and telling me that, by suggesting ways to go about our garden chores and duties, I always was a power and control freak. This blaming was her standard operating procedure in our relationship over many years. In order to not appear to be groping for control (which I wasn't...was I?), I simply gave in and hoped we would just work things out as we went along. Within a short time, however, Colindy had somehow managed to take over and reduced my participation to doing small tasks that she assigned to me. I went along with it.

"Soon, Colindy started to have a hard time getting along with the other volunteers. Until this happened, I hadn't ever accepted how controlling she was, not just with me, but with everyone—always needing to get her way and not able to tolerate any feedback from anyone. Without realizing it, I had served as a buffer between her and others for decades. Maybe I'd been doing this all my life. Now, one by one, the volunteers began to drift away. Eventually, Colindy found herself doing almost all the work herself. At one point, complaining that her health was deteriorating, she asked me to take over as director again. I agreed and began working on getting everyone back on board. I was also in a more heightened state of observation about what went on between us. This time, I was going to figure it out once and for all.

"Several weeks later, it was announced that the Zen Roshi [prestigious leader] would be coming for a visit. Colindy called to remind me that, '[she'd] never relinquished her position as manager of the garden, that I must have gotten it wrong'—and that she would be there to greet the beloved guest and give him the garden tour herself. I told Colindy that this was definitely not my understanding, but by the time the discussion was over, I had backed down again. Colindy reinstated herself just in time to take all the credit for how beautiful the garden looked. At least, I finally saw how she operates and how impossible she truly is."

REWRITING REALITY

The essential common theme in both Heather and Raelyne's stories is that *reality cannot be fixed in one spot*. It keeps shifting. Heather and Raelyne, both earnest overfunctioners indeed, worked very hard to accommodate their family members. Regardless, no matter how hard the women try to be flexible, they go down to exhausted, painful defeat. Heather ends up being blamed for her "selfishness." Raelyne loses the post she had enjoyed and recognition for her accomplishments. Because they were always trying to be understanding, often to the point of self-blame, they rendered themselves powerless. They didn't challenge these intractable reality re-writers, even in their own minds. Until now. Both are finally beginning to see that they are dealing with an IP. And, therefore, to stop overfunctioning, that they must take unilateral limit-setting action to change the intolerable situations.

> ✍ Always trying harder can be hazardous to your health.

Narcissists ("It's All About Me" people), in particular, externalize everything. You know, it is always somebody else's fault, never theirs. If you take issue with this and indicate that responsibility is shared, they get very anxious. This state they cannot tolerate, and so they turn on you in anger and righteous indignation. You end up blamed, often shamed. Sometimes, under this pressure, you surrender to their point of view and apologize, as Heather and Raelyne did repeatedly.

🖐 It's tough to stand up to Narcissists. They know that they're always wronged, never wrong. And they'll rewrite reality to prove it.

Overfunctioning women are highly susceptible to the grip of these IPs, and we have a particularly hard time breaking away. Rejected by one or several, many of us are so shaken that we are drawn to get involved with yet another in order to finally "do it right"—we will be found worthy this time! In the end, IPs will devastate those who remain attached to them. Sooner or later, the only role you are permitted to play with narcissists is that of poor, foolish Echo, and she went down to weary, humiliating defeat! It's impossible to maintain genuine power or personhood in such relationships. You become a mere repository for their needs and fantasies, allowed for a time to serve them or bask in their light. Even though the room may be gilded, you have actually been kicked into the servants' quarters. Eventually, despite all your devoted efforts, you will displease. And you will be punished. The peril of losing yourself looms large. The only smart, healthy strategy is to exit the relationship.

🖐 There is no winning the Narcissist Game except by ending the game.
🖐 The best defense against Narcissism is prevention. RSVP "NO" to the initial invitation.

Still uncertain whether your partner, friend, or parent is a dyed-in-the-wool Impossible Person? Or reasonable facsimile? Here are two short assessment tests so you can ascertain reality clearly and nip in the bud engaging with these dangerous types.

IP Brief Test I: If somebody does not inquire what you are up to; if someone does ask you, but swiftly gets self-referential; if, after a few weeks or months, something begins to feel strangely hollow and confused inside yourself; if you notice that conversations often seem to get twisted, spun, and rewritten; if you find that every encounter turns into a competition, that *if you've been to the moon once, they've been there twice;* if you sense the pressure to praise constantly, even when you don't want to; or if you are NEVER right, you've probably caught a Narcissist/Me-Person on your line. You can confirm this hypothesis by intentionally taking up a topic important to you and trying to stick with it or begging to differ about something. See what happens.

IP Brief Test II: Imagine the person you're testing is authoring a play or movie. What character is he or she and what part has he written for you? For instance, is it *Gone With The Wind*? He's Clark Gable and you are Vivian Leigh? Playing the parts of Rhett and Scarlet might be great temporarily, but you probably wouldn't want to sign a long-term contract. Some scripts are very good for peak experiences, incredible moments, or weekends, but not for building a life. If the plot is really melodramatic, contains one dominant star and it isn't you, or your leading role is tightly scripted by him/her, you may well be embarking upon the stage with a Narcissist/Me-Person. Know that since you are not the author, the plot outline is <u>unchangeable</u> except by insisting on exercising your right to quit the show.

Learn to do these tests early in the game. If your initial results prove inconclusive, set up several yellow flags of caution for yourself. Return to redo the assessment frequently until you are sure. Search for more signs as you go, and go slowly, systematically, no matter what the person in question urges you to do. His reaction to your sticking to your own pace will also supply telling data. For example, does he quickly turn your stance into some variant of "Oh, please don't put me through this pain!" Notice the ME-ness of this statement and do not get hooked by the "flattery" and conclude that he wants you so much he can hardly bear to wait.

One's capacity to "see" accurately fogs over quickly in the presence of these people because they distort and manipulate with such skill. They are often either seductive or guilt-inducing or both. As time passes under their influence, you may lose so much clarity that you even lose sight of the door, give up the belief that you are entitled to leave, or lose the willpower and self-esteem to make it out.

Don't yield to the temptation of writing an overfunctioning script for yourself based on thinking you will be "the One"—the Perfect One—who can do the impossible! "No, he's never been faithful to anyone, but with me it will be different." Or, "She's always been displeased with everybody, but I'll change it. I'll make her happy."

✂ Know that you can never change a Narcissist/Me-Person, regardless of how clever, cute, strong, weak, sweet, assertive, passive, compelling, pretty, sexy, supportive, or overfunctioning you may be.

If the IP Brief Tests come out positive and you still can't leave, you need to face that you are in a trance. Try to force yourself to wake up out of it by pushing yourself to ask: "Why do I persist in punishing myself by tolerating this sort of personal jeopardy? What purpose is this person serving for me? What induction from the past makes me willing to become the ultimate sufferer, victim, pleaser, or passive Echo? Why do I take on mission impossible?"

Or, are you driven by "I feel basically frightened and helpless, but I now shall become a queen. I've found someone to create the magical kingdom for me. And shutting up, obeying, and fading away are okay prices to pay for a stylish temporary rescue." If you are still not budging from your trance, enlist the help of your friends or a professional.

PRESCRIPTION:

Overfunctioners need to learn to have their radar up for Impossible People. Noticing situations in which communication isn't occurring (a firewalled situation) can help you to protect your sense of reality from being twisted.

Even those small, just annoying encounters can be insidiously energy-draining. Sally encountered one of them, just trying to order:

A Hot Cup of Tea

"It was at a fast-food restaurant on the highway. 'I'd like to have hot tea with four creams, please.' The young man asked, 'Four creams?' 'Yes.' 'For tea?' 'Yes, thank you. I'd like to have four creams with my <u>hot</u> tea.' He brought me back a huge plastic cup of cold, brown liquid and no creams. 'This isn't hot tea,' I said. He said, 'It's tea.' 'You're right,' I replied. 'But, it's cold.' 'It's tea,' he repeated himself. 'But, I asked for <u>hot</u> tea.' 'We don't have that,' came the response. I looked up at the sign. Maybe I was wrong. I could have sworn I've ordered hot tea hundreds of times from this fast-food chain over the years. I pointed to the sign, 'It says on your sign 'Hot Tea, $1.19 cents.' He didn't move, didn't even twitch.

"This is the point where I should have just walked over to the fast-food operation next door. But, no! I launched into overfunctioning, albeit minor, but overfunctioning none-the-less. 'You see,' I began to explain, patiently, 'Iced tea and hot tea are two different things. You have given me iced tea and are charging me the iced tea price, $1.69. I did not ask for iced tea. I asked for hot tea.' 'It's tea,' was all he replied. I thought about explaining it to him again. I could have asked in another language, but he clearly spoke English. I thought about going to the manager to straighten the situation out. By now, I was salivating for hot tea. It could have been easily remedied by talking to the manager, but I might have humiliated the young man behind the counter. My mind raced through various scenarios in an instant. Finally, I caught myself. I'm overfunctioning to get a blankety-blank cup of tea! I sighed, looked at the guy, shrugged my shoulders. 'Thanks anyway.' I walked out, scanning the landscape for where to get that cup of hot tea and a little peace of mind."

It's easy to see from this story how small-impact situations set you off-balance and throw you back into traditional overfunctioning accommodation mind-sets. They drain energy and, not to mention, make you feel temporarily frustrated and nuts. Once you are an expert in identifying when what you are saying is <u>not</u> being heard, you will raise a red flag swiftly. Twenty-five seconds max is about all you will spend on an encounter like this.

Getting off the points on the TT—and staying there—require knowing how to deal with what matters to you. "Deal with" means bring it up, attempt to communicate about it, talk it through. Tell the truth: "I feel (about this thing or this person...)" whatever your feeling is. "I think..." whatever you really think. "I want..." "I do not want..." "I will not..." "I will..." (words simple enough for a three year old to understand).

Because talking this way (which, again, doesn't necessarily mean agreement) typically involves saying something that may be unpopular and cause upset, disappointment, or anger, it may feel like a *counter-intuitive* move. This does not make it the wrong thing to do. You may have to tolerate some discomfort, nervousness, or fear. Can you? These feelings do not necessarily signal that you are wrong or doing something poorly. Instead, it may be the signal that you are breaking new ground. Good and unfamiliar ground, which is progress.

Of course, speaking out doesn't always guarantee that what you say will be heard, but at least you will know that <u>you have done your best to communicate</u>. The other person's response will give you good feedback with regard to who he/she really is and the level of healthy communication capacity he/she possesses.

If you are dealing with a truly Impossible Person (the Narcissist, the Me-Person, the Reality-Rewriter, or your run of the mill firewalled person), you will discover that your feelings don't matter to them anyway. You will have the urge to set the record straight. You will have the urge to say your piece, but it will only backfire if you try.

TO THE POINT

As you become an effective communicator, when, in certain circumstances, you realize you can't create or facilitate dialogue, your diagnosis of whom you have on the line will be complete and you will act accordingly.

Because you may have to reevaluate some important relationships, this process of assessment and action can be daunting. Once you stop your customary overfunctioning (accommodating, taking the blame, working harder at it, "Echo-ing,"), the truth will out. Once you no longer protect the other person, you will get to see if you have an IP in your midst. Remind yourself that you cannot change such people, even though many of them hold prestigious, lucrative positions of power in the world and are intelligent, witty, and charming. This only makes them more dangerous.

> 🖐 Narcissism is a serious, deep-rooted psychological condition. No matter how good an overfunctioner you are or no matter how healthy and good a communicator you are, you will not satisfy these people.

DAMAGE CONTROL

It's not always necessary or possible to quit and run. In some situations, things can be handled with a goal-oriented, self-protection strategy laced with ingenuity. Focus on <u>not</u> getting reactive and <u>not</u> letting your buttons get pushed. Do not look for praise, connection, or kindness; recognize that these responses, if they do come, are temporary at best and most likely manipulations—scripting to keep you firmly in *your* place in *their* script.

Limit your interactions to getting the common task done. Or select an activity that is free (relatively) of the toxic dynamics. For instance, Raelyne can have fun going to the movies or the ballet with her sister. If she keeps the relationship limited to such things, she's okay. This form of damage control is a valuable option to have in your overfunctioning kit bag—particularly in the workplace, with some members of your family of origin, and with others where survival circumstances (yours) preclude an exit option. Damage Control does consume precious emotional energy, and it never feels particularly rewarding. However, it can serve a practical purpose when needed; it can feel good enough.

If containing the damage becomes a big job (overfunctioning), eroding your time, energy, and self-esteem, you need to consider a more bold approach. For example, leave the job or the person. If this is not realistic to do all at once, develop a strategy of steps to take towards that end. While engaged in this process, you'll have to tolerate a high level of anxiety (See Chapter 7). You will need to ask friends to help support you as you go along.

Watch out for *unexamined assumptions* and fears that throw you off. They can keep you from acting in your own best interest, prevent you from heeding your own yellow warning flags: "The highest pay-ing, most prestigious job is always best." "Without this job, I'll face financial and emotional ruin." "If I leave him, I'll be alone forever." "If I draw a line, people will think I'm controlling, mean, bad, or high-maintenance." Stop to ponder whether these beliefs <u>are</u> true or just <u>feel</u> true. Consider the price of continuing to play a role which inevitably makes you overfunction and feel confused, weak, and small.

Think about this: Here's the Treacherous Triangle:

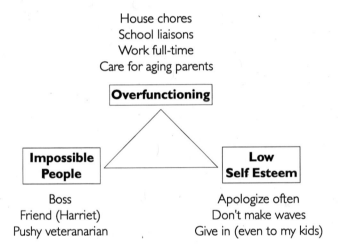

Take a moment to review its design and structure. You may be looking at your life.

Your Turn! ON GUARD FOR THE FIREWALL DIAGNOSIS

Topic: How to quickly assess situations in which communication is not happening

Purpose: To learn how to protect your time, energy, and heart

A) Recall several occasions when you were forever trying harder and harder and feeling worse and worse. These can involve your job, family of origin, friends, lover, spouse, or extra curricular organizations such as schools, clubs, boards of directors, and carpools.

B) List the impossible people and impossible groups you were involved with there. Try to remember well enough to estimate about how long it took you to extricate yourself and who, if anyone, helped you to unchoose these dangerous liaisons. Think through the detrimental short- and long-term effects of the encounters (particularly with bosses, parents, and lovers). Note these carefully. You probably will discover that it took you more time than you thought to get away. Do you allow yourself to feel some compassion for the distress you have experienced and endured?

What factors make it hard for you to assess "firewalled communication" and move on? For instance, what are you consistently afraid of that stops you dead in your tracks? "I'll be a quitter, a loser, a louse, a weakling, a _____." What illusions are you under? "I can charm him/her, get him/her to love/marry/notice me (even though no one else ever has managed this feat)." "If I'm just prettier, more fun, thinner, more _____, less _____, he/she will see me." Or, "My mother always discounted what I said. So, I'm re-creating this now and tolerating it 'just like family.'" Or, "Not much I can do about it. That's the way it is. I don't deserve much anyway. Oh, well."

C) As you go along in your thoughts, notice the difference between static, chronic suffering ("oh, well...") and forward-motion suffering (the anxiety accompanying the risk you're taking to do something differently, to experiment). Who, in your life, can you count on to help you to move from the first form of suffering to the second? Count yourself as one. How might this other person help? What do you think you need from him or her?

D) And...just to check...just in case: Do you have any firewall tendencies yourself? Pause and reflect carefully about whether your "hearing" is in good working order. Identify any "loaded" situations in which you know you have a tendency to shut down or close off a little. Checking yourself for firewalling is an area of self-exploration in which there is no substitute for a trusted friend, one who will be candid with you. Take your trepidation in hand and talk with that friend. Sample questions you might ask: Do you have trouble getting through to me? Sometimes? A lot? Rarely? What do I do/say, or not do/not say to make this so? Even when I don't agree with you, do you feel I really truly hear you out? Do you think I distort things very often? You know...reach a point beyond just my normal slightly dramatic flair. I mean serious distortion. Do I ask questions to draw you out and show my interest or caring? Absorb the feedback, like it or not.

E) We have focused, so far, on the destructive "firewall" put up by IPs as part of their personality make-up. Look now at firewalls—the constructive and positive type. These are very different. You must build them to protect yourself adequately. They will form a necessary defense that you will deliberately employ when faced with impossible situations (those that include IPs and impossible jobs, of course). These positive firewalls are conscious and made of sturdy stuff, like saying NO, changing your course, or setting limits in your own behalf. These firewalls are temporary and custom-designed for emergencies and specific needs.

✂ A healthy individual is neither defensive nor defenseless.

4
WE KEEP BUYIN' WHAT THEY'RE SELLIN'
Quick Fixes/Faux Formulas

From the *Wall Street Journal's* "Work and Home" column:
"...'integration,'...it's the hottest work-life buzzword since 'juggling.' A behavior ascribed to people (mostly women) with multiple but disparate roles, 'juggling' denoted a circus-like act that allowed little sustained focus and was destined to fall apart. It has fallen out of favor...as a solution to anything.... The newer idea, integration... means drawing the world of work and home closer through technology, workplace flexibility...so people can move seamlessly between the realms...forecasters...call the convergence of work and home life one of the top 10 trends.... Tina, a vice president, says she gets 50 percent more done both at work and at home since she and her boss agreed on a plan for her to integrate.... She limited her work at the office to seven hours a day, but is available a total of 12 hours via pager, phone and PC...home by late afternoon...to prepare dinner, often taking work calls at the stove. She also works during lulls in her school volunteer stints.... A voice-mail message she left for her boss included the remark, 'Yes, Honey, it is a blue truck,' an aside to her toddler....

"...Among the ways Donna, a computer specialist, integrates her life is by taking work to her son's sports practices. But she takes pains to watch when her son wants her to. 'It's read this, look up, read this, look up.... [Integration] requires mental disciplines, too: Schedule personal time thoughtfully and assign it as much importance as work. Communicate skillfully to let everyone know your plans...."[5]

How do you feel when you read this? Does it make you laugh? wince? cry? Even as some of us doubt the validity of trying to do so much, we read articles like this in respectable places and feel guilty and demoralized. The admiring tone is grating. Alluring words like technology, workplace flexibility, and seamless mask the destructive effects of overfunctioning, and we're hooked into believing that if we aren't managing this well, and if we aren't happy to be doing it, we've got a problem. That's not the problem!

Seductive yet superficially pleasing examples make it easy to miss what is <u>not</u> addressed in the article. For instance, what is Tina's two-year-old son learning about his importance in the family while his mother acknowledges his blue truck as an aside while she cooks dinner with her neck crooked into the telephone for a business call? The toddler has, no doubt, spent his whole day at day care, while she was spending her mere seven hours at the office and looking ahead to five more hours "on call" at home. Tina says she gets "fifty percent more done at both work and home." Is this a formula for success or disaster?

How does Donna know exactly when to look up from her work? Does her son call out to her every time he wants her to watch? Can she achieve genuine satisfaction or a reasonable level of concentration on either endeavor? Does her son feel special and valued from his mom's split attention at his game? Instead, the sales pitch is that "integration" or "sequencing," or however it's fashionably framed today or tomorrow, creates more freedom and is somehow equated with "QUALITY."

Slicker and more insidious versions of the quick fix are offered. "Schedule personal time thoughtfully...assign it as much importance as work," "Communicate skillfully...let everyone know your plans...."[6] HA! As for this advice, it's laughable and patronizing. These ideas are easy to say and difficult if not impossible to pull off with any consistency. Exactly where is the time available to schedule...? Maybe, Donna and Tina know. We haven't seen it for years! Although when we read such articles, written so glibly, we think it should all be simple; and it is only we who can't seem to pull it off.

A LESSON IN SEAMLESS INTEGRATION

Meet a master of the Module Principle and Integration and see where she goes: Bev is another star. She's got a pedigree education—Yale, Harvard—and a pedigree job. When we encounter her, she's concentrating her efforts focused on her annual Christmas cooking project. Uncomfortable with feeling upset, she zooms right back into the fast lane about her "little disappointment" that seems to center around pectin—or does it? "Just a tiny setback, that's all," she claims. In the moment, Bev suffers less than Anna Jen did (Remember Anna Jen's daughter's birthday party preparations from Chapter 2?) And, the following event was not enough to jolt Bev awake even for a moment. Like the many things she accomplishes, she does it by:

Applying the Module Principle

Tough, feisty, petite Beverly leaves for work at about 7:30 a.m. and returns home generally at 9:00 p.m. or later. She runs before work to keep in shape. She is the mother of an energetic four year old and an excellent cook to boot. She thrives on her intellect and enjoys being the determined, focused person that we see. "Breakneck is my routine speed," she quips.

"At Christmas time, I always make marmalade for family and friends. It's my yearly tradition. Everyone expects it. But this last Christmas, I was so busy at work, I failed to realize that I didn't have enough pectin until I was in the middle of the process of cooking. It's a timing thing, you see, and the pectin really does need to go in at a certain moment. I also didn't have enough time to buy more and didn't feel comfortable asking my husband to go get some for us since he was working in his studio downstairs. So, I used what I had and cooked the ingredients twice to force it to work. It didn't work. The organic orange peel floating around in it gave the marmalade a festive appearance, but it was runny. I even tried a fancy packaging strategy by wrapping the jars with beautiful ribbon.

"When I passed them out on Christmas Eve, I tried to joke about it, 'I have a product disclaimer to announce. It's a little thin. We failed to meet the production deadline. Sorry,' I laughed. To be honest, I was embarrassed. I really only had myself to be angry with, right? I had only slotted in one half-day to handle my yearly holiday ritual and didn't allow for any production contingencies."

Bev was gypped of the magic of her holiday tradition, and so was everyone else. She applies the Module Principle, which is about planning, no...make that squeezing in things in perfectly timed slots throughout the day. It's an efficiency concept and it just doesn't work.

No matter how well-designed modules are, they don't allow much, if any, room for error. And they certainly don't allow for the time needed to enjoy or savor the activity. Only Bev had the power to insist on taking the time she needed to make the marmalade properly. Something else would have had to go. Perhaps she would have had to ask her husband to go to the store and buy more pectin, but she didn't want to disrupt whatever he was doing (no doubt important) and let her miscalculation show (no doubt her fault).

> ✂ It is clear that the To Do List is long and contains many important things. What isn't clear is when we became our To Do Lists.

TO THE POINT

Stuck in the prevailing mode, we cannot fathom that there is time to choose something now and something later, or to unchoose multitasking, integration, and whatever else has managed to overwhelm our To Do Lists. As women, we have retained from our female history the tendency to blame ourselves; we sincerely believe that failure to accomplish everything we set out to do well must be our own shortcoming. We cling stubbornly to the Module Principle in an effort to fit it all in and keep our self-respect intact.

Disheartened by this insane way of managing life, many women take a slow and very private journey to disenchantment, sometimes talking to their best friends or partners, sometimes talking to no one. Some suddenly sink into disaffection, taking even themselves unawares.

Making matters still worse, we often feel at fault, ashamed, and isolated. We do not feel we have any right to speak up. Like Bev, we might have solved the "assertiveness" issues in the boardroom, but not at home. Our self-esteem fluctuates wildly, several times a day because the critics and peer pressure continue to loom large....

Near the end of the twentieth century, when Jane Swift was running for Lieutenant Governor of Massachusetts, she became pregnant. While answering the many queries related to issues about serving in public office, she was also questioned about her child-care plans. Swift replied, "This whole debate about whether or not women should be able to combine work and family—I thought we'd moved past that at least several decades ago."[7]

Well, we hadn't then and we haven't now. Imagine treating a male candidate this way, asking that prospective father about his parenting intentions or stance in the breast-feeding versus bottle-feeding debate.

Time has passed. Ms. Swift's babies have grown. We've had a woman as the Majority Leader in the United States Senate. More women are running for President. Yet, women are still being harangued with patronizing, sexist questions to account for their choices.

The cultural conversation loudly speaks about the worth of families, but does nothing to help women with children who need or want to work. *San Francisco Chronicle* columnist Joan Ryan quotes a *Time* magazine cover headline: "Babies vs. Career. Which should come first for women who want both? The harsh facts about fertility." It's not about fertility! How Ms. Ryan counters this is eminently quotable: "What about the harsh facts about the workplace?"

> "...the message...women...are guilty...for counting on fertility technology to make them mothers in middle age.
>
> "You know why so many high-achieving women have no children? ...It isn't their bodies that have betrayed them, but their bosses. ...In 21st-century America, a place of gaudy reverence for family values, we still see child-rearing as an individual problem rather than a societal one.
>
> "...women don't need the next generation in fertility drugs, [they need]...workplace legislation."[8]

Even in the face of these astute insights, polarization, competition, and judgments still persist within our own ranks. With the pressure always high, as we struggle against confusion and lack of resolve, it's all too easy to criticize each others' choices. This error is costly. It keeps us on guard, a destructive kind of hypervigilance that sets us up as overfunctioning adversaries.

> ✂ The same old race is on. To risk running or risk not running, that is the question

⌂   Okay, rant time! Since new mothers make up the largest percentage (65%) of people going into the work force, companies have taken up the topic of breast-pumping at the workplace in the usual sensitive fashion—"supporting" women to breast-feed their children for longer. Statistics show that women who work outside the home tend to give up on breast-feeding their infants after about twelve weeks. Why does Corporate America care? Because it "discovered" that breast milk actually produces healthier babies and that breast-feeding mothers take less time off work (three days less a year to deal with their sick children). Millions of dollars on health care costs and lost days of work productivity can be saved if the babies drink more breast milk and less formula. Talk about faux formulas for families! Holy crow!

The business plan? Give mother-worker the right to one hour off (unpaid!) in every workday to pump in privacy. But where? ... the bathroom stall? her cubicle? her car? We can trust that committees will be organized to work out the proper etiquette: an option to bring your own pump perhaps? Strikingly, ample statistics support that there is a difference for both mother and child when breast milk comes from a bottle provided by a caregiver and when it comes from the interaction between a mother and her child, but these data aren't getting much press.

High Price at the Pump

As we go to press, Sophie Currier, a new mother with a doctorate in neuroscience from Harvard, has taken her plea for time to breast-feed her four-month-old baby during her medical board exams to the Massachusetts Supreme Court. The request for additional time (an hour per exam day) has been denied! The argument *against* giving her more time is that "forty-five minutes is sufficient" (it isn't) "…for a nursing mother…to eat, drink, and use the restroom and to fully and properly express breast milk using an electric pump two times over the course of eight hours."[9] We think that the position of the National

Board of Medical Examiners is completely wrong-headed. Even the inventors of the mechanical milking devices themselves did not intend for the expression of breast milk to be an express-lane experience. The breast pump may have its place in modern society, but the product does not compare with, as they say in their own product's press release, "a human baby, whose lips tend to move rhythmically as the baby suckles...[thereby stimulating] the discharge of milk."[10] It could be argued that the Board's insistence on forcing this new mother into an overfunctioning Milking Module in the midst of her important exam merely pays lip service to their own creed: *First Do No Harm.*

> ✂ The corporate measuring stick creates an occupational hazard—reluctance to advocate the human measuring stick.

TO THE POINT

Many aspects of women's lives are under siege. We fret even about our effectiveness at home. This used to be our one clear domain, a low-status place, but a familiar one that we ruled and treasured. For a number of decades, it became more and more trivialized and devalued by us. Now, regardless of whether we want to be there or not, we find ourselves home less and less. Yet, we feel responsible for how it isn't all working out. Social critics, of course, are quick to point their fingers in our direction. We'd better hurry and solve it. Their oversimplified suggestions like "Just integrate; schedule personal time thoughtfully; communicate skillfully..." and quick-fixes like the module method for micro-managing life propel us into guilt. So we anxiously overfunction to get it right.

Anna Jen summed up the truth, "It doesn't matter how efficiently you go down the wrong road."

PRESCRIPTION:

Take stock of which over-simplified stuff you've bought into that you could consider dumping.

Your Turn!: No structured exercise this chapter.

Instead, experiment with the following: Do something that is fun and aimless. Or, do nothing at all. See if, over a short time span (10 – 15 minutes), you can pass from uncomfortable/restless with this to comfortable/restful. If not, don't beat yourself up. You can do it again some time.

✄ Calm got lost long ago and may take a while to find.

5
THE INVISIBLE DRIVER
How the Overfunctioning Trance Got Behind the Wheel

"Now! Now!" cried the Queen. "Faster! Faster!" And they went so fast that at last they seemed to skim through the air, hardly touching the ground with their feet till, suddenly, just as Alice was getting quite exhausted, they stopped, and she found herself sitting on the ground, breathless and giddy...The Queen propped her up against a tree, and said kindly, "You may rest a little now...." Alice looked round her in great surprise. "Why, I do believe we've been under this tree the whole time! Everything's just as it was!" ..."Of course it is," said the Queen. "What would you have it?" ... "Well, in our country," said Alice, still panting a little, "you'd generally get to somewhere else—if you ran very fast for a long time, as we've been doing...." "A slow sort of country!" said the Queen. "Now, here, you see, it takes all the running you can do to keep in the same place. If you want to get somewhere else, you must run at least twice as fast as that!"[11]

If you want to get somewhere...

The Red Queen proclaims, "It takes all the running you can do to keep in the same place." Initially, Alice feels giddy and exhilarated, "skimming through the air hardly touching the ground." But, before long, she becomes breathless and bewildered and then frustrated, disappointed, discouraged, and spent. Eventually, she complains, "We've been under this tree the whole time! Everything is just as it was." Her Majesty is not sympathetic.

It gets worse. As the Red Queen matter-of-factly admonishes Alice: "Of course, it is!" ...to get somewhere "...you must run at least twice as fast as that!" She explains nothing. Alice must simply yield to the Queen's "truth." Alice is being indoctrinated into the rules and norms in the version of overfunctioning practiced in Wonderland. The Red Queen's pressure on Alice to accept what she herself believes to be the right way to live is inscrutable and unrelenting. "It takes all the running you can do to keep in the same place." There is no opportunity to consider the merits or meaning of these procedures. There is no choice but to obey.

A similar phenomenon occurs in families and society. Children are as vulnerable to the adults in their lives as Alice is to the powerful queen. When someone in authority asserts something, reasonable or not, it sticks. Over time, we gradually understand *what is expected and respond automatically, regardless of what we might think or feel.*

The Red Queen acts as if all her ideas are completely logical, sensible, and correct—even when they appear quite illogical and confusing, even weird, to Alice and to us. For example, she dismisses Alice's concerns with a belittling judgment: "[your country is]...a slow sort of country!" In this interaction, the Queen conveys a basic rule to Alice: complaining and questioning are *not* okay in Wonderland. In our family life, too, we learn lessons to act, speak, and feel in certain ways established by Mom and Dad (or other powerful people). Their messages can be communicated visually, audibly, or behaviorally. Comments, gestures, and facial expressions and judgments, punishments, and rewards all constitute programming devices, particularly when we are young.

Some indoctrinations are openly expressed; many indoctrinations are covert. Although never stated directly, we get the meaning loud and clear. Mom gave us "that look" or made the loaded little remark in "that" tone of voice. Family directives, no matter how subtle, put us into trance-like states in which we absorb the messages and automatically behave according to the "rules." Core programming varies from household to household and may include: "You're the best." "You're the worst." "You'll be loved only if you meet the following demands." "I'm always right. Don't question that. Think the way I do." "Blame someone else for everything." "Blame yourself for everything." "I'm too fragile for you to contradict me."

Because trances form a large segment of everybody's emotional memory bank and reflexes, as adults, we fall prey to being re-entranced. Even when painful, that same old stuff feels oddly comfortable— it's so familiar, after all. It feels like intuition, just doin' what comes naturally; but it's "bad intuition." A tidal wave of hypnotic messages from the *Overfunctioning Woman Trance* crashes over us: "Be thin." "Do more." "Just do it." "You can do it all." "If you want to get somewhere...you must run...twice as fast." "Juggling is out. Integration is in." We are always at risk.

As a culture, women are on a socially accepted *Overfunctioning Automatic Pilot* governed by: "I ought to because my husband needs me to. I ought to because my children need me to. I ought to because my mother told me to. I ought to because the boss is waiting. I ought to because my agent said so. I ought to because the sisterhood of women is depending on it. I ought to because this is what everyone does. I ought to because some of this is really interesting (though, I'm not sure anymore which of it is really interesting to *me*). I ought to because, if I don't, *I'll lose ground.*" What exactly "losing ground" means is vague but is accepted without questioning.

We have misgivings about the content and pace of our lives, but stopping to consider this may lead to unwelcome conclusions and feelings. Therefore, we embrace the cycle of overfunctioning, though it's a vicious one, and continue to buy the payoffs: glory (sometimes, but not always), money (sometimes, but not always), and a sense of satisfaction (sometimes, but not always).

> ✍ We are driving and driven in every sense of the word.

As we gain momentum on this downslide of disenchantment, very serious consequences catch up with us, eventually bringing sadness, irritability, a lack of real passion about anything, fatigue, depression, and, sometimes, physical illness. Most scary of all is feeling almost nothing—a kind of numbness and detachment.

Let's look more closely at the *Overfunctioning Woman Trance* and listen to these stories from the perspective that people are acting like hypnotized subjects on autopilot. Rita, a wife, a mother, and an escrow officer, is another one behind the wheel. She is moving so quickly, fueled by her heady pace and rush of adrenaline, that she has no time to question things. These feelings are, no doubt, familiar to us all: pressured, proud, important, exhilarated, exhausted, burdened, frenzied, frayed, fried, frazzled, trapped, excited, breathless, cocky, scared, indispensable. This is Rita as she:

...Be Comin' 'Round the Mountain

"Because I want my children to grow up in the country, I drive to the city twice a week and stay in an apartment for a few days in a row for work. This time, I left before the sun went down on a Sunday evening in order to avoid the Monday morning traffic. I was listening to my book on tape because, well, it's actually the only time I can fit in some pleasure reading. But even that didn't keep me awake. It was a hot summer afternoon and I dozed off. I hit a tree head on. The car spun around and ended up over a steep cliff in a dark forest.

"After careening down the mountainside, bumping wildly into trees that knocked the car from side to side, I finally came to a complete stop. It took me some time to orient myself. The sun was setting, and the lights went out in my car. I heard a faint drip-drip-drip sound. Too much TV, I guess, but I couldn't shake the emerging concern that the car might blow up. I stretched my arm behind me into the backseat and fumbled around quickly for my shoes. Though worried about the car exploding any second, I actually took the time to reach into the glove compartment for my cheques (in case someone found them down here in the gully, like anyone had been down here for a hundred years). What was I thinking!?!

"Then, I swung my legs around, stepped out, and dropped into four or five feet of loamy soil. This was virgin forest. I swear, I don't even know how anyone would get down here. I felt an urgency to get away from the car, which was still dripping. My heart was pounding as I fought my way through the deeply carpeted forest and crawled up, up towards the top of the mountain with my purse flopping off my shoulder, and dusty tree debris filling my mouth and lungs. What a mess!

"When I reached the road above, covered with dirt, pine needles, and redwood bark, I flagged down a passing car. I must have looked like Sasquatch. A man got out. When I saw him, I panicked. EEEK! I was alone on a deserted road with a stranger. So I started to run in the opposite direction. Seeing my fear, he set his cell phone down on the ground and yelled, 'Here, it's okay, Lady. Use my phone. I'll wait in my car.' When the policeman came, he asked if I needed to go to a hospital. Of course, I said, 'No, I'm fine. I just bumped my chest.'

"As I proceeded to describe where the car had gone over the cliff, I looked down and saw that, in my haste to leave home, I had forgotten to make sure that my shoes matched. 'Oh, my God,' I thought. 'My shoes don't match!' All I could hear, as the policeman spoke, was my mother's voice, 'Leaving for work without checking to see if your colors were coordinated...Rita, how could you?' A bolt of embarrassment flashed through me.

"The next day, someone at the office stood up and announced, 'Oh, by the way, Rita can't be here today. She drove off a mountain and won't make it to the meeting. But, she's okay!'

"The doctor told me to take a week off. I allowed myself two days. Then I told myself I had used my *leisure time* up and needed to get on with it. Of course, I went back to work because it is what is expected. If I don't, I'll lose ground. It is what I do. You do what you have to do. You take care of it. In a way, it's a life philosophy of *'you are self-sufficient.' There isn't an option of not doing it.*"

After her could-have-been-fatal accident, Rita brushes aside her feelings quickly—too quickly. She just whimpers slightly and moves back to her breathless pace. Speaking from the depths of her trance, Rita states, as if it were a fact: *"There isn't a question of not doing it."* She feels she has to do it all herself. She thinks she ought to. She knows she must. *These are the internal conversations of the Overfunctioning Trance.* What she, Rita, wants to do... nobody knows, especially Rita. We suspect that she is experiencing, unawares, those contrasting and conflicting emotions characteristic of the overfunctioning trance state: from indispensable to trapped and everything in between....

TO THE POINT

Rather than examining her assumptions, Rita is run by them. Finally, we women are big players in the big game. We temporarily gloss over our self-doubts. Our expanded opportunities and important work keep us too busy, too proud, and too pressured to think about them.

> ✋ When you are overfunctioning, you can't feel much.
> You can't think clearly either. Your self-esteem is always on the line.
> And you're always on the move.

Anna Jen recalls a time "…when I had it close to perfect, both in terms of performance and my total loyalty to the 'program.' I was on autopilot all the way, and I didn't know it. Overfunctioning, all the way, and I couldn't see it. Numb and wasn't feeling it. My performance was flawless, but I wasn't enjoying my life, and I didn't know that either." Anna Jen is:

⌂ Torn Apart and Doesn't Notice

"One morning, (7:30 a.m.), one of our three children was sick. My husband said he was booked up and rushed out the door without further discussion. He assumed that because I have a home office, I was 'at home' which, of course, translated into 'she's available.' Actually, I had a very important meeting to attend thirty-five miles away and a project deadline that I needed to work on at the computer. But, rather than dealing with Ken (that's another story) or (not to mention) my boss, I just took a deep breath and, ever efficiently, moved into action…

"One: Postpone the important client meeting until 4 p.m. and do this charmingly, without a hint that anything is on the verge of unraveling. Two: Spend twenty minutes pulling project materials together and faxing them to my assistant to polish and deliver to the conference room, where I will need to be present via table top intercom phone for the meeting. Three: Call the doctor (not until 9:00 a.m. when the office opens) and set up an immediate appointment for my sick child. During numbers 1, 2, and 3, I am comforting her on my lap. Four: Dress child and self while singing to her to soothe the pain and distract her. Five: Drive child to the doctor. Six: Get prescription filled (long line, new cashier unfamiliar with cash register…Figures!) and return home. Seven: Continue working on the project; while Eight: Periodically changing tapes for daughter to listen to and heating soup for her to eat and hugging her. Nine: Call a babysitter to be in the house while I... Ten: Take the conference call at 4 p.m. and do well (of course.) P.S.: It all went without a hitch. Not a comma was out of place on the paper, and, though no one could see me, barely a hair was out of place on my head. My sick daughter finally curled up to sleep. Then, naturally, my other two children came home and it was time to cook dinner!"

Both Rita and Anna Jen are exceptionally adept at overfunctioning—they are members of the Ideal-Awesome Overfunctioning Group, like Jaclyn. They have it down! But, don't you find it curious that Rita doesn't think to allow herself time to heal even after driving off a cliff! That Anna Jen neither experiences exhilaration nor perceives her solo victory as strange and empty? That she doesn't even try to enroll her husband to help with *their* sick child! And, knowing Anna Jen will handle things just fine, he doesn't even bother to check in during the day or get home early enough to prepare dinner or help out with the children.

Also, let's not forget the other adult players within the larger context of these two competent, astounding women. Rita's husband, a really nice guy actively involved in child-rearing, urges her to slow down for a few days, but this has no impact on her. Rita's manager, in a blasé manner, sums up the situation: "SHE DROVE OFF A MOUNTAIN, BY THE WAY.... And she's fine." His operating assumptions are apparent! The boss is in the same trance, barely skipping a beat over Rita's serious accident as he rushes to his next meeting.

✂ When you're in the *Overfunctioning Trance* and help is available, you don't notice it.

When asked why she didn't call on her husband to help out, Anna Jen replies, with resignation, "Because it would have eaten up too much time to explain what needed to be done. Since it was obvious, I resented having to explain. Then there's the part of me that yearns and desires to take care of my own child, no matter what, not just to be a mother, but *to mother* in the deepest sense of the word." Anna Jen's bosses never even knew she had a problem—they didn't think to ask why she needed to attend the meeting by phone. She, in the most professional way, did not let on. She covered her tracks (and her emotions) seamlessly.

TO THE POINT

It's upsetting to finally realize that, for years, you've been walking around hypnotized in many aspects of your life. At the same time, breaking out of trances is frightening because it leads to those unwelcome feelings. It is normal to have strong emotional reactions when you begin to stir into awareness. As you identify your trances, try to recognize and accept all feelings that emerge, however intense they may be. Anxiety and anger are very likely to appear. They are healthy responses to your discoveries. But, they may seem strange and unhealthy to you.

> ✋ Your self-esteem so depends on overfunctioning that you're scared to drop anything, even temporarily.

Prioritizing—as the slogan goes—eludes us because we need first to discover what's stopping us from figuring out what matters most to us. In light of this, it is easy to see why advising women simply to "learn to prioritize effectively," as so many periodicals and books do, is misguided. It's premature; no wonder we can't do it. This is the point: Only when you can see *what is influencing* the choices you are making, can you make different choices, ones which might better resonate with what you personally and truly value.

> ✂ Feelings of comfort and discomfort about doing something come primarily from old trance messages; they're unreliable.

"Now, here, you see, it takes all the running you can do to keep in the same place. If you want to get somewhere else, you must run at least twice as fast as that!" says the Red Queen, inducting Alice into the frantic Wonderland trance. "There isn't a question of *not* doing it..." says Rita, long ago inducted into the *Overfunctioning Trance*.

Before taking important actions, examine your (automatic) inclinations. What we call "intuition" may well be based on dubious programming. It can serve as a short-sighted comfort zone, setting up a wall against newness, risk, and the unknown, all the things that generate anxiety—and growth. You can trust intuition only after you've tested it against habits, trances, and paths of least resistance.

PRESCRIPTION: It's imperative to know when to trust an automatic reaction and when not to. Force yourself to pause. Begin to evaluate whether the intuition (feeling within) you are following will likely produce more status quo (often bad intuition) or a positive change (often good intuition). Assessing this will help you to make decisions based on current data and present circumstances, not past programming.

Think about this: AUTOMATIC PILOT. Are you still attracted to a giddy, wild ride like Rita and Anna Jen were for so long? And Bev still is. Or, are you ready to get behind the wheel and drive differently?

Your turn! AUTO-DEFINITIONS
Topic: Automatic assumptions and consequent actions
Purpose: To dissect these assumptions and reevaluate their appropriateness in present time

A) Are there any specific phrases that pop into your head associated with immediate action? For example, as Rita would say, "There isn't a question of not doing it." Examine closely what these phrases actually mean.

B) List some auto-definitions that are important to you.

C) On a separate piece of paper, set up new definitions for these internal commandments.

D) Picture your particular version of the TT. Now, fill in names and actions at each of the three points, like this:

```
_____
_____
_____
_____
```

Overfunctioning

Impossible People   **Low Self Esteem**

```
_____                    _____
_____                    _____
_____                    _____
```

E) For instance, with "There isn't a question of not doing it," why isn't there a question? ...of not doing it. Or, the question ought to be "Will I do it or won't I do it? Or "Must I do it?" And, if so, "Why must I do it?"

6
TAKING THE WHEEL
Good/Bad Intuition and Relationships

Take a deep breath… Let it out S-L-O-W-L-Y….

Seize the Day by Sofia Haas (age 17)

Pluck each day as if it were
a succulent peach…
gently, gracefully.
If the precious cargo of the highest branch
entices,
let vital energy transport you.
Reach and attain an unsurpassed zenith
—a summit of delight.
Refuse to listen to that voice
raspy and thin
which disclaims, defies your dreams.
Relish in the pungent flesh of that
sweet sphere that Nature brings.
Glide into the clouds on whim
without begging leave
of those who came before.
Let dawn's new sun offer joy
and hope
to your bedraggled being.
Don't abandon life
empty, crumpled
by the road.

Seize the day! Most likely, the To Do List is so long that it's impossible to get time and space for plucking those succulent peaches. Ten-year-old Ashley couldn't glide into the clouds on whim! If a ten year old doesn't have time and space for this, how can we expect that for ourselves? Or worse, have we stopped thinking we deserve something so…so…lyrical, poetic, frivolous, whimsical, imaginative, magical? Caught in the TT, it's difficult even to see the sky. Glide into the clouds on whim? Not a likely option! Must we "beg leave" for our joy?

Overfunctioning is built on pleasing/accommodating lessons taught to little girls: "Don't be selfish." "You're the girl." "Don't upset your father." "You need to make him (father, uncles, grandfather, boyfriends, husband, bosses, teachers, any other males around) feel important." "You're Daddy's little star." "Help Mom." "Dad's been working so hard." "Let's not tell him that just yet." "It's unbecoming!" "Why don't we ask your father if this is okay?" "That's not OK for a girl." "Don't bother him with something so trivial." "That's not lady-like!" "Don't be so loud!" "Don't upset your mother." "Mom's been working so hard." "Don't be so smart." "Show some respect." "Go help!" "Don't be so aggressive." "That's not nice." "Watch your language, young lady." "Why don't you go *help*, honey?" *Statements such as these become trance inductions and determine our actions in the future.*

HOW TRANCES ARE FORMED

When family members send distress signals, as girls and women, we frequently "cope" by accommodating (obeying) their requests. We respond to whatever is being sought, even if it means interrupting something that is very important to us. Even though it's often at our own expense, we remember, "Don't be so selfish!" Distinctions blur between contributing our fair share (with chores and other kinds of help) and sacrificing all, on demand.

Mary Pipher has analyzed this phenomenon in her brilliant book, *Reviving Ophelia*. She observes: "Girls become 'female impersonators' who fit their whole selves into small, crowded spaces. Vibrant, confident girls become shy, doubting young women. Girls stop thinking, 'Who am I? What do I want?' and start thinking, 'What must I do to please others?'"[12]

A message commonly sent to us is that some key family member's anxiety is rising. This is the SOS for us to rally into action by helping out; we must make that discomfort go down or keep it from going higher. We will endure practically anything that will take this family member's attention off what feels threatening.

From early on, these placating themes predominate. They form the basis for those autopilot responses which drive us in later years. Our responses will feel natural—intuitive—but they would most aptly be described as *trance behavior*. Taken to the extreme, one may be expected to guess what to do without being asked, and, oddly enough, this too feels perfectly natural. It keeps us in a state of hypervigilance and hyper-doing (overfunctioning), which, ultimately, contributes to our stress and fatigue—our *bedraggled being*.

Unless we recognize this trance programming and its specific inductions, this type of caretaking, more often than not, will remain part of our Job Description for life. The trance-driven sense of "knowing what's right"—that is, making decisions based on what feels right (intuition) —can be characterized as following "bad intuition." This is not a reliable basis for taking action because it can lead to costly mistakes. This then leads to overfunctioning which obstructs and narrows our ability to see our own goals and paths to fulfillment.

🖐 We've been inducted into saving the day, not seizing it.

When the underlying motive is to do it for *them*, even achieving something wonderful can feel lousy, driven, tense, or even desperate. Under pressure to save the day, our actions bring us, as achievers, no substantial joy or comfort. "I *have* to get those A's, that field goal, that lead in the play, that date, to reassure and/or rescue him, her, them." There's no choice really, and the stakes are high, especially for a child or young adult. In this way, accommodating and overfunctioning become linked. Our true interest in the accomplishment gets foggy and, at a certain point, it becomes no longer relevant.

Because trances are so powerful, it's hard to see them and harder still to budge them. Learning to recognize when you are "under the influence" of your trance can help you begin to break its power over you. Trances are pervasive in our friendships and marriages, and in our choice of mentors, real estate agents, investment advisors, therapists, you name it.

The following is an example of a how a trance induction develops. It may sound funny, but look how Merry's childhood "pink trance" carried forward as an overfunctioning accommodation pattern in her adult life. Merry is:

Into Pink

Merry always adored pink—or thought she did. In fact, it was her mother who favored the traditional girl color. The child "loved" pink and also most everything else her mother liked. The induction was happily announced and repeated often and warmly, "Merry's favorite color is pink! Let's buy pink curtains, bedspreads, clothing, birthday cake icing...." So, of course, Merry carried the pink banner always. She had the pink room, pink dresses, pink ice cream, pink crayons.... In the presence of others, her mother would chant, "Merry and I are similar in so many ways, don't you know." The far-reaching significance of this often-repeated, deeply imbedded mantra only became clear over many years' time.

"If it was pink, I'd gravitate to it," Merry reflects. "I only became aware of my 'pink trance' in stages. First, when I went shopping to select the bridesmaids' dresses for my wedding... I was 24. Naturally, Mom came along. She beelined for the pink ones. To my surprise, I knew immediately that I didn't like them. This was the first time I ever saw a relationship between my mother and my believing that I loved pink. Always before, choosing pink had felt easy, natural, true. I thought Mom was just supporting me. In that instant though, I felt like pink was being shoved down my throat. When I told Mother, 'No thanks, I want my bridesmaids to wear teal,' I felt really tense. Sure enough, she was offended and gave me a hurt look. 'But you've *always* loved pink!' she exclaimed. I did end up picking the color I wanted, but I felt really guilty about it.

"During the next few years, it slowly dawned on me that my marriage, which also felt *perfectly natural*, was based on my submitting to my husband's opinions about everything [old mother-trance at work]. Even though he was always remarking about how much he and I were on the same page, in actuality, he was always telling me how I should think and feel. I was uncomfortable with many of his opinions but would always acquiesce to his pronouncements even if it meant I had to go to extra lengths to accommodate myself to them.

"Then, one night, while taking a bath, I was staring at a bar of pink soap. It reminded me of my mother's chant, "Merry just loves pink, don't you know. Merry and I are similar in so many ways." I experienced a wave of sickening discomfort and then got really upset. 'No, Merry does not like pink, damn it!' I thought to myself. There I sat in the tub, pissed about pink. I realized how I was such a wimp with my mom all the time and then how I had rolled right along to do the same with my husband. I did not sleep well that night. The next morning, like a wild woman, I began grabbing all pink possessions and dumping them out of my life. Ten bags for Goodwill®. For the next few months, all sorts of connections and implications kept coming to me. I began to look at my marriage and saw all the ways I accepted my husband's point of view and demands and didn't even consider my own."

TO THE POINT

The Pleasing/Accommodating Trance, which so many of us share, has enormous significance. It can easily lead to a lifestyle of overfunctioning and surrendering our self-esteem to the approval/satisfaction of others. We offer our entire personality to the needs of others. And, of course, this makes us great prey for IPs, just like Merry was. The TT thus locks us tightly in its grip.

Placating and accommodating responses sound like this: "Of course, I'll do it." "I don't mind." "I'm very sorry." "It's really okay." "Is it okay with you for me to do this?" "I see you're feeling bad. I'll help." "I won't do it if you don't want me to." "I guess it doesn't matter that much." "I'm wrong. You're probably right." "Is there anything I can do?" "It's my fault." "Whatever you want." "I was probably irrational." "Oh, I feel so guilty." "Did I behave badly? I will really try to be better." "It's probably PMS. I'm not myself." "I know I was reacting emotionally." "I'll try harder." "I'll work harder." "Don't worry. I'll take care of it...them...you...." "I'm very sorry."

When you look at it from this context, it's easier to see how knowing what *we* want—what matters most to us—can elude us. Actually, knowing what we want becomes a liability because it could make us conflicted and discontented. And, it most certainly would upset the status quo. Then, we'd really appear uppity.

⌄ Let's examine another personal trance induction, given to Alma Mae from her cradle on. Her task has always been to shore up a fearful, insecure woman—her mother. Alma Mae is told:

"You Don't Really Want To"

"My mother would always say, '*You don't really want to* do that Alma Mae.... *You don't really want to* eat that cake (age 2).... *You don't really want to* go out for Halloween (age 5).... *You don't really want to* go to that party (age 13).... *You don't really want to* go to a college out of state (age 17).... *You don't really want to* write that controversial article (age 26)....' My doing any of these things would have made my mother anxious.

"So, I decided to become an accountant. Mother was happy because it is safe and prestigious. But I hate it. I've considered changing careers, but I don't know what people will think. I'm overscrutinous about any decisions I make. I really don't know what I want, and I feel too guilty to really go for it anyway. So I just keep trying to make my life work as is, but I'm not happy."

Alma Mae entered a career that initially *felt* right ("intuitively" felt right, get it?), but it sprang from her mother's needs. Her mom's inductions can be summarized as: "I know what you want better than you do. Don't do anything that might make *me* uncomfortable. Keeping my anxiety at bay supersedes everything else." Alma Mae's Pleasing/ Accomodating Trance has pervaded her life. She overfunctions because she is over-solicitous—always wondering what others think and fearing their judgments. Guilt and worry dominate her thoughts.

We assume that the price for dumping the typical, accommodating overfunctioning trance will be high. The notion is anxiety-producing, disorienting…We'll lose our place, our role (in the family, other relationships, our jobs). So we just grind on with what we know how to do, even when it's clear that we're not happy with it.

Sometimes, a person breaks out of accommodating in quite dramatic fashion. One hears the occasional story of a woman everybody knows is placid, meek, unassuming, and cares what the neighbors think, who suddenly gets up one morning and leaves her partner with no warning. Or a person who turns on her good friend, bursts out with a long list of grievances, and severs the relationship. Things have accumulated over the top, and the first authentic action taken (probably in years) is extreme and often irreparable.

Both Merry and Alma Mae overfunction (while walking on eggshells) in order to reduce the anxiety of someone they love. It becomes a way of life.

Both women must become aware of what is throwing them into these automatic pilot responses. Only then can they stop and see themselves capable of thinking differently and doing things differently. If you develop good intuition, you will drive yourself out of the Treacherous Triangle. *This is a very important point because you can't stop overfunctioning until you can figure out what is keeping you on the automatic pilot. Only then can you begin to articulate what you'd rather be doing with yourself, your time, your energy, your life.*

🖐 "Women often know how everyone in their family thinks and feels except themselves." ~ Pipher[13]

BAD DRIVING/GOOD DRIVING

Intelligence, level of education, and sophistication will not protect you from family or societal trances. It takes Dr. Chris Landis a long time to awaken from the trance induced by her mother's indifference towards her. She fashioned herself into an overfunctioner in an attempt to gain attention in her family. In this story, Dr. Landis recognizes her old trance programming playing out, overshadowing her good judgment in present time. In the end, she is no longer willing to turn:

A Blind Eye

"As a girl, I always had my sight set on becoming a veterinarian or a doctor. I was the youngest of four, an only girl with three older brothers who were jocks. My mother herself was an avid sports enthusiast. My brothers would be playing basketball and Mom would bring lemonade to the court. The delivery service stopped there.

The tasty treats never made it back to my little animal hospital in the backyard. I didn't feel any specific disapproval from her; I just chalked it up to the fact that some people get queasy about wounded birds…things like that. Yet, I did go out of my way to try to gain some recognition, like making my family sit through detailed presentations. They would endure my little 'animal shows' (with various taunts and teasing), but the conversation would quickly turn to which team or player was doing such and such. I always tried to brush it off with good humor and would fuel up even more for my next show. At last, I hoped, I would surely astonish them....

"After medical school, I interviewed for a research fellowship, working for a well-known doctor. Though he was rather cold and formal, I felt very much at home from the get go. Even though I was the only woman, I wasn't intimidated because I'd been tops in my graduating class and was used to being the lone female recipient of dumb male jokes.

"Hard-working as always, one day I discovered that there was a flaw in the design of the study. When I mentioned it to one of the other doctors with whom I had developed a level of trust, he dismissed my concerns with, 'I'm not in a position to question the design and neither are you. And besides, I doubt it's very serious.'

"Several other colleagues, though mildly sympathetic, also shrugged me off. 'Surely, the top guys know better, even though you're a smart cookie,' one of them commented. I didn't get angry, of course. I just turned my frustration into trying even harder, and gathering together everything I could to demonstrate that the team should be concerned about this finding. No one was interested. Finally, I mustered up the courage to bring the design problem to the attention of the lead doctor. He thanked me for my 'insights' and the conversation stopped abruptly. He was already looking down at his papers. As I lingered there, he looked up briefly and added, 'We've got it all handled, Miss... I mean, Doctor.'

"Something inside jolted me. Just then, I realized I'd unwittingly (and eagerly) walked into a reenactment of the family in which I had grown up. It was obvious to me now why it all felt so 'right.' Dr. N was my cold, dismissive mother all over again. The other doctors were my oblivious fraternity of brothers. It was all a repeat of my never-ending story of trying harder to get Mom's attention and being summarily dismissed by my brothers. I suppose that I really didn't expect anyone to respond because, fundamentally, I didn't think I deserved it. And, here's the catch: I thought I could work around it. After all, I was just the brainy girl who sat on the sidelines while Mom shown the spotlight elsewhere.

"At this point, I decided to stop the rerun. In spite of how it might look on my resume, I left the position."

In her childhood, Dr. Landis had to go to great lengths (overfunction) to get noticed by her own mother! In this work situation that resembled home (which she unconsciously recognized and chose enthusiastically—bad intuition), history repeated itself. Dr. Landis tried harder and harder, overcompensating as a way to cope with the insults and discounts she was receiving. Finally, she woke up. She was able to make a conscious decision about how she deserved to be treated. From then on, she was more alert to this particular trance that had driven her to overfunctioning in adulthood. Looking clearly at her situation, she knew she needed to extract herself from it. She was then free to develop her good intuition and follow it.

We willingly enter the fire of our old trance-based reactions from childhood. These often form the foundation for our overfunctioning responses in adulthood. To get safely out of the destructive force field that trances create, often we must act in a way that can seem counterintuitive. Though she had entered strange and anxiety-ridden territory, Dr. Landis could sense she was on a new and healthy track.

Remy, however, takes overfunctioning to a masochistic extreme. Imprisoned in the TT, suppressing her negative feelings, she literally—physically—becomes:

Her Own Worst Enemy

"I was a marketing executive in the advertising industry, and I'm also the mother of a small boy. My job was stressful and demanding. The company was going through hard times. Customers were leaving us in droves, and I was at the eye of the storm, responsible for all customer correspondence. At the time, I was married to an artist. He was talented and charismatic. I believed in him and his work. To me, his art was so much more meaningful than my career. I guess it's something I had secretly wanted for myself when I was younger, but did not pursue it because the risk was too great. I grew up on the wrong side of the tracks, so to speak, in an otherwise highly intellectual, cultured, and wealthy town.

"Like many artists, he struggled to make money. And because, having been brought up on a reservation, he came from a truly depressed culture, I somehow found myself both resonating with his struggle and charging in to save the day. Marketing wasn't his long suit so I took over for him the business part of being an artist. I created mailing lists. I developed a marketing strategy. I set up appointments for him. I took all of this on, along with working my usual 60 hours a week and commuting 10 hours.

"After a while, I began to resent the pressures on me. I was covering my husband's lavish personal spending habits as well as the business debt he had taken on. I was helping him with marketing and customer relationships. But when I'd try to tell him what I thought ought to be a priority and how to follow through, he turned a deaf ear. He spent his time doing what he wanted. I spent my time trying to bail out his sinking boat. I had almost no time for my son and not a minute for myself.

"Inside, I was seething, *but I wouldn't let myself feel it.* Instead, I tossed and turned at night, waking early to go for a joyless run. One day, I went to the hairdresser, and she pointed out a bald spot on my hairline about the size of a fifty-cent piece. It was only a few short months later that my hair was falling out by the handful. It took some persistence to find a doctor who could give me an accurate diagnosis. In the end, it seems that I had created such a distortion of my immune system that it began attacking my hair follicles. There was nothing to be done. Within six months, I was completely bald, like a space alien. As if that weren't a bad enough blow to my self-esteem, my husband left me too. The irony is that he ended up with a woman who is completely dependent on him."

✄ If you can't access your feelings, you can't identify what's wrong and take the steps to change it.

We women can pay dearly for continuing the role dictated by our trances...shaken self-confidence, apathy, passivity, vagueness, depression, insomnia.... At its worst, we can suffer from chronic stress and fatigue syndromes or immune system weakness (like Remy did). Eventually, we can lose our vibrancy and nerve. Routinely, when we seek help from our doctors with an array of vague complaints and/or physical symptoms, they offer us a smorgasbord of mood-altering medications. All too often, this is another attempt at "the quick fix." Although medications have their place when physiological tests confirm a chemical imbalance, drugs can otherwise disconnect us further from our feelings and authentic selves. We can end up even more lost. Inevitably, some of us turn to even more meds.

GOOD GIRL/BAD GIRL ⌂

Overfunctioning trances commonly exhibit themselves in two forms—the traditional "good" girl making nice (as described in earlier examples) and the "bad" uppity girl making trouble, shouting "I'll show you; you can't mess with me." These styles appear to be opposites. However, they are two sides of the same coin because both are driven by the need to be *reactive*, usually to men or women in very powerful positions. We either please them (comply) or defy them (rebel). Neither position involves making <u>free</u> decisions, independent of their desires. Both lead to the same result: overfunctioning to make it work and losing touch with what one truly feels—one's authenticity.

Dumping the placating/accommodating mode makes it possible to feel better than you ever have. Little by little, full of trepidation, Alma Mae shook off her mother-trance and began to explore and own her likes, dislikes, and priorities. Yes, her mom got upset. Alma Mae, despite her own fears and anxiety, survived all the fuss. Merry also woke up to herself, made lots of waves with her mother and husband, and found Merry. Dr. Landis has since set up her own pediatric clinic. Remy used the loss of hair and husband as a catalyst to start a self-reflecting journey away from the TT. All three women broke out of the family trances that had run them for so long and gradually learned to take actions that balanced pleasing themselves and helping others.

Sometimes it's very difficult to see what you are doing—even if you can see the poor results over and over. It may take therapy or counseling to help you crack your own personal trance code and move permanently away from it. In the world of *feel better fast* and *go for the short run, not the long term*, psychotherapy can be tough to stick with. It is a hard sell because it may, initially, make you feel worse before it can help you feel better. But good counseling can be an invaluable tool. It can make the difference by waking you up enough so that you can deal with your issues.

PRESCRIPTION: Consider what was conveyed to you when you were a child (directly and subtly) about having personal interests, being uppity, getting help, setting limits, getting annoyed, getting angry, or making a loved one angry.

Who was the leading authority talking to you and what behaviors were modeled for you? Sometimes, the trance induction is as simple and subtle as watching and imitating the important adult women in the family. They have traditionally held that all-important responsibility of preserving the peace or, at least, the status quo. Your answers will reveal some rules and "commandments" into which you have been indoctrinated (entranced). There may likely have been different expectations for males and females, children and grown-ups. Ponder whether communication of these key directives in your family was primarily done in an overt or covert manner.

Finally, spend a few moments clearing your mind of "stuff" and allow yourself to reflect on the invitation within the poem that began this chapter. Join the young poet and begin to reprogram yourself:

"*Pluck each day as if it were a succulent peach...,*" the poet proclaims. This is hard work. But it's not like sitting in traffic listening to a language tape while creating the day's grocery list or saying "I'll do it myself" about everything that comes up in your life. This is about being in touch with yourself and engaging your feelings and, from this place, moving about the world. It's a different kind of *hard work* than what you tend to think of. It is working to stay connected to yourself and "let" that count.

"*Refuse to listen to that voice, raspy and thin, which...disclaims, defies, your dreams...*" You aren't required to please everyone else at your own expense or sacrifice yourself. You don't have to be perfect or go along unquestioning and accommodating and of good cheer all the time. To wit: You can reclaim your dreams.

"*Glide into the clouds on whim without begging leave of those who came before...*" You aren't required to humble yourself in order to get someone's approval. You don't have to feel guilty or punish yourself for your shortcomings or for falling short of the expectations of others. You still deserve to take times of pleasure and freedom. Key words: glide, clouds, whim, pleasure. Key actions: no begging; no guilt.

"*Let dawn's new sun offer joy and hope to your bedraggled being...*" We are, all of us, worthy. Every one can join in, regardless of endowment. This is not just for the rich, super-talented, super-bright, super-thin, or privileged, a specific culture or favored race, or the overfunctioning woman.

"*Don't abandon life/empty, crumpled/by the road....*" Find your guiding voice of good intuition, which comes when you are free from the trances that run you.

Think about this: DETECTIVE WORK: As you are starting a new Book of You, it may help to get re-acquainted with the you of the past. Pull out some old photos of yourself at different times in your childhood. Line them up and jog your memory. See what surprises turn up, what intense emotions and forgotten events. Can you remember your slide (a la Mary Pipher) into trance? For instance, do you appear more vibrant or feisty at five than at ten? Leave the photos out for awhile so you can continue to notice and recall.

Your Turn! AUTOMATIC PILOT TRANCE EXERCISE

Topic: Trance inductions and intuition

Purpose: To recognize automatic pilot efficiently and reduce its influence; to distinguish between bad and good intuition so you can head in the direction you really want to go

If feeling naturally right could likely be bad intuition and is therefore not a trustworthy gauge for action, what is?

This is a long exercise. Go at a slow pace. There is no expiration date and the warranty won't run out.

A) Try to recognize when you are going into a trance. Can you figure out the key induction words, looks, or actions that put you under (entrance you) and make you react automatically? It will probably help to write them down. Re-create in your mind your role as a child and the rules you were following.

B) Attempt to see yourself, as if from a distance, as you act robotically. Consider whether what you are doing makes sense *in present time*. In the first few rounds of trying, your accurate perceptions may quickly fade, and you will go right on doing what you're doing. The challenge is to not feel guilty or like a failure about this. You are engaged in a re-learning *process*, not a race. The idea is to hold onto the "seeing" for longer and longer periods until it becomes obvious to you when you are entranced. At these times, you are probably repeating old dynamics with the same negative results.

C) As you get progressively more aware of when you are on Automatic Pilot, you can begin to experiment with stopping it in mid-flight. This will, of course, feel unnatural and uncomfortable at first. This is to be expected because you are changing very entrenched, bone-deep habits.

D) Questions to think about: "Is my intuition leading me towards reaching a goal I cherish, an outcome I desire? Is it addressing something that is chronically not working or something I want or need to change? Or is it leading me away, consistently failing to bring me closer to what I want?" If it's leading you away, it's probably motivated by avoidance of anxiety—wrong direction.

E) Trance-driven intuition will always lead you astray. Keep reviewing your trance list. Be persistent. It takes time to identify this phenomenon and gain control. When you do, you will find personal and societal "hypnotists" obvious and, of course, objectionable. Your self-esteem will get strong enough to resist and disengage from IPs. Can you identify some IPs in your present environment? Do you see how they keep you hooked with trance inductions, like the men at her job did with Dr. Landis?

Imagine yourself gradually loosening the hold of the TT.

BREAKING FREE
OF
THE TREACHEROUS TRIANGLE

7
WELCOMING ANXIETY
Let Your Discomfort Be Your Guide

Fable: The Sleepy Family

There once was a regular ordinary sort of family with a mother and a father and two children. At night, the mother sang the children to sleep with her special song. It always worked. One night, after a particularly long day, the children settled into their beds, but the mother couldn't recall her song. She was puzzled at first and then concerned. The children were very unhappy. The dad looked worried too. The mother, tired though she was, immediately got up and announced, "I've lost my song. I must go and find it so that the children can go to sleep."

She set out into the village to look for her song. Along the way, she met a number of nice people. They all had wonderful songs which they were happy to share. "I have lost my song. Perhaps you know it," the mother would say. "Well," said the shepherd, "at night, when my lambs are restless, to get them to lie down, I sing them this one." All very different, each melody was lovelier than the last, but none of them was _her_ song. She thanked each person in turn and continued to search for several hours until she became exhausted and discouraged. Reluctantly, she turned towards home. Walking wearily, she noticed the air begin to stir. First, she felt its cooling effect, then she heard the magical sound of the wind. In it, she recognized her song. Excited, she began to hum along with the wind so that she would not forget. Her pace quickened.

Still humming, she came into the house, expecting mayhem. But everything was very quiet. She walked upstairs, saying to her family, "It's all right! I've found my song. I can sing to you now." There was no reply. She entered the bedroom. The children were fast asleep. "I've found my song," she repeated softly, somewhat amazed at what she saw. The father was sitting very still, half asleep himself.

"Oh," he said, "that's terrific. But the children have already gone to sleep." Mystified, she asked, "What happened? How can they be asleep when they didn't have my song?" "Oh," replied the father, "I sang to them." "But you can't sing!" she laughed. "And you don't know any songs for children." "Well," said the father, "that's what I did. I sang. Wait, I'll sing for you." And he began.

Truly, he couldn't carry a tune, and his song was unsonglike. But the father continued. Within a few moments, the mother's eyes became heavy and began to close, and she too fell into a deep and peaceful sleep.[14]

TO THE POINT

When you combine the promising payoffs for doing it all with anxiety about yielding control, particularly in the domestic domain, the result is that a rock-solid grip on everything needs to be maintained.

Despite our claim that we *want* others to share our responsibilities, for a variety of reasons, we're still reluctant to give up certain functions or split the tasks: For one, it's just easier to overfunction simply because, as Anna Jen remarked, "It would have eaten up too much time and I resented having to explain." Or, as Bev, our marmalade-maker, comments, "It makes me crazy to watch him fumble through it." Most of us know just what she means. Also, we still retain the heartfelt notion that, as in *The Sleepy Family* story, some of these things are exclusively our territory.

Even when someone offers or agrees to help, our experience suggests that doing it our way is best. This puts our nearest and dearest in a perplexing and unfair position. The Sleepy Family mom started out feeling like this. "What? He sang? And, it worked? Impossible!" Eventually, she moved beyond this position, but it was not immediate and not something she initiated. This is where we often get stuck. We're afraid we'll lose our crown of indispensability if we relinquish control. It is better, we convince ourselves, to stay fatigued and to overfunction than to take *that* chance! So, we continue to give double messages: "I would like you to take over and do more around the house." At the same time, "I don't like the way you do anything around here, so I'll do it myself." In short: "Do it. Don't do it." Let's face it, no one can expect good results with communication like that!

In addition, we're reluctant because of adverse female programming about "help." The internal voices simultaneously chorus: "I don't deserve the help;" "I shouldn't need help;" "They'll probably refuse to give me help;" "If I open this thing up, it could create conflict, and I don't want to be the cause of that; I can't handle that." Thus, though grumbling about it, we remain too anxious to relinquish our monopoly on doing it all ourselves.

Sally's friend, Lourdes, is proud and competent, but beginning to get frayed. This is how it plays out for her in the arena of "help me; don't help me." Lourdes does the:

Overfunctioner/Underfunctioner Tango —Sally ⌂

On Sundays, she takes their two kids so that her husband can attend his martial arts class. She works full-time and is the main breadwinner for her family. That day, she and I went to the beach in my car because it has room for three car seats.

By the time we were driving home, the kids were tired and hungry. I suggested to Lourdes that we put her car seats on her garage floor rather than taking the extra time to hook them back into her car. This would expedite getting the children into the house quickly. "Oh, no!" she replied, "I should just put them in my car now."

"But," I protested, "listen to them. They're crying. The kids have had it! Go on in. Your husband can put the seats back when he gets home." "*He won't do it,*" she said, without missing a breath. "What do you mean he won't do it?" I asked, puzzled, "Can't you *ask* him to do it?" "He won't remember," she shot back. "Forget it. I *know* he won't do it." She was getting upset with me, but I pressed on, "How about *insisting* that he do it? You took the kids all day so he could take his aikido class." "No," she replied, "I'll just do it. It's easier. He won't do it."

Why does Lourdes, usually such a reasonable, easygoing, tuned-in person, insist on letting her children, tired and crying, wait even a few minutes more after a long car ride while she puts their car seats back into her car? We all know why! But does it make sense? From within the confines of the TT, voices can be heard:

Bev: "...because it's simpler to do it all. What you have to go through to 'get' (beg, persuade, manipulate) 'them' (anyone but me, of course) to participate is too exhausting, frustrating, or insulting." *Bev automatically assumes asking will be a stand off of some kind, rather than a friendly encounter.* (That's her trance!)

Jaclyn: "...because it takes less time and energy to do it yourself than to coordinate and cooperate with somebody else. It's either too slow, too fast, or they just don't do it right. They overlook something, do it in the wrong order. It's just inefficient." *Jaclyn feels, "The only person who can do it my way perfectly is me." She's right about that and it keeps her stuck. Even if someone else is trying to do it her way, he or she will never succeed completely. All parties will inevitably end up frustrated.*

Rita: "...because it's frightening when, sometimes, unexpectedly, 'they' do it well." *Many of us operate with the idea that "You are what you do." So, it is no wonder that Rita feels little joy or relief when they succeed at her tasks. With her rocky self-esteem, she's caught up in worrying about losing her crown—oh, Irreplaceable One!*

Remy: "...because I'm a martyr. I know it. I hear myself saying, 'I always have to...' 'I'm the only one...' 'I can't stop because it will all fall apart...' 'The lot in life I bear...pity poor, overburdened me....' I'm embarrassed to admit, but it's habit-forming." *Remy's onto something. Playing the victim (or the Superhero) has its rewards. For instance, it provides a certain inner comfort, a constant source for conversation, and frequent "strokes" from others.*

Alma Mae: "...because we ought to be doing it anyway because we don't want to be convicted of dropping the ball or get told we are too inept to handle it." *In other words, Alma Mae doesn't want to risk being criticized or failing in her Job Description."* (Trance driven? You bet!)

Lourdes: "Some guys are great when it comes to diaper-changing or other things that used to be only women's business. But, they still don't usually see the big picture. They need direction." And what would happen if we didn't give them any idea of what to do? (Unthinkable?) *Would they, perhaps, be compelled to figure it out?*

Laini (you don't know her yet, but she's coming up): "...because we infantalize these men. Then, we resent them. We don't tell them things that threaten them. We protect them from all that partly because we fear their reactions. Certainly, there's no comfort to be had from them. They would likely just think we're high-maintenance, and nobody wants to risk that! And when they can't cope with something...like if I'm anxious about my yearly mammogram, I can't/won't/don't talk to him about it because it trips up all *his* fears about getting sick or old. We don't want to have to handle their not being able to handle it. So, we suck it up and carry on. It's a vicious circle." *Laini's right—it's a vicious circle.*

Anna Jen: "At least in the old days, they used to be gallant, protective, but we resented the inequality and the condescending aspects of that. So, we pressured them to stop it. Now, when we want some of those things sometimes, because they feel sweet and comforting, you know, like holding a door open for you or helping you with your coat... we can't admit that we want or would appreciate it. Worse, however, is the shocking fact that many of them either don't recall how to be gracious in these ways or they never learned in the first place. We may have signed up for the worst of both worlds here."

Merry: "Nor have we developed any back and forth with this like, 'I'll do it for you sometimes, too.' It doesn't have to be about weakness or gender. It could just be about nurturing." *Merry and Anna Jen make an important point. We've never clarified for ourselves that being on our own and being treated well are not mutually exclusive. Since we're confused, inevitably, so are most guys. They fear they can't do it right, so they don't try at all.*

If your identity is tied up with being indispensable, and this is combined with "I ought to," a pull to protect others from themselves, or the need to do every task beautifully to the amazement of your family and friends, it's going to be difficult to let anybody do anything for you. You will get uncomfortable when these automatic assumptions are tampered with. It will increase anxiety. Moreover, the "they can't do it well anyway" is a self-fulfilling prophecy. No partner or family member can gain competence, let alone mastery, when you rush in to take over. Or if you let them try, but stand on the sidelines with vibes, they're doomed to fail. Thus proving your point. If they somehow manage to do well, as Rita points out, their competence creates another problem—this, too, makes overfunctioners nervous.

In *The Sleepy Family*, the usual balance is upset. The dad comes forward to help, and he does the job in his way with great success. It's interesting to see how the singing mother copes with this unexpected occurrence. Initially, she reacts with skepticism and defensiveness because what he did makes her anxious. But then a remarkable thing happens. She moves through these feelings and is able to acknowledge that her husband has created something valid—different, but fine in its own right—in an area of responsibility where she has always reigned supreme (putting the children to bed). Though she expresses her doubts in the moment, she doesn't put him down when he offers to sing his song to her. Instead, she listens.

The singing mother rides out her sense of being threatened and feeling anxious. She reaches a state of mind in which she takes pleasure in her discovery about him. This creates the opportunity for both partners to feel good—and get a good night's sleep! Thus, the Sleepy Family is also the happy family. This is not sweet fairy-tale magic: it's psychological magic that is within our grasp to learn and do. Accepting anxiety and relating to it differently is necessary to move forward in relationships. It weakens the TT.

Failing to accept that having anxiety is part of healthy living locks us more tightly into going forward with unquestioned assumptions in automatic pilot, which leads right back to the overfunctioning, placating-servant role (trance) to IPs and the TT.

Laini finds herself caught between what she says she wants and how she actually avoids asking for what she wants. Unlike the singing mother, she's completely immobilized by the standard *anxiety-avoidance trance* and the standard anxiety-avoidant partner. Laini can't:

Go There, Girl!

"I found out that I had cancer of the cervix. My fiancé was planning to go to graduate school. He was leaving in two days. He said he was concerned, that he'd stay longer to help out, but I knew that his school started next week and he needed the time to settle in before his classes began.

"My girlfriend, Carmen, took me to the hospital for the surgery—a cone biopsy. The doctors did it as an outpatient procedure because I didn't have any health insurance. When Carmen dropped me back at my apartment, Rick came by to bring me dinner. But I didn't feel well enough to eat. I was bleeding heavily and feeling very weak. I told him I thought it would be better if I were left alone. I was embarrassed for him to see how heavily I was bleeding.

"As soon as he left, I called Carmen to pick me up another package of jumbo absorbent pads.

"'You've already gone through all those pads the hospital sent home with you?' she inquired. 'I thought that they gave you enough to get through tomorrow.'

"As it turned out, being alone was dangerous. When Carmen got there, one glance at me was sufficient. I looked 'scary pale,' as she put it. She called the hospital back and described how fast I was going through the pads. They told her to bring me back in at once. By this point, I was so weak I could barely make it down the steps to her car.

"We got to the hospital and, apparently, I needed to be re-stitched. Also, I had lost so much blood that I needed a transfusion.

"Carmen said, 'I'll call Rick and let him know where you are.'

"'Oh, no, please don't do that,' I said, 'I know it will freak him out. Then, I'll end up feeling guilty that I've upset him. I just don't have the energy to take care of him. I just can't go there.'

"'Okay, I understand. I'd be pretty hard-pressed to go there if it were my boyfriend, especially if I felt as weak as you do right now.'"

Laini keeps the whole life-threatening ordeal to herself. She doesn't ask her boyfriend to help her. She spares him the embarrassment of going to the store to buy her more absorbent pads, and she doesn't cry on his shoulder about what she is going through. Instead, she bucks up, politely asks him to leave (which, amazingly, he does), and then she dials up a girlfriend. Carmen immediately comes over to save the day—what a pair! And she admits that she "wouldn't go there" with her own boyfriend!

We have to dare to "go there." It really doesn't matter what age you are. These kinds of interactions are so commonplace, accepted, and pernicious that we don't even see them. We consistently come to each other's aid in emergencies, but we have a hard time encouraging each other to require this action from men (and sometimes other women!).

It's embedded in how we talk to one another—our conversation about men includes <u>not</u> including them in a variety of deeply human circumstances. They get to underfunction because we willingly overfunction. The first necessary step forward is to do exactly what makes us anxious. It will help break the pattern of infantilization, protection, and resentment of men.

ANXIETY HAS A BAD REPUTATION

Historically, anxiety is a loaded word with negative associations: confusion, weakness, shame, alarm, panic, loss of control, and pain. Indeed, anxiety can be mental and physical; pain of some intensity does play an intrinsic part. However, <u>we</u> have created the <u>artificial connection</u> between anxiety and weakness or shame. A dictionary definition characterizes the confusing emotion of anxiety in a simple way: *A painful or apprehensive uneasiness of mind usually focusing on an impending or anticipated ill.*[15]

Unfortunately, even in its milder forms of uncertainty and feeling unsettled, anxiety stimulates big fears in most of us: "It is a sign that I can't cope!" "It means failure." "It might not ever stop." "I will die from it!" In short, experiencing anxiety makes us anxious; just thinking we might get anxious makes us anxious (you know—uptight, stressed out). Yet, it is tolerance of anxiety that is key to shifting overfunctioning dynamics and making significant (meaningful) changes.

✂ We've linked anxiety so tightly with breakdown that we miss its value for breakthrough.

PRESCRIPTION:

Take it on. There is a dosage of anxiety that is beneficial, even for children; it compels us towards mastery and growth in all areas.

Though you may not realize it, you already know a lot about anxiety, and how to raise and lower it. Anyone who has ever watched (or been) a mother helping a toddler learn to walk, for example, has seen a demonstration of someone adjusting an anxiety thermostat, yours and the toddler's. Let the baby have the freedom to experiment and to take some risks—teeter, sometimes even fall, and try again, pressed to the edge of his (or her) learning curve and your tolerance zone for danger. At the same time, you don't allow the child to fall hard or head for dangerous spots. Your thinking goes something like this, "Don't overprotect him and swoop down on him, but don't let him be flooded out with panic either. 'Saving' him from all frustration will impede his learning process. He won't build confidence in himself and won't feel that great sense of competence. However, if I let him go too far, he could get hurt physically, become discouraged or perhaps traumatized, give up, or feel defeated." This familiar interior monologue that we all talk ourselves through frequently with children, whether they're our own or not, is actually a calibration of anxiety, a search for that best balance.

✂ When adjusted well, anxiety supports and challenges simultaneously.

Avoiding discomfort (anxiety) wreaks all kinds of havoc. It drives you to overfunction to avoid the pain (ironically, exposing you to worse pain, like the hell of the TT all over again!). Avoidance may drive you to act impulsively, with a likely negative outcome, or not act at all, exposing you to staying stuck. You will inevitably behave in destructive (self-defeating) ways, such as hooking up with the wrong partner just to hook up ("I'm so glad I'm not alone and unchosen."); staying with the wrong people in personal relationships or at work in order to not make waves ("Thank heavens, I've escaped the angst of being alone and the guilt I would have if I were to leave."); allowing yourself to be a doormat in relationships so "they" won't be upset or threatened, like Laini did with her fiancé.

Other telling signs of ducking anxiety include chronic inertia, "checking-out," spacing out, drifting, chronically procrastinating, going blank at times when it's important to be alert, or being passive and letting someone else decide something for you. What are the payoffs of all this? "At least I am not making a fool of myself or having to take responsibility for a potentially bad or unpopular choice. I'm so relieved that it's not my fault."

To gain a temporary respite from anxiety, we often trade long-term power for short-term power. We micromanage moments and over-control things to ensure our indispensability in relationships. This hearkens back to that original legacy: Wrapped too tightly not only in corsets, but also in household chores, tied down to babies, alternately put on a pedestal and put down... We were taken for granted but were also depended upon absolutely.

We use overfunctioning as a way to stave off anxiety—overbooking, heaping up stimuli, and filling our time keeps us too busy to feel much. It seems like a solution at first. After all: *Being busy means I'm accomplishing something and finding satisfaction. Right?*" Stuffing oneself by overeating can't be equated with satisfying dining, and overfunctioning, a form of stuffing, doesn't produce genuine fulfillment either. Instead, it increases fragmentation and dissatisfaction, which leads directly back to feeling anxious. To dodge this, we race back to even more overfunctioning.

✂ Tolerating anxiety is essential to all authentic change.

Consider carefully the different forms of anxiety (stress) in your life. You need always to make a distinction between:

1) anxiety (stress) attached to taking an appropriate risk—this is constructive; and

2) anxiety (stress) caused by you're doing too much with too many deadlines—this is destructive.

POSITIVE NOTE

Rosalyn comments: When training to become a psychotherapist, much time is devoted to studying techniques to raise and lower anxiety levels of clients. If anxiety is too high, it stops people from taking action (changing), and they retreat: placate, accommodate, suck-it-up, feel guilty or become depressed or immobilized. If anxiety is too low, they will be unmotivated to change and will also stay stuck or in retreat. Step outside the office, and exactly the same patterns exist. If you're too anxious, you can't change. If you're not anxious enough, you won't change.

Anxiety has great value as a little signal to alert you to pay attention and search for a message. It often indicates that you should shift your way of dealing with someone or something. In order to think clearly about those major goals that are eluding you, you will have to let yourself be anxious. It's worth it. Not feeling anxious does not necessarily mean all is well. It can mean things are stagnant and need to be shaken up.

✂ Anxiety brings us to the edge of our learning curve.

Your Turn!: USING ANXIETY WELL—BEGINNER TECHNIQUES

Topic: Anxiety as a key for change

Purpose: Turning anxiety into a personal power tool

A) Assess your typical anxiety style: As you go through your days, are you one who tends to feel too much anxiety or too little? Even if you've never conceptualized things in this way before, if you stop and become still and quiet, you will probably be able to figure this out. If you can't, ask someone who knows you well for help: Do you think I am excessively worried and uptight, or not worried and nervous enough even when circumstances warrant it? Do I play it too safe to grow?

Choose the "B" that fits you:

B1) If you identify yourself as a person who tends to be highly anxious, trace your usual path of escalation and try to identify which things send you most over the top into immobilization or panic. Kids have blankets, teddy bears, and bottles. Consider what small, pleasing things you have to comfort yourself: a cup of tea in a patch of sun or by the fire, a walk around the block, a special song, popcorn, calling that good friend, lighting many candles in the middle of an ordinary day. Gather these treasures in your mind and examine whether you are using them to help bring down your anxiety to a good motivating level. If your nurturing inventory is skimpy, work on expanding it. No need to throw a lot of money at this, just a bit of time, thought, imagination, and patience.

One can, of course, use comfort items in excess, as stall techniques to preserve the status quo. If you are reducing anxiety too low to keep you motivated, you're too comfortable. You won't be willing to push yourself, shake up a stagnant or negative element, or shift it. Check this out.

B2) If you identify yourself as a person who typically experiences too little anxiety and is clever at avoiding it, list two or three things that you guess might make you anxious if you were to dwell on them. You can recognize these because, when they come up, you start to feel a little edgy. Your automatic response to this signal is to promptly begin your dousing tactics. Consider the maneuvers, activities, and tactics—busyness, lists, TV, junk food, alcohol, etc. Do you notice that you behave as if anxiety will kill you? (*It won't.*)

Trace your path of avoidance, and see if you can identify the earliest moment when you begin bailing out. Play a *Minutes Game*. Take five minutes. See if you can purposely generate an unsettling, scary feeling. Though this will seem odd and counterintuitive, stay with it. Be exact about the time by using an alarm clock or timer. You can build your anxiety tolerance gradually by this method. Increase your time by one more minute each day for five days. Don't exceed ten minutes. Force yourself to hold the feelings even as you notice yourself starting to use your escape repertoire. Get to know your main anti-anxiety ploys so that you can spot them in the heat of the moment and choose not to use them.

Do this short exercise frequently until you gather a list of things that do indeed make you anxious.

B3) Some people are, of course, hybrids. They get too anxious about some matters, not anxious enough about others. If you are like this, discriminate between your "too much" and "too little" as clearly as possible. Practice adjusting anxiety up (B2) and down (B1) as relevant.

(continued on next page)

C) Look for themes or patterns that lead you to avoid anxiety. It's usually helpful to write them down. For example: "I avoid making waves because, whenever I do so, I get really worried that someone is going to criticize, humiliate, or even abandon me." "I tend to get somewhat uncomfortable when I have to face any *new* situation, whether at work or even with a friend." Recognizing and staying with anxiety, even just for five or ten minutes at a time, is a victory. It's helping you prepare for changing a pattern that is blocking the accomplishment of important goals. If the anxiety gets to paralysis level, don't stay there lamenting that you can't act. Instead, bring your anxiety down to a level that actually motivates action, like the mother does with her toddler.

D) As you pursue this course, rewards are plentiful. Your skills in using anxiety well will enable you to stay in touch with how you go about things in your life, to take appropriate risks, to create time, and to prioritize wisely. You will discover that not everything makes you equally anxious. *Recognizing where a variety of things fall on your personal anxiety continuum will assist you in fine-tuning your own anxiety-regulating skills.* Keep your list going over time. Add items when you think of something. Read and reread it often. Can you see things that you really want to do, say, or experience that make you anxious? Pick a few of them to try, carrying your anxiety with you. You do not need to let anxiety inhibit you from your chosen goals. Having anxiety just means you're being ambitious and/or breaking out of a trance. It's a great sign of progress. Do not wait for anxiety to go away before you act.

✄ Anxiety accompanies all growth spurts.

PARENT ALERT!   ⌂

Note one of the latest poor-parenting routines, now practiced very widely: Rushing to prevent little Johnny and teenage Suzie from feeling anxious. How do misguided moms and dads do this? By constantly smoothing everything out so that their children will not be frustrated, even for a few moments.

This is producing troubling results:

—Spoiled, entitled children and young adults who expect to be given everything with little effort of their own.

—Young adults, phobic of anxiety, who have no idea how to handle even mild set-backs or problems. Scared, overwhelmed, and incompetent to deal, they rush to call home at the slightest challenge to have you take care of it (and them) as you have always done. And more and more, lately, they actually come home to live. (Part of this is economic; but, part of it emotional.) Bad for you—overfunctioning forever; bad for them—emotionally helpless to cope with life's inevitable slings and arrows. As for their self-esteem—very low.

In order for us to parent well, we must learn to accept and use anxiety well ourselves and teach our children to do the same.

✂ "Rescuing" your children from anxiety disables them.

8
HANDLING CRITICISM
Strengthen Your Personal Empowerment

✂ Sticks and stones may break my bones, but names will never hurt me.

Well, let's see about that. Here's a basic list of **Intimidating Labels** for women:

Emotional, lazy, bitchy, broad, old-fashioned, on a power-trip, clingy, ball-buster, pushy, demanding, pig, dog, fox, chick, smart ass, greedy, whore, virgin, hot, needy, skinny, stupid, pre-menstrual, menopausal, old, dependent, frigid, loose, sentimental, domineering, prude, inadequate, pathetic, castrating, controlling, bimbo, dumb, know-it-all, Barbie-doll, cunt, pussy, smarty pants, weak, flirt, flighty, manipulative, mean, wimp, big-mouth, clueless, unattractive, incompetent, big boobs, loud-mouth, aggressive, witch, fearful, dizzy, lightweight, blonde, baby, fat, thoughtless, high-maintenance, childish, high-strung, uptight, selfish, failure, broad, snake eater, slave, girlish, naive, foolish, mousy, quitter, flat-chested, thunder thighs, old hag, dyke, pushy, fragile, airhead, silly, perky, on the rag, ice queen, slut, fool of a woman....

Did we leave anyone out?

Criticism has long been a way of frightening, controlling, and disempowering women. Criticism is a powerful trance inducer. Be it from others or from oneself, it can keep us on the Treacherous Triangle treadmill. Some insults are universal. Some are gender-specific. But they're all damaging in that they can actually stop us from doing what we think is best. We dwell on criticisms and obsess about what we've been called or what we might get called. This inhibits not only our independent assessments of the situations we're in, but also our spontaneity. It can stymie change. We surrender (our power) to those who label us because certain names have a hypnotic effect on us, literally placing us in a trance.

Labels hurled at us by significant others trigger old trance reactions, causing us to respond in present time to past experiences. If you react disproportionately to the current circumstance, the present moment is likely distorted, triggered by the ancient label. You are not dealing in the NOW. Automatic feelings of self-recrimination can get stirred up. A panicky inner voice says, "I don't want to be a bitch (naive, selfish, whatever... fill in the blank with your personal nemesis words); I must not be a bitch..." followed by, "I probably really am this—a bitch, demanding, stupid...." Up rises anxiety, guilt, uncertainty, or shame. Self-esteem plunges. Placating/accommodating/overfunctioning behavior revs into high gear.

Trying to avoid labels is always a losing proposition. Examine the list and you'll see why. For instance, if you focus on making sure you are *not* joining the *demanding* group (domineering, castrating, bitch, smart ass), you will, by your actions to sidestep, expose yourself to accusations drawn from the *dependent* group (wimpy, foolish, passive, needy, childish). Remember that vague promise that if you just juggle well enough, are innovative enough, or try hard enough, you can find that perfect path between the demanding and dependent stances? This seductive notion is a clear hook that leads back to accommodating, to abandoning your authenticity, and to overfunctioning. Can you feel the grip of the TT clasping you again?

"Good labels" can also play an equally insidious role. Needing to hold onto praise in order to boost your flagging self-esteem, avoid painful self-knowledge, and dodge potential criticism can lead you to act in self-defeating ways. "She's so nice." "So low-maintenance." "So good-natured." "So easy." "Such a lady." Better keep those press releases coming—at any cost!

> ✍ We carry the false hope of finding that minuscule magic perch from which everything flows seamlessly into a perfect balance...as long as we sit tight right there.

Labels control us and cloud our judgment, so dealing with them is essential. Dodging them gets us into serious trouble. Consider what befell Sally. When, in her early twenties, she admitted to her mother that she'd been sexually active prior to marriage, Mom immediately shot back with, "What a stupid, naive little girl you are!" Her mother died shortly after this conversation, and this harsh judgment froze into permanence for Sally—stupid, naïve little girl.

Some years later, Sally was suing a former business partner for fraud. She recounts, "I felt…"

…So Stupid and Naive

"Every lawyer I interviewed asked me, 'How could you be that stupid and naive?' Except for Thor, who told me point blank, 'You are the most naive and stupid person I've ever met.' While peering intensely at me through his thick glasses, he periodically reminded me of my folly throughout our initial meeting. I hired Thor, ostensibly because he seemed to be the most fierce, aggressive, and honest advocate. But Thor, God of War, clearly fit the bill for what I needed in more ways than these.

"During the course of the lawsuit, Thor never missed a chance to say, 'You couldn't be have been that stupid and naive!' Well, I had been. Finally, after a few months, his relentless negative barrage began to feel to me like adding insult to injury.

"One day, Thor called me in to say my case was in jeopardy. He had failed to catch a clerical error. This oversight put things out of proper legal order. I could, if I so chose, sue him for malpractice. Then he broke the terrible news that he couldn't represent me anymore because we were potentially adversaries. I felt flooded with panic, wondering how I would proceed with my case. I began to cry. Thor insisted, 'You don't need to do that. This is indeed 'a tough break,' even though 'it isn't my fault' and 'there's *nothing* I can do' except advise you to find another lawyer.' He took this opportunity to again remind me that if I hadn't been so stupid and naive in the first place, I wouldn't be in this position now, and neither would he. So, you see, it really was still all my fault!

"I couldn't stop crying. The tears just poured out of my eyes.

Thor gazed past me through those glasses, agitated by my emotions and trying to dismiss them. 'It's just a lawsuit. I really do wish you good luck,' he stated, as if to summarize everything. But, to my surprise, I blurted out, 'How would you feel if you had lost your home, your life savings, and then the lawyer you hired informed you that he could no longer represent you because of *his* clerical error? How would you feeeeeeeeel? You think I can go out and find another lawyer just like that? Do you have any idea what position this puts ME in? This means two lawsuits! You made a serious mistake ! Yet, *you're* still reminding *me* how dumb I am?'"

Why does Sally take months of abuse from Thor? Partly in "exchange" for his legal brilliance, partly because she was entranced by the names he called her. Though negative, they identify her in a familiar way. She does feel ashamed, weak, and pathetic. Secretly, she agrees that the labels "stupid" and "naive" are apt. After all, Mom said so. Sally cowers and cringes, and accommodates to Thor's assessments of her.

It takes an enormous new crisis within the ongoing crisis for Sally to shake free of Thor's trance-power over her. At this moment, she speaks up in defense of herself and her personal values and against his stance—the "I know and you don't;" "It's never my fault;" "Feelings are irrelevant and unacceptable;" "Because feelings make me (Thor) nervous (anxious), you (Sally) are forbidden to have them. I make the rules here in my kingdom." By asserting her right to have her emotions (whether they upset him or not), insisting that Thor take some responsibility for the new mess, and expressing herself honestly despite continuous criticism, Sally reclaims her voice, autonomy, and self-respect. His tyrannical reign is over! At the same time, so is the tyrannical reign of the negative label.

Although Thor continues to call her the same old names for the rest of their lengthy association, this never again inhibits Sally from speaking up; it never again puts her "under."

✄ Enduring discomfort is key to solving Label Paralysis.

Now, consider Andrea. Formerly, her marriage was characterized by an imbalance of power and chronic bickering. This was combined with placating and the accumulation of resentments on her part. But Andrea tried a new tact. She held the line in the face of a poisonous label her husband, Richard, had periodically hurled her way, a name that he knew would stop her in her tracks. When she changed her response to it, she shook up a major dynamic of the relationship and shifted the status quo between herself and Richard. When something that's been stuck is destabilized, a window of opportunity and hope opens. Habitual interactions can be dumped and better ones created.

Andrea is VP of a consulting business; Richard is a building contractor. Andrea is the one who holds the family schedule together. As logistics coordinator, she carts the kids around to and from school and to their afterschool clubs and sports. Andrea repeatedly does more than her share because she can't bear being called "selfish." In the past, her siblings and mother routinely called her this name. Over the course of her fifteen-year marriage, her husband has almost always been able to immobilize Andrea with this loaded label—selfish.

When, finally, she analyzed a typical conversation with Richard in detail, she was able to compose a new delivery. She prepared a different set of lines to say in the same old scene. She knows she will feel nervous, but accepts it because she realizes it is not a signal that she's off track; she's breaking solid ground. She realizes that the dreaded criticism, "Andrea, you're so selfish!" might apply to her at times. She decides that she can live with this. She's scared and uncomfortable but feels a sense of freedom when tackling the conversation with a different strategy. Andrea holds on to that:

Hot Potato

"A very important client wanted my husband to stay late. Well, my boss needed me to stay late, too. The kids needed to be picked up. In order to make the rest of the family's schedule work, I would have had to tell my boss that I couldn't do it. If I stayed the extra half hour and picked the kids up later, the traffic would add an hour and a half to my already bursting day. If Richard would just tell his client, 'No, I'm sorry, I can't stay at the job site any longer today. I have to get my children. My wife has to work late. Otherwise, she and the children won't get home until 8 p.m. I don't want to put them through it.' Then, I wouldn't be going through this.

"But I knew the drill. Before even trying to see if it could be done, I knew he would icily say, 'You are selfish. You are making me do extra work. And you know my job is very important. So, stop being so selfish, Andrea!' In the 'good old days,' that would have been enough to freeze me. I would have done anything to prevent being condemned as 'selfish.' But, in this instance, I was too angry to endure a repeat performance. 'Enough!' I said to myself. Though it was in a wimpy voice, I did say it.

"I battled it all out in my head in advance because I could imagine exactly how the scene would play out—how his voice would grow more stern and mine shakier. Desperately, I tried to think of something I could do to make the logistics work without him, while not absorbing the usual rearranging of my job and the children's schedule. But I just couldn't see any way around it.

"I held the concept and sound of the word 'selfish' in my mind and immediately began to squirm. I noticed I was becoming mildly nauseous. I waited a few minutes, concentrating hard on the point at hand. Then, I mustered up my courage and said, 'Will you please tell your client that you simply cannot stay today?' 'Aren't you being a bit selfish?' he instantly accused. Hearing this made the hair stand up on my neck, but I focused on producing a clear voice. I felt as if I had just stuffed that hot potato in my mouth. It was sticky and uncomfortable to talk. But I replied, 'Maybe you're right. Suppose today I am being selfish. With any luck, tomorrow I'll be less selfish.' That was pretty good; I congratulated myself. Though still shaky and feeling queasy, I felt surprisingly energized. It occurred to me to debate with him about who is more selfish—pass that usual hot potato back and forth between us for awhile. But I decided against this too familiar skirmish. It never led anywhere. Instead, I continued to chew on the potato myself and, you know, it wasn't so bad. Guess what? After shaking his head a few times, he did it! He made the call! His client said it would be fine.

"It worked out more than fine for me. For the first time, that 'selfish' label did not produce internal paralysis and lead me to give in.

And it never has since. My marriage? It survived very well. Got better, actually. So, my advice is: Don't pass that hot potato!"

PRESCRIPTION:

Imagine an effective interior monologue to neutralize a label-intensive interaction.

Examining Andrea's process, we can see that she is very distressed. However, she shifts her focus and makes her request. To her amazement, she gets what she wants. When you can do this, things can change. What others might think of you or label you no longer stops the action. You make the dreaded call for the job interview, go to the adoption agency to get that baby, tell your partner to change his/her appointment, audition for the choir, try a new activity, give up an addiction, or tell that friend that you are angry.

You will gradually see that even when you feel like you are going to panic (you may well be too anxious to take any useful action at this point), you will not die from it. By practicing, you can become skilled in the techniques for adjusting these feelings to a manageable, motivating level of anxiety, just as you would the thermostat to regulate your body temperature.

Because Sally and Andrea faced their demon labels head on, they never again found themselves at the mercy of words or phrases that were formerly poisonous to them. Their success re-emphasizes the importance of mastering anxiety modulation skills and underscores the capacity to do so even after years of being stuck.

Think about this: CAN YOU SEE A LINK between labels that make you most anxious and certain criticisms from important people in your past? Do you see how this connects to your trances and weakens your self-esteem?

✁ Creating a different interior monologue will change the dialogue.

Your Turn! OVERCOMING LABEL TYRANNY

Topic: Labels that take your power away from you

Purpose: Desensitizing yourself to the effect of labels so you can protect yourself

A) Pick out the particular labels that have power over you. They can be single words, phrases, or a cluster of ideas, like "You're not a team player." Going down your inventory, choose the top ones and some lesser ones. Think in present time: How often does this labeling come up in your current relationships? What are the worst results for you? Use Andrea's story as a model of a good discovery and planning process to break out of the pattern.

Labels can disempower you totally as they did Sally when she related to Thor and Andrea with Richard. To avoid getting called that certain name, you cringe and twist and obey. You will overfunction and sell yourself down the river to keep the label at bay. For example, "you are a mean mommy" stops a lot of mothers from setting limits that they know in their hearts are good ones. We know a woman who is an exceptional preschool teacher, adept at making appropriate rules for her young students and following through on them. At home, she is completely paralyzed, unable to discipline her own child. Her daughter, Belva, screws up her face and says, "I hate you!" Mom caves immediately. Inconsistent, anxious, exhausted, and unhappy at home, she flees to school to do extra "but important" work. Belva is neglected as well as underdisciplined. At age six, the child is completely unable to control herself and completely able to control her mother. The situation will only get worse over time unless Mom can stop being triggered by the critical labels Belva hurls at her.

B) Develop your list into an instruction sheet for those closest to you. Let your family members in on the expressions and criticisms that disturb you the most.

Yes, this will make you more vulnerable to them. They will have precise and powerful ammunition against you. Yet, there's a positive side. The various choices of things that they might call you can be fine-tuned to reflect the level of frustration they actually feel towards you. For instance, they can select a small firecracker label instead of a large bomb because they will know which is which. Otherwise, attacks on you will be much less exact. Someone could step on one of your landmines unintentionally. Unfair to you; unfair to them. After all, being called "stupid" minimally affects Andrea, but devastates Sally. Meanwhile, Andrea withers at "selfish," whereas Sally flicks it off like a small mosquito. Invite your family members to give you their Label Instruction Sheets.

C) Withstand the label. You can protect your power and take charge of your self-esteem by bearing the criticisms as Andrea and Sally learn to do, acknowledging that the label is probably true some of the time—"chewing, even swallowing it," as Andrea puts it. You no longer hear it with shame or defend against it. "Oh, no! I'm not a bitch!"...followed by seven well-argued reasons why you are really wonderful, demure, and nice doesn't do it. That's still fighting the label! You're still terrified! You are continuing to try harder to prove that you're not whatever "it" says you are. Instead, take it on board. "I know I can be selfish sometimes, but being selfish doesn't disqualify me from feeling the way I do and making my requests. Maybe I am selfish today, but we both know I'm not that way every day."

✂ Stand firm and you will soon stand liberated.

9
DRAWING YOUR OWN LINES
Find Your Right to Say NO

The Little Red Hen ~ an old folk tale

Perhaps you remember that old story from childhood about a hard-working little hen named Red? She was one of the original overfunctioners. Used to be that this tale was told as a matter of course to children. These days, not everyone has heard it. So, her tale bears repeating here.

Picture a quaint little barnyard with chickens, pigs, ducks, geese, dogs, cats, cows, sheep, and what not. In this pastoral setting lives one feisty, brave chicken—the Little Red Hen. She is quite the industrious lass on the farm, we might add. We meet Red in the springtime, when it's time to plant the garden…

"Who will help me sow the seeds?" asked the Little Red Hen.

"Not I!" said the duck.
"Not I!" said the goose.
"Not I!" said the cat.
"Not I!" said the pig.

"Then, I'll do it myself," said the Little Red Hen. And she did.

And, so it went through all the stages of the harvest…

"Who will help me thresh the wheat?" asked the Little Red Hen.

"Not I!" "Not I!" "Not I!" "Not I!" came the response from the animal chorus.
"Then, I'll do it myself," said the Little Red Hen. And she did.

"And who will help me carry the wheat to the mill?" asked the Little Red Hen.

Oh, dear me! Met with the same response!

"And, who will help me bake the bread?" asked the Little Red Hen.

By then, the Little Red Hen knew the answer to that one!

After she took the loaf from the oven, it was set on the windowsill to cool.

The delicious smell of it wafted over the barnyard.

"And now," asked the Little Red Hen, "who will help me eat the bread?"

Suddenly, the animals sang a different tune! They all wanted to eat it, of course!

"I will!" said the duck.
"I will!" said the goose.
"I will!" said the cat.
"I will!" said the pig.

"No, I will eat it myself!" said the Little Red Hen.
And she did.

We circle back again to "I'll just do it myself." There are two things going on here: First, can you ask for help? Second, when you don't get the help you've asked for and deserve, can you get indignant?

Here are some advanced questions: Can Red get angry about not getting some help without then quickly feeling scared and guilty? Can she hold her line without, possibly, backtracking and apologizing? How would you rate *your* ability to set limits? Do you think the Little

Red Hen is self-protective, selfish, or both? Can you tell the difference? Is it all blurred because you are looking out from inside the Treacherous Triangle as, busy and selfless, you put up with enduring and accepting impossible people (or animals)?

IN PRAISE OF WOMANKIND

"I'll do it myself!," the motto of the Little Red Hen, is the Overfunctioning Woman's mantra. The folktale reveals the dilemma women face, their courageous persistence, some solutions that work, and some that don't. We love this story because the choices Red ultimately makes can be viewed as a bright antidote to the helplessness that women have suffered through the ages—the helplessness of being ignored or trivialized, getting minimal or negative responses, having to go it alone even in the midst of a crowd, and being responsible for so much.

At first, the Little Red Hen is a quintessential overfunctioner: She plants the wheat all by herself, reaps it all by herself, takes it to the mill (to have it made into flour) all by herself, and brings the flour back home to make bread, which she then prepares all by herself. But she also does something important that the overfunctioning woman often fails to do: she expresses her needs and desires directly, unapologetically, and repeatedly. A lot of overfunctioners would have stopped asking for help long before Red did—if they ever asked at all.

Though her requests are met with the same negative response many times, the Little Red Hen takes "no" with dignity. The others' responses do not diminish the validity of her project in her eyes, and she avoids some of the reactions an overfunctioner might typically feel: sulking, getting defensive, placing blame, feeling victimized, guilty, embarrassed, self-doubting, or crazy.

"Who will help me thresh the wheat?"
"Not I," said the duck.
"Not I," said the goose.
"Not I," said the cat.
"Not I," said the pig.
...to which she replies... "Then, I shall do it myself!" And she does.

> ✂ Learn to take "no" as an answer; otherwise, it's not safe to ask for what you need or want.

The hen's approach is deceptively simple. She says what she wants in—you guessed it! —words easy enough for a three year old to understand. Her self-esteem and self-respect hold because her inner voice confidently assures her, "This is legitimate and I'm okay." She doesn't need to run off and be rescued (for instance, to seduce the miller; maybe she'll marry him, maybe she won't). Instead, she stands her ground and achieves her chosen goals.

What is her secret? The hen, though little and perhaps a bit dowdy, sees herself as BIG. Because of this, she has no problem admitting she wants help. (*"Hey, Pig. Please come here and help me, would you?"*) She's has picked her priorities, feels entitled to her vision, and acts accordingly—whether or not others validate her. Finally, she moves about the farm at a pace that is copasetic to her. Her confidence is fed from within and isn't diminished by external circumstances.

Her strengths are numerous, and all of them are within our grasp!

TO THE POINT

Look at what overfunctioners do: We, too, persevere but rarely act with such clarity. We're often confused and uncertain about what we're entitled to. For many of us, the very act of asking, even if our requests are small, triggers fear and guilt. We then hastily back off. We fall prey to the trap that we shouldn't admit that we need or want help. If we ask, we'll seem weak, incapable, or ineffective. And the other person could say "no." Or, we might lose our role as that easy-going, pleasant gal who can always be counted on to get the job done. Or, we could be dumped entirely. *The anxiety that surrounds the asking produces an automatic response—not asking.* This anxiety results in more and more overfunctioning.

> ✂ Those who feel intrinsically good about themselves are comfortable asking for what they want. They do not feel diminished in doing so.

> ✂ If you can't request help, you will inevitably be stuck in overfunctioning.

When the bread comes out of the oven, the other animals eagerly wait to be offered a piece. At this point, the Little Red Hen does another remarkable thing. She feels angry and she shows it: *"Oh, no you won't! I made it. I'll eat it myself!"*

At this point, she learns from previous mistakes. Up until now, Red has not expressed any measure of displeasure or frustration about the shabby treatment she has received from the other animals. Many overfunctioners are like this, believing that anger is wrong, and, furthermore, don't have the bandwidth to deal with something so loaded and time-consuming. Not until the others are standing in line, expecting their portion, does the Little Red Hen stand her ground. When she *finally* sets her limit—"no" to sharing ("no" to being exploited one more time)—it comes out somewhat clumsily and imperfectly. But, most importantly, it comes out honestly.

At first glance, the hen's decision to keep all the bread may seem selfish and mean. Yet, because she has been taken advantage of, she believes she has the right to enjoy her rewards without guilt. After all that has happened, giving in to the animals would likely lower her self-respect and build up chronic resentment. The hen's attempt to verbalize her true feelings is indirect and a bit underhanded (she does set them up and trick them). But it is admirable that she tries at all.

"Oh, I'm soooo sorry I got mad. Please have some bread. Sit down. I'll go get it for you." (All with a big smile and, perhaps, a little laugh…) That's the well-known "make nice" overfunctioner's backtracking. But Red doesn't do that. What a victory! We sense she wouldn't weaken in her stance even if she were met by the wrath of the animals. She wouldn't knuckle under just so they would like her. This is impressive. This makes all the difference.

> *"You selfish bitch! Give me a piece of bread!"* quacks the duck.
> *"I'm sooo hungry,"* whimpers the goose.
> *"I neeeeeed you,"* howls the cat.

"You sure are a lousy leader. It's all your fault! You really ought to share. You set us up. And, besides, I'm feeling sick," guilt-trips the pig.

TO THE POINT

There's a prevailing expectation that people—particularly women—shouldn't get angry because it isn't feminine. When women dare to express their displeasure openly, they frequently get their hands slapped. Fearing judgments and conflict, quickly they undo the anger and crawl away, often back into accommodating. Instead of retracting or pretending that nothing is wrong, we women need to engage in genuine dialogue—speaking up with feeling, however unpopular the message.

> ✂ The best protection against being taken advantage of is to stop avoiding conflict. Learn how to express your anger and to take it from others. Claim the right to set limits, to say "no." We must.

OFF TRACK

Carolina, a successful entrepreneur, does not feel she has a right to express her anger. When she does and someone calls her on it or is annoyed with her, she retreats hastily and returns to placating.

Oh, That Was Harsh!

She's a woman who walks with confidence. She's tall, understated, hip. Though generally reserved, she reveals a certain flair with the unusual earrings that peek out from under her shoulder-length auburn hair. She prides herself on being understanding, nice, and smart, but never pushy, even in her industry, one notoriously unfriendly to women.

At last, Carolina thought that she was in a promising relationship with a man she met through work. They were having fun, talking frankly, saying heartfelt things to one another. She even expressed trepidations about the big business deal she was putting together; it was significant enough to make or break her career, she felt. These fears were something that she would normally have kept to herself. But, she risked revealing her worries. He seemed to like her blend of reserve, candor, and sparkle. One morning, she called to wish him well before a surgery he was to have that day. Less than 24 hours later, he called back and said, "We're going too fast; I am considering reconciling with my wife." Then he hung up the phone.

In spite of her heartache (stalwart Little Red Hen that she was), she concentrated on the project she was working on. After much anguish and cliff-hanging, things were completed in her favor.

Although the boyfriend had a clear understanding of what she was up against, he neither considered this in timing his good-bye, nor did he contact her during the final days of the negotiations to find out how she was doing. He *never* offered to talk to her about the break-up. She, of course, did not insist.

Ten days later, Carolina called him to get a professional referral for her cousin. One might wonder why she did this, why didn't her cousin make the call himself? "Naturally, I didn't think to suggest that," commented Carolina, "and neither did Cousin Jay." The ex-boyfriend remarked, "Oh, and by the way, how'd the deal go?" Spontaneously, Carolina replied, "I closed it, but if you really cared, the time to have asked was last week when I was in the thick of it, not now." His response: "Oh, that was harsh!"

After Carolina hung up the phone, she was convinced that a) being rid of this man was a blessing, and b) she had overstepped some forbidden line by making her honest, "mean" comment. This left her deeply shaken.

Her close women friends applauded and urged her to stand firm. But Carolina called the ex-boyfriend back several days later to explain her behavior! She said (GROAN!) she'd "been under a lot of pressure and, therefore, on edge." She "was very sorry." In short: "It was all my fault. I was just being an emotional, hysterical woman." Subtext: "It is not okay to get even mildly annoyed or have someone displeased with me, even if he is a creep." Her rationale for calling him back was that because they were in the same profession, she didn't want to burn any bridges. Underneath this was her fear of his anger and disapproval (and her own)—in spite of the fact that *she* no longer had a high opinion of him.

Carolina was caught being angry. So horrible was this to her that her focus shifted from the inexcusable way in which the guy had dumped her to feeling out of line for her mini-outburst.

In a song entitled "Ferret Said" by Charming Hostess (a Klezmer-punk/Balkan-funk band), the lyrics go: *"Ferret said, 'I've had enough of your shit-eating grin.' She walked out. She was back the next day, saying, 'I'm sorry, honey! I'm sorry, honey!'"*[16] How many of us are on board Carolina and Ferret's guilt and backtrack train?

JUST REWARDS

The more skeptical or tentative among us might wonder if the consequences of getting angry and setting limits are too formidable. Did the Little Red Hen simply trade a loaf of bread for a one-way ticket to isolation, loneliness, and despair? Maybe the price of taking personal power is just too high. So, we shy away.

Look at Red at the end of her tale. In some versions, she is pictured by herself; in others she is with her chicks (children) relaxing and savoring her achievements and her leisure, feeling at peace. She may be reading in bed, munching bread, or sketching by the fire. And though this story appears in dozens of versions and in many countries, she is <u>never</u> depicted as feeling guilty, isolated, bitter, hopeless, depressed, agitated, ashamed, defeated, martyred, desperate—or compelled to quickly search out an eligible rooster or start an affair with a married one.

One reason many of us consistently sell ourselves out is that *being alone seems like defeat.* Red does not buy into this one. In addition, she is not immediately driven to take on more work, to throw herself into overfunctioning to drown out her angst. Having accomplished a lot, she has a sense of inner satisfaction, and she takes the time to enjoy it. All is well!

> ✄ "It's strange, but saying 'no' to people has started to feel so good, energizing even, like blocks of wood being lifted off my shoulders." ~ AJ

PRESCRIPTION:

Think about heroic Red's story.

We see that she exhibits many qualities and beliefs that could serve us well. She feels sure she possesses a number of *inalienable rights*: to take up space; ask for help; pace herself; have a vision, goals, and independent opinions; disagree with, or sometimes reject, the majority point of view; set limits; get angry, however awkwardly; make mistakes; learn from her mistakes; be imperfect and still like herself; take time off; enjoy herself and the pleasure of her own company.

Start to grasp the notion that anger is always mean and nasty in the moment, but essential for living a life of integrity. Red figures out how to give it a try. She does not beat herself up for it as we might: *"I expressed my anger so poorly." "I didn't say it soon enough." "I didn't approach them right. I'm a rotten team-builder." "I'm sorry. I'm stupid." "I'm so disappointed that I couldn't get them to cooperate. It ruined everything." "I should have seen what jerks they were and found new friends long ago. I messed up." "I'm messed up."* Instead, our Little Red continues to like herself. We, too, continue to like her, even though she has flaws. Why don't we extend ourselves that same acceptance?

Red keeps her priorities straight. She believes she deserves (has the right) to relish in the fruits of her labor; she stays free from guilt and shame. She gains insight <u>over time</u>, realizing, after some initial confusion, that she *is entitled to protect herself against being taken advantage of.* She does so by getting angry and setting a firm limit. She says "no" and she sticks by it. The Little Red Hen stays true to herself. She is big on the Alice Measure, but not "bully" big. She is self-protective and willing to take the risk that people may label her as selfish.

Limit-setting, taking risks, conceiving and achieving personal dreams, safeguarding the right to have and not have or the right to do or not do—many women find these nearly impossible challenges. Saying "no," even when it's about something sacred (our bodies, our souls), is tough. Holding onto "no" is tougher. In general, we are not convinced that we have the right to say "no." "No" is an uppity, defiant word—not for nice girls. Remind yourself that enduring anxiety is inevitable while changing old habits that perpetuate the TT. How far are we on this journey?

✄ Rights: You have the right to have a Guilt-Free Zone.

⌂ OFF TRACK

Meet Lisa, another typical overfunctioning woman in a terrible fix. Lisa, like Carolina, fears setting limits because someone might get upset or accuse her of being angry. Unable to express or deal with (receive) anger, especially from her own child, Lisa becomes easily immobilized. Lisa is:

The Guilty Mother

"All the way back to our car, five-year-old Alexa pulled on her mother's arm, screaming, kicking, biting, carrying on. And Lisa dragged her along. We'd already been through a half hour of trying to eat sandwiches at the deli, with Alexa demanding to sit where Lisa was sitting, and Lisa, ever compliant, jumping up and down to accommodate Alexa. It was like musical chairs with no music. It was like lunch without eating. I finally put a halt to it and ushered us all out. Now we had a new game that included making a scene all the way back to the car. 'What would happen if you said 'no' to her?' I (Sally) asked. 'Can you see a connection between your inability to say 'no' and her failing to develop the ability to say 'no' herself?'

"'I just feel so guilty about the divorce,' Lisa replied, forlorn. 'I can't deal with how upset Alexa gets when I tell her 'no.' 'Lisa,' I replied, 'Do you think she will die if you say 'no' to her? Actually, she will only get unglued temporarily.' 'I'm sorry, I really can't stand it!' moaned Lisa. 'It makes me so upset!'"

Lisa is perpetuating an unfortunate pattern. It makes her anxious when her child becomes anxious or angry. With her own behavior, she is teaching her daughter that 1) experiencing conflict and expressing anger is to be avoided at all costs and 2) being manipulative and out of control pays off. Alexa won't die (or hate Mom permanently) if Mom sets a clear limit. In fact, it would be good for her. After initially being furious with Lisa, Alexa will feel secure and relieved. Lisa won't die either. If she could tolerate her own anxiety about her daughter's angry feelings, Alexa would have a safe place to bump up against and she'd learn how to manage her frustration in a healthy way. But express-ing anger, even feeling it, is not maternal. Only shrews and bitches do it, right? Isn't that what we believe? So Lisa can't do it, and Alexa spins out of control.

> ✂ Conflict and anger aren't signs of failure and should not be avoided. They are natural by-products of all relationships, even happy and contented ones—simply because no two individuals are identical.

TO THE POINT

Because many women have not learned to handle anger comfort-ably, they are beset by long-held unexamined assumptions and worries about it.

"If I express my anger,
no one will like me
others will retaliate and escalate their anger, and maybe they'll
   dump me
I am being immoral
I will become unfair, too controlling, a bad person
other people will fall apart, and I will destroy them emotionally
other people will get angry and call me awful names
I'll get so upset that I will fall apart
it will feel good and that will be frightening and confusing
it will get out of control and I will never be able to stop—
   perhaps I will hurt someone."

These beliefs about the negative effects of getting angry lead to the most common of women's woes: fear, guilt, depression, and anxiety. "Will I be rejected and abandoned?" a woman asks herself, followed by, "Will I have to undo this outburst endlessly and repent forever?" and perhaps worst of all, "Will I have to leave him because I will discover that the relationship doesn't work anymore for me?"

Something big can happen when you change your anger-avoidant and "no"-avoidant behavior. You may lose an important (but unhealthy) relationship. You will *not* lose a healthy relationship because you set a limit and/or get angry. In fact, heated disagreement handled cleanly can lead to an unexpected positive outcome, improvements in communication, and increase in the level of understanding. Think of Andrea and Richard. Expressing independent opinions sometimes may indeed lead to anger and arguments. But many of these will prove resolvable. Speaking freely is a prerequisite for growing, being lively and relaxed with others. You become Alice-big, but not Alice-bully.

Surrendering to various fears and running from anger—ours or theirs—can create something even worse than losing someone. It can shrink you to a very tiny size on the Alice Measure:

"I can't ask 'cause they'll get mad."
"I can't say no when they ask 'cause they'll get mad."
"I can't get mad 'cause they'll get madder."

✂ Own your own self. It's a valuable purchase.

Here's the story of Mary who always minds her manners. She completely deserts herself to avoid facing her negative feelings. She becomes hollow and limp. She's barely registering on the Alice Measure. Mary is:

Never Contrary!

"My mother had the Irish temper in the family. Whenever she wanted her way, she'd just flare up, throw things, tell us she didn't love us, or poke our hands with her fork at the dinner table. I coped with this volatility in my family by being the consummate placating child.

"When I grew up, I found myself a husband who was equally controlling. Though his 'style' was different, I always felt afraid of his anger. (The Automatic Pilot and bad intuition were operating in this selection.) He was a big flirt and eventually had some affairs, which he didn't hide. I felt so hurt and angry, but was too freaked out to do anything about it. In fact, the more humiliated and resentful I got, the more I felt that silence helped me to maintain my dignity. So, I said nothing but suffered terribly within.

"One of my girlfriends suggested that, at least, I beat pillows to express my feelings. All I could do was roll my eyes. Like I was going to lower myself to the point of showing my anger in any way—not to him, not even to myself! It would be far too unbecoming. I would *never* consider it."

Because Mary's mother controlled the family by tyrannizing them with her endless uncontrollable outbursts, Mary confuses anger with two things more dangerous—rage and tyranny. She equates showing anger with lowering herself, with being a "bad, classless" person. As a result of this inability to face her contrary side, she allows herself to be victimized and increasingly becomes depressed. The fear of being abandoned probably also plagues her, but ignoring her feelings leads her, ironically, to abandon herself. In the end, her husband left her anyway. With her dignity trashed by him and her own unwillingness to stand up for herself, she will likely remain in the TT indefinitely.

✂ It requires boldness to go beyond the programming that defines anger as forbidden, wicked, or unfeminine.

Your Turn! IT NEVER HURTS TO ASK, OR DOES IT?

Topic: The "Don't ask/Don't need" Overfunctioning Trance

Purpose: Ascertain your issues with NOT getting help, even when you know you want or need it

A) Over the period of a week (or, if you are over-overfunctioning, try two days), keep a record of the simple, clear, and direct requests for help that you make and to whom you make them...you know, the kind that a three year old will understand (though not necessarily do). "Will you take out the dog?" "Will you please call the insurance agent, the baby-sitter, or the piano teacher?" "I would like you to help me pick up the toys or dirty laundry." "I want you to take a bath now before bedtime." "Can we talk?" "Can we go have some fun?" "I want to spend some time tonight telling you what's bothering me, okay?" Check in a column whether the requests are accepted or rejected.

B) Now note:
1) Are the requests easy or difficult to make? Does it depend on the type of request—those that are for *me personally*, for the *family* or the *pets*, for some serious *good cause*?
2) How easy or hard is it for me to state my request <u>directly</u> (even to children)?
3) How hard is it to accept <u>refusal</u> and not start feeling guilty, wrong, or <u>too</u> demanding for asking?
4) How hard or easy is it for me <u>to accept help</u> and not feel guilty, wrong, inept, inadequate, or selfish for needing or wanting something?

Notice who, if anyone, in your life says "yes" to your requests often. Who is particularly easy to ask? particularly difficult to ask?

C) If you have made very few requests for help, maybe it means you don't know how. This can be learned. Or are you <u>insisting</u> on doing it all yourself? If so, why? "Am I wrong, weak, foolish for requiring help? Is it uppity and controlling to ask? Are there "commandments" written in the Book of Me like "Thou shalt not ask for help because..." Realize that such items are ancient history and need updating.

D) Keep company with the Little Red Hen and try updating a few commandments here and now, just for fun: It is fine for me to... or I shalt.... This begins your process of creating a personal "Bill of Rights."

10
DEMYSTIFYING ANGER
Discover Anger's Constructive Uses

"...our anger [is] a guide to determining our innermost needs, values, and priorities..." ~Harriet Lerner, Ph.D.

* * *

Sugar and spice and everything nice.
That's what little girls are made of!
~ Nursery rhyme

In the last few decades, well-meaning but misguided attempts have been made to help people "deal with" or control their anger. Workshops and books teach us to talk <u>about</u> being angry while, ironically, encouraging us to avoid expressing it. Here's where anger-management classes fail. Various tranquilizing devices (pills, even excessive exercise or excessive meditation) throw a blinding blanket over the damaging effects of refusing to accept conflict as normal. We must welcome anger as a full member of the family of emotions. Denying anger its place can produce unfortunate results for several reasons. First: not dealing with it head on leaves people more afraid of it than ever. Second: we are missing out on a most effective tool for communication, self-knowledge, and getting our needs met.

IS ANGER RAGE?

To change the pattern of anger avoidance, we must first get Rage separated from Anger. The Random House dictionary defines anger as: *a strong feeling of displeasure and belligerence aroused by a...wrong....*[17] It is linked to exasperation, ire, and wrath. Whereas, Rage is: *angry fury, violent anger.*[18] It is linked to frenzy and madness.

Rage and Anger do have components in common—both are upsetting, not nice, and can be irrational. However, after some scrutiny, one realizes that the <u>differences</u> between the two emotions are far more significant than the similarities. Rage is often physical and violent, always extreme and relentless, and it careens out of control. It can appear to arise out of nowhere—randomly. It does not diminish with time or conversation. It may seem to dissipate, only to flare up later with equal or greater virulence. Rage is first cousin to Abuse. Anger is temporary and merely mean—a very distant cousin.

Anger results from frustrated communication and is stimulated by a desire to interconnect and communicate better. Rage stems from and is stimulated by a desire to control and/or punish. When anger is successful, it leads to reconciliation on an equal footing with others. "Success" with Rage—if you can call it success—is measured by power, intimidation, domination, and a sense of entitlement to more rage.

Enraged people have a definite personality profile. *They are consistently bullies, consistently unreasonable, incapable of trusting, listening accurately, or empathizing. They cannot put themselves in the place of others or allow those others their own feelings and the right to disagree.* Though enraged people sometimes express regret, their apologies have a hollow or manipulative quality, lack substance, and are short-lived. Anger passes relatively quickly after it is expressed and is replaced by a sense of fairness and a willingness to hear the other side and reconnect. Rage festers and thereby feels sinister. Rage is always dangerous and should not be tolerated. No one has the right to rage; it interferes with the safety of others and their right to pursue life, liberty, and happiness. Professional help is mandatory to deal with it.

The distinction between Rage and Anger cannot be overemphasized. The two can be graphed as follows:

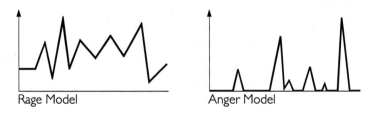

Rage Model   Anger Model

If Calm is the baseline, Rage is <u>always</u> up over that line and never comes down. In contrast, Anger rises quickly while being expressed and then comes back down to Calm within hours or days, having been completed. Anger always is stimulated by a specific catalyst in the here and now; sometimes, it also taps into past experiences, creating <u>over</u>-reactions.

Snit Fit—Andrea again

"Anger...? Well, for example, Richard reading the newspaper while I am trying to talk to him. My father and grandfathers always did this. Growing up, I never felt like I got their full attention. So, tonight, when Richard did this, I became very angry at him instead of just mildly annoyed. Imagine! Richard, who really is a great listener and consistently responsive to me! He shouted back, 'Dammit, I was listening. Don't be so super-sensitive!' Within seconds, I recognized that I had definitely over-reacted, but I stomped off sulking anyway."

Rage may or may not have a cause in present time. However, it is inevitably exaggerated to the extreme, and someone gets blamed and threatened. Here's an example of rage leaking out. Jenna is unaware of what is simmering beneath the surface when she's waiting for her:

Taxi!

"Another woman and I were standing silently under an awning in the rain, both waiting for a cab. It had taken a long time to hail one. I had been there the longest, and when the cab came, I started towards it. Before I realized what was happening, the other woman bolted in front of me and tried to take my cab! I was totally furious. Everything flashed red, and I knocked her briefcase out of her hand so she'd have to go reach for it. Then, I screamed loudly in her face and she backed off. I jabbed at her with my umbrella and managed to kick her briefcase further away. I no longer really cared about my taxi cab...except I sure didn't want her to have it! When I jumped in, I told the cabby to 'step on it.' What an outrage! Imagine the nerve of that bitch messing with me! I hope she ended up in the gutter, soaked along with all her important papers!"

Whoa! What happened here? Both women seem out to get each

other even though they are total strangers. Stealing a cab is a fairly minor offense in the larger scheme of things. Yet, Jenna doesn't hesitate to get physical, grabbing and throwing the other woman's briefcase into the wet gutter. She even goes on to kick the briefcase out of reach. The original point—to get a cab in a timely fashion—is quickly lost in the overwhelming stampede of the violent emotion. (Why doesn't it occur to either of them to behave in a mature way? How about an offer to share the cab, for instance?) Though Jenna appears calm and pleasant at first, the moment she is frustrated, she becomes furious, and enraged. The other woman was rude and obnoxious—no more, no less than that. A more healthy angry response from Jenna might be, "Hey, I was here first, Lady!" or (in a loud voice) "Wait a minute! You're pretty damned rude. I believe this is <u>my</u> cab!" It is also significant that, as she narrates her story, Jenna shows no remorse for or insight into the inappropriateness of her overreaction. In fact, she remains indignant long after the event, delighting in the telling and retelling of the drama and proud of herself as she continues to enjoy her nasty fantasy of woman and briefcase wet in the gutter. Securing the cab clearly wasn't enough of a victory for her.

Compared with rage, anger may suddenly seem manageable and containable. This can make it less frightening. When we can grant ourselves and others permission to be angry without guilt, we can begin to consider how this misunderstood emotion works as a constructive tool. We can feel safe in its presence.

> ✂ Anger is indispensable for calling someone's immediate attention to a temporary state of distress or pain.

TO THE POINT

Anger is not: polite, nice, pleasant, fun, fair, sensitive, rational, tepid, accommodating, thoughtful. It is also not endless, unsafe, or physical.

Because our culture is preoccupied with antiseptic modes for handling anger, most families have lists of what is <u>not</u> permitted when somebody is upset. However, there typically is no list at all or only a short, vague one for what one <u>can</u> do. If there is no acceptable (non-punishable) way to express yourself passionately with words, communicating intense negative feelings becomes tough. What can one do? For instance, may you shout? Insult? Use ugly words? Curse? Give the finger to your elders? When there are no recommended guidelines and nothing is considered healthy or acceptable, people make dubious (often unconscious) choices. They pretend not to have the feelings; feel ashamed, guilty, and bad about having them; get them out in a sneaky, covert, or confused (passive-aggressive) manner; simmer chronically with them; or internalize them deeply.

WHAT WOMEN DO

Women often quickly convert feeling angry into feeling hurt, sad, depressed, or vaguely ill. These emotions are much more acceptable to us because they fit with our families and our culture. They draw empathy, sympathy, and care from others. They are largely passive, not aggressive. They can be easily turned against the self into quiet personal agony. That way, no one else's cage gets rattled. They can also be used covertly to fire up guilt in others. "Oh, I'm just so hurt. I'm sad, but it's okay," is more palatable than "I'm pissed! And, you're the one I'm pissed at!" The meaning of a "hurt" statement depends heavily on the tone of voice. Said meekly, it can readily be passed over and discounted, and nobody feels threatened. Said with an edge, it's the guilt-trip jab. If confronted, however, any hostility can be denied. *"Oh, no. I'm just feeling bad about myself. I wasn't criticizing you. I wasn't mad at you."*

If you've ever been around a seriously depressed person, you know how much space he or she takes up, while sincerely claiming to want to take up no space at all. Depression dominates the environment and all those in it. Therefore, depression can become an undercover form of control, power, and unexpressed anger. This is tragic because everyone, most of all, the depressed person, suffers profound pain. Often, the underlying problems do not get articulated or appropriately addressed.

> ✂ Anger plays a part of honest, candid, intimate communication between self-respecting equals.

TO THE POINT

Anger has a key role in helping an individual be seen and heard—two essential components of a healthy relationship. "I am hurt, upset, scared, put out, shaken, frustrated, disappointed, and feel he/she/it has done me wrong. Ideally, I have already tried being assertive in a neutral way, and the other person has failed to notice or respond adequately. Now, I feel stymied. That's what drives my need to speak up in anger, to alert the other person by communicating my state more vividly (sometimes in words both ugly and shocking) and to insist on my right to be heard." Anger is a form of reaching out to someone when you are in a psychological emergency—to assert, by extreme means, your opinions or feelings. Later, you will desire acknowledgment and fuller consideration. However, at first, you'll settle to waking someone up just to see and hear you. *Deep down, anger is well-intentioned because it is motivated by wanting something to get better.* It is not about forcing agreement. That's being a bully. When you think about it as a way to improve things, the concept of anger is both logical and functional.

✂ Insist on being taken seriously. You may need to do it in a loud voice.

As with doing most things (cooking, singing, chairing a meeting, writing, playing tennis) expressing anger well is a skill. Yet, we overfunctioners, otherwise so willing to take on mastery of anything and everything, shy away from mastering anger. This is because of the pull of our cultural and familial trances. After all, we are expected to perform seamlessly and pleasantly. Getting mad doesn't fit the picture.

Expressing anger openly and directly is the only way to prevent sinking back into overfunctioning more—we are busy, busy, busy and, all the while, covering up what we are really feeling. Not expressing ourselves directly causes us to act inauthentically—we revert to accommodating as opposed to seeking an understanding with others. The TT closes in.

PRESCRIPTION:

With practice, you can learn healthy anger delivery.

The process consists of three essential steps. At first, since recoiling from anger is a habit, approaching it may feel daunting, definitely unappealing, and counterintuitive. So, try this method <u>with</u> <u>someone</u> <u>who</u> <u>is</u> <u>also</u> <u>interested</u> in practicing good anger-expression technique. This could be a close friend or anyone with whom you feel emotionally secure. Because, as a culture, we still maintain a pervasive fear of expressing anger authentically, this technique needs to be done with mutual consent.

Step One—Delivery of Feelings: This may include a loud-voiced ⌂ verbal outburst or a quieter nastiness, but it definitely consists of proclaiming grievances with passion. Flapping your arms, showing a scowling face, crying, and pacing around suit some people's styles. *Remember, you are speaking up and out.* Being illogical (at least, to some degree) and heated (emotional) are all part of a successful delivery. Otherwise, you are probably talking about anger, not being angry; anger once removed will prove insufficient. All people involved must have an opportunity to perform this first step for the process to be complete—the accuser, the accused, and anyone else who is relevant. This may take place in one or several rounds.

Step One is, by definition, unpleasant. Its positive purposes, not obvious but essential, include getting someone's attention, removing blocks to constructive consideration of the problem, release of pent-up pressure, stalemate, or misunderstanding. Paradoxically, only by permitting yourself and others to act irrationally can you get to a state of mind in which you can be honestly rational and cooperative. Step One is a prerequisite for sorting out upsetting things well. You can fix the problem adequately later on only because you've gotten everything out (expressed yourself) now.

Step Two—Personal Interlude: After Step One, which requires interaction, comes this private, individual piece—the active pause for reflecting and mulling over. This is an opportunity for increasing self-knowledge. "Slow down," says Harriet Lerner, in <u>The Dance of Anger</u>, one of the few good books on the topic. She astutely advises us to learn to use "our anger as a guide to determining our innermost needs, values, and priorities."[19] Whereas Step One was almost purely emotional, in this phase, your mind *and* emotions should be engaged. In Step Two, work solo on the issues that were raised from the fight.

Meanwhile back to Andrea and Richard's marriage, a work in progress. In the case of the newspaper, Andrea, after storming out of the room, enters Step Two. She reflects on her intense condemnation of Richard who, overall, is innocent of the crime of not listening to her. Therefore, she identifies her stuff rather quickly. She will acknowledge how she appreciates her husband's usual sensitivity towards her, so unlike her father and grandfather. She also will revisit with Richard his tendency, when rattled, to hurl mean labels her way. In a perfect world, when he gets mad, maybe he could just say, "Damn it, Andrea. Stop that!" instead of calling her insensitive or selfish, those A-bomb labels that put her *under*. Richard will likely see this as a reasonable goal for himself. They both will probably agree that this isn't a huge deal, that Andrea is learning to field the labels better, and that neither of them wants Richard to inhibit his anger.

In Step Two, like Andrea, you will ponder what events (comments, behaviors, etc.) brought on your upset and frustration in the first place. Where in the original interactions did the other person go astray? Where did you go off? How does what just went down connect to past painful encounters with this same person or with others?

Gather internal information about your sensibilities in the matter. Hypothesize about the other person's sensibilities. In relation to the incident, consider: 1) precipitating events to the moment of the angry outburst; 2) relevant past history; 3) essence and details of the basic issues in contention and in need of resolution in present time; 4) explanations useful to express to the other person and explanations you may wish to request of the other person; and 5) possible solutions or options going forward.

In this private process, you may raise questions or painful revelations about yourself and someone else. You might simply get a new idea. You may identify a false assumption with which you or the other person has been operating, or you may discover that you have overreacted or misplaced your upset onto the wrong person. You may recognize a familiar shortcoming in yourself or another. If you become convinced that you have aimed the ball the wrong way, an apology can be planned. You may identify what you are afraid of or see that you want to ask what he or she is afraid of. Even if you only "recognize that…(you) are not yet clear about something,"[20] this is significant. Personal realizations and insights from this middle Interlude (Step Two) constitute valuable data to bring into Step Three.

Step Three—Regrouping and Problem-Solving: The task of Step Three is to access your rational capabilities, including your flexibility, open-mindedness, and concern for the other person as well as yourself. Now it is time to tackle the controversial issues. Real problems usually drive anger; these still exist, demanding attention. The heated emotions have been aired, and you've had time to reflect. You can now achieve a blend of mind and feeling—the best of yours and the best of theirs.

This may occur anytime from several hours after the Interlude to several days. If you attempt it before at least an hour has passed, that may be too hasty to work. You may just be covering up the exposure and calming the discomfort that Step One generated. If so, the resolution (or re-solution) will not last. Sometimes, a number of days is needed to move with authenticity to Step Three. Some people require more time than others to make the transition from being angry and receiving anger (Step One) to dealing with the issues involved that caused the feelings (Step Three). Some need lots of time to ponder and sort in the Personal Interlude. There is no virtue or vice here, no extra points for moving on more quickly. The slower party does, however, need to acknowledge the delay so the other person won't feel punished, toyed with, ignored, or worried. If no explanation is given, taking extra time may be a form of acting out more anger in an indirect way. It's the Ice-Prince/Ice-Princess: "I'll freeze you out and control/punish you with my silence" routine. This behavior indicates that Step One is incomplete and must be revisited. The anger has not been cleared out sufficiently.

You will succeed in Step Three if you acknowledge any irrationality you have displayed in Step One. The literal words, "I'm sorry," are not key; accepting roughly 50% responsibility (in almost all situations) is the essence of the matter. A small number of conflicts really are more one person's doing than the other. However, beware the relationship in which this is claimed more than about 15% of the time, with one party either absorbing or slinging most of the blame.

During Step Three, you must continue to work hard. Problems should not be ignored, even in the midst of a seductive and welcome calm. The good news is that you return to the table as teammates rather than as adversaries. You attempt to reach clarity, and perhaps consensus, even if it is only to realize you still disagree with each other. You can agree to continue the struggle or get comfortable with seeing things differently.

A healthy relationship was well-characterized by E.M. Forster, in the *introductus* to his novel, <u>Howard's End</u>: "They never always saw eye-to-eye, but they were always looking at the same things."[21]

Great opportunities present themselves. Now it is time to bring up <u>tactfully</u> what you feel is the other person's "stuff;" exchange information, even secrets, from the present or past, and develop new ideas. Build a coalition, a compromise, a restructuring of things, a plan, a new perspective, a better and deeper mutual understanding and respect, and an expanded sense of trust, love, and closeness. Only within this structure will genuine fairness grace your primary relationships. Anger can then become a constructive tool for intimacy and personal growth.

THE FOUR ATTRIBUTES

An ability to a) listen accurately, b) self-reflect, c) receive feedback, and d) empathize is essential. These four attributes sustain relationships and make them fulfilling. Without them, the danger of overfunctioning and sacrificing yourself is always high. Those who do not possess these abilities are likely IPs.

Skipping any of the three steps of the Anger model will produce less than satisfactory results. Completing only Step One (delivery of emotion and pressure release) creates chronic resentment, smoldering mistrust, and more anger. This can potentially turn into rage and/or permanent bitterness because nothing really gets settled. Many people grow up in such households, overhung by a poisonous cloud of negative feelings. They come into adulthood convinced that if anger is dished out, nothing can ever get fixed, and life will be lived in perpetual tension, sadness, or fear.

Some people try to skip Step One. Instead of getting angry in a vivid, direct way, they try to self-reflect while still full of frustration and upset. Here, mulling will rarely prove productive because it gets skewed through the lens of unexpressed negative emotion. Some people leap into Step Three (Problem Solving)—"let us make nice and reason together." Often, books on "fair fighting" fall into this trap. They provide elaborate, constricting Do's and Don'ts that inhibit participants from expressing themselves fully. Since, as we have explored, anger is, by its very nature, unfair, irrational, and not pretty, this method encourages an intellectualization of anger. Inadvertently, it reinforces avoidance and fear of the raw feelings. It's the release of Step One that does the cleansing. Without it, your capacity to think clearly and fairly or to feel empathy is impaired. So you may tend to bury things and get stuck in the superficial or walking-on-eggshells life. In this landscape, lasting solutions can't be reached.

Step Two also should not be omitted. The Interlude provides the possibility for a personal growth spurt in perspective, insight, and wisdom which will contribute both to a positive shift in Step Three and to improving your ongoing relationship.

Think about this: WHAT ARE THE RULES about anger in your cur- △ rent environment? Can you risk stimulating anger in order to change the patterns you believe need to change? Can you risk being seen and heard? Ponder if you are willing to get angry in order to protect yourself and safeguard against the TT.

Your Turn! ANGER RECOGNITION EXERCISE

Topic: Anger: a complex, loaded emotion— up close and personal

Purpose: Develop your own Anger Profile

Learn the ABCs of your own relationship with anger. A: When does it occur? B: What causes it? C: With whom does it happen most frequently and most problematically? Now, break this down into manageable parts:

A) First, become Anger Aware. Know when you're feeling it or worrying that it will slip out. Check in several times a day and search for it in case you have brushed it away automatically. Look carefully at the usual suspects: feeling hurt, sad, bummed out, listless, or uptight. See if anger is lurking behind these emotions. Observe whether you tend to "see" other people's points of view very quickly— too quickly. You may be uncomfortable with not doing this because you fear their possible anger.

What do you typically do with your angry feelings? Stuff them away? Try to distract yourself? Blame yourself? Sulk? Tell a third party about "their" outrageousness and your victimization? Take it out on someone weaker—your child, the dog, your employee? Yell and scream for long periods of time? Lecture? Nitpick? Forget something important they asked you to do?

B) Come up with three or four things that make you the most angry and upset on a fairly predictable basis. Which of these things are you most frightened to mention directly? "I would never dare tell my mother that I was so angry when she did..." "I was too afraid to speak out when my friend stood me up again." With whom do these emotions most commonly occur—partner, child, mom, boss, employee, neighbor? Who are the people you feel most afraid to get angry at? Who are the people you feel most afraid to receive anger from? Why?

C) Do any of these individuals seem to be very poor selections based on the four qualities on the Attribute List? However difficult, face this squarely. Even if you cannot completely divest yourself, try to reduce your sense that the difficulty with this person is always your fault and that you must overfunction to fix it. Develop your confidence in recognizing IPs and placing a firewall of protection around yourself. Note: this is the positive side of firewalling.

11
OPERATING RULES FOR ANGER
Maintain Self-Esteem in the World

In Persian Sufi lore, there is a comical character named Sheik Nasruddin. He is always getting into trouble. Here we see him mishandling his emotions in a way that makes us laugh…until we remember that Nasruddin needs to accomplish something important and he can't. We empathize.

Nasruddin needs to plow his field, but he doesn't have a plow. He decides to borrow one from his neighbor. He gets on his donkey and as he's riding, he starts thinking: What if my neighbor doesn't want to lend me his plow? If my neighbor doesn't want to lend me his plow, then I won't be able to plow my fields! If I can't plow my fields, my crops won't grow and I won't have any food and I won't have the money I would make from selling some of my harvest! What if he won't answer the door when I get there? If he doesn't answer the door, I can't ask if I can borrow his plow. What if he does open the door but won't speak to me? Nasruddin goes on and on like this working himself up. When he arrives at his neighbor's house, he pounds on the door, spitting mad for all of these perceived injustices. His neighbor opens the door, happy to see him, but Nasruddin is so angry that he yells at his neighbor, "How dare you not talk to me! How dare you not lend me your plow! I never want to speak to you again! How could you do such a thing? You, my closest neighbor!" And he storms out, leaving his neighbor perplexed.

Nasruddin suffers two big fears: He's afraid of receiving anger or NO and he's afraid of asking for help even when he approaches a friendly neighbor. Add to his burden, a fear of *getting* angry and, worse still, *showing* it, and you have the predicament of most women. Even in neutral situations, we become fellow travelers with Nasruddin. We get so anxious about expressing ourselves assertively, particularly declaring our opinion or pain or asking for a favor (help) that we twist reality around and behave strangely—leaving our recipients stupefied and ourselves out of options. It's a wonder that we can move around in the world at all.

No wonder that many of us long ago have run away from our feelings. Clearly, that doesn't work. Typically, anger was the first emotion to get dumped, even less acceptable to us than anxiety. But, where to turn… We must reawaken <u>all</u> our feelings in order to grow into our power and effectiveness in any area of life. What now?

As always, clear definitions of key terms will help us out, will lower our anxiety to a good octane level. *Power* is another loaded word, especially for women. It's useful to define power carefully. As with many loaded words, what it does <u>not</u> mean is as important as what it does. Note that power does not mean aggression or hostility. It means strength and taking up some (equal, but not all) space.

> ✂ You cannot NOT teach your children. If you don't teach them good habits, you will, by default, teach them bad habits.

TO THE POINT

You can't avoid negative emotions without paying a high price. Not convinced? Consider which of the following consequences you would prefer to an angry exchange: giving or getting the silent treatment; withdrawing or being withdrawn from; chronic forgetting (by you or the other person); being picked on and picking on; being cheated on and cheating on (financially or romantically); being lied to and lying; being talked about behind your back or doing the talking; performing poorly at work, at school, or at home; getting dumped or dumping (seemingly out of the blue).

Or would you prefer someone else expressing your anger? A child, perhaps, will have an outburst on your behalf because you are pretending you're not angry. How about becoming despondent and depressed, or turning to alcohol or drugs, or sleeping all the time? Some people suffer from migraines, backaches, insomnia, digestive problems, chronic exhaustion, immune suppression, or even something worse.

These conditions can often be anger-related. For sure, *someone* will carry the negative feelings. Remember Remy!

People often mistakenly link anger to disrespect: "You can't say X because it means you don't respect me." Actually, respect has nothing to do with whether you get angry at somebody and call him or her names. Respect means holding someone in high esteem and regard, and taking his or her viewpoint, priorities, values, feelings, and advice seriously over time. Think about this in relation to people you know you respect. You do not experience them as impressive every single second of every day. Nor do you relate to them without ever disagreeing or getting frustrated and upset. You even hurt their feelings from time to time and they hurt yours.

A KIND OF WORKING CAPITAL

Within families, creating good operating rules for expressing anger is important: you must establish clearly *what is permitted without punishment*. Only then can everyone feel emotionally safe and free to occupy equal amounts of space. These anger concepts apply widely in both domestic and work areas. Those of you who are parents have the great opportunity to support your children in developing a stable, robust Alice-size for life. Getting the anger mechanism in good working order with a clear instruction manual is crucial.

Marriage researchers have stated that for a union to thrive, negative communications need to be outweighed by positive ones, approximately five+ to one. At first glance, you might think that these findings indicate that getting angry can be dangerous to the stability of a relationship. However, upon deeper consideration, it becomes evident that the expression of anger in a clear, direct fashion (as in the model presented in Chapter 10) stimulates positive communication. This, in turn, produces genuine warmth, hope, and good feelings about one's significant other. People are inspired to relate in a more support-ive, tender, connected, joyous manner. In comparison, relationships weighed down with holding back, secrets, and "protecting" the other person by avoiding frank communication about difficult things become dreary, sad, and tense, even when no one is being overtly negative.

✂ Unexpressed anger erodes intimacy.

Child-Parent Anger Rules are among the most challenging to figure out. It works like this for Marion and her fourteen-year-old daughter, Ariel. In this family, expressing emotions emotionally is:

The Insurance Policy

"Ariel frequently hurls insults my way. Things like 'I hate you!' 'You're a terrible mother.' 'I'd like to run away from home.' 'You don't understand anything!' 'You're a bitch! Go to hell.' Whoa! These comments sting badly and upset me very much. But I trust Ariel and our history together and our love for each other. So when things erupt, first I try to stay silent and take her feelings in. I also raise my voice at times and tell her a thing or two like, 'I'm not your damned servant. I'm a person too. Do I look to you like Cinderella before the ball?' And 'You need to take more responsibility around here.' 'Why didn't you....?' My daughter's flare-ups are related, of course, to the shifting of roles from mom-and-child to mom-and-adolescent. Since neither of us has made this transition before, inevitably, it gets awkward and bumpy at times. Misunderstanding and hurt occur as we try to find our way. In between, we still laugh together, enjoy each other, and help one another.

"Even in my distress, I always know that this anger business is okay. I'm the one who taught her how to do it! My husband and I are the ones who established that it is acceptable to say mean things, and even curse and call the other person names. In our family, there are no punishments for <u>anything</u> said in private, regardless of how caustic or outrageous. We believe that releasing anger is constructive. All words are okay. No double-standard for what adults can say versus what kids can. Only physical expression is not okay. These are our rules.

"Harrowing as it is while it's going on, I am convinced that this method is helping to ensure, for Ariel and her younger sisters and me, a good relationship for life. A lot of trust and closeness develops when you are free to speak your mind. Upset as I get and angry and hurt—and I do—I don't worry about my children respecting me.

In fact, *I'm confident that their respect for me increases every time I respect them enough to let them express themselves fully.* Although this may seem like unorthodox behavior, their father and I are convinced that it serves our goals with our children."

✂ The right to express anger must be granted to all.

This exact plan is not for everybody. Each set of parents has to find a zone that works for their family. What is acceptable to you in the anger department? Not easy, not comfortable, but *acceptable*. Most of us were raised with poor anger models. So, bad intuition most often prevails in our initial attitudes towards this topic. As usual with intuition, you need to examine it and trace it back to its roots. Just because a certain procedure feels natural doesn't mean it's a good one.

PRESCRIPTION: Think through the results you are getting with your current anger program (provided you even know what your program is). If you don't know your rules of operation, start here and figure them out.

You must challenge and question your automatic/unexamined assumptions about anger. Find something verbal that will allow your children to get their feelings out passionately. Marion adds: "Many of my friends have disapproved of my no-words-barred method. Recently though, a number of people have been commenting on how easy an adolescence all three of my kids seem to be having. And they want to know my 'secrets for success.' Our Anger System surely is one of them. I think it's worth pointing out that our children tend to curse in public far less than their friends. In fact, overall, they behave in a very responsible, straight-forward fashion; you know, no little white lies, staying out late, or other rebellious acts. I think all this is related to the fact that cursing and other rude, ugly utterances are <u>not</u> <u>prohibited</u> in my home. When there is a rule against it, cursing (and the like) become juicy temptations, perfect tools for defiance. After all, defiance and acting out are just anger in different clothing—one, more dangerous than mere words."

✂ Anger, well-processed, buoys relationships up and blows away the clouds of revenge.

Not every situation is a ripe playing field for the kind of honesty we are talking about here. Unfortunately, in many work environments, just like many domestic ones, clear methods may exist for anger control and/or suppression, but not for anger expression. In such environments, launching your anger can be very risky. You could lose your job. Often, the boss/leader/parent/adult/male is allowed to get angry, and everyone else (subordinate/child/female) isn't. In these settings, overfunctioning workers, because they are so competent, efficient, or reliable, frequently get taken advantage of by bosses and co-workers. The rules in organizations for how to handle situations that stimulate anger are typically vague or non-existent.

It's easy to overfunction in the workplace because there's always too much to do. With the trend in cut-backs and outsourcing, American workers feel less safe and are now more likely to accept unreasonable demands on their time. If this isn't bad enough, there will always be co-workers who blithely count on "the team" to pick up the slack for them. Tess, a consummate Little Red Hen, found herself in such an untenable situation:

The Over/Underfunctioner Work Dance

"Janet was hired because she had worked in a prestigious agenting house in Hollywood as a script reader. She didn't have nearly the experience that I did in editing scripts for television, but she was hired to edit them for our production company. Her position was above mine. Though I had worked at the company longer, she was paid more than I, solely on the basis of her background. She was very protective of her copy and wouldn't let anyone touch it. She also took time off that no one else took and often worked from home. All this made her unavailable for things that came up in the office. This annoyed many of us in the department, but we tolerated it. What else could we do? Worst of all, when deadlines hit, Jan's copy would never be ready, and the task of finishing up her job always fell on the rest of us, checking her facts and so forth. Not surprisingly, I felt used. But also no surprise, I didn't think I had the right to say anything to the boss. It seemed like tattle-taling (shades of junior high school), and this would reflect badly on me. Finally, after I had endured many late nights, I did say something, second-guessing myself all the way. Fortunately, my boss immediately agreed that it was egregious and took action. I was relieved, but, you know, I still feel terribly guilty. Believe it or not, even knowing that what she was doing wasn't fair didn't make it easier for me to speak up. Old habits sure die hard! I'm positive Janet thought I was a backbiting bitch. But with her blatant disregard of others, I have to ask myself, why do I even care what she thought?"

To avoid becoming easy prey to excessive demands and commands of others, hone your skills in saying "no," protesting, showing anger about seriously bad treatment, and receiving anger (or other more subtle pressures) when you do set limits. In many systems (except thoroughly tyrannical ones), authorities will often come to respect you if you respect yourself enough to refuse to be treated badly. You are not a failure if you do not do it all. Shake off your overfunctioning trances. When Rita proclaimed, "I can't afford to lose ground!" she wasn't really consider-ing what this phrase meant. Don't turn into Rita. Since her accident, she has changed. In fact, she now laughs about her story: "Can you believe I did that to myself?"

TO THE POINT

The main challenges in a job will always surface when you get to know the unique subculture within the organization—the rules by which it operates, both overt and covert. We recommend first figur-ing out the rules structure as it relates to power, conflict, and general communication. Then, as particular situations arise, you will be able to hone appropriate tools and successful strategies.

In dicey work environments, sometimes the mature decision may be to say nothing. Though these times are relatively rare, they do exist and should be honored. Keep your own counsel or talk to a friend. More often than not, reasons for deciding to be silent are based on personal fear and rationalizations.

Keep in mind, as always, the four attributes needed for healthy conflict resolution—the ability to: a) listen accurately, b) self-reflect, c) receive feedback, and d) empathize (not in the heat of Step One, of course). Remember Dr. Landis. If she had used this attribute list as she was applying for that research job, rather than just going into the *trance* of "it feels like family," she might have made a different choice entirely. As it was, only after hitting the wall did she awaken to the fact that she would *never* be taken seriously in that setting no matter how hard she worked at it or how intelligent she was.

It's hard not to fault yourself and descend into guilt and self-doubt as Dr. Landis and Tess did. For the sake of your internal sense of stability, it is important to make suggestions and express your ideas, even if positive feedback is minimal. In doing this, you will be supporting your self-esteem and gathering useful data about the health of the organization. If a system is seriously dysfunctional, people will react with defensiveness and closed minds. Even so, continue to speak up in a diplomatic fashion. Your frustration level will diminish because you aren't permitting yourself to go passive and invisible. In this way, you will prevent yourself from shrinking to a tiny slip-through-the-key-hole Alice-size.

You may be surprised to discover that just understanding the dynamic of the particular anger system (even a dysfunctional one) will help you to feel less crazy or wrong. You will know that it's "it," not you. This sense of sanity will enable you to function more efficiently if you must remain at your post. It will be easier to maintain distance from the drama and to take some pleasure in certain specifics of your job. Set limits when others push you to overfunction. Remember Tess! Practicing this sort of damage containment becomes an effective firewall—in this case, a form of positive self-protection. In adverse circumstances, save your resources of time and energy for other parts of your life. Guard them as the treasures they are.

As a culture, we handle anger reluctantly and incompetently. This is one reason why more rage keeps developing. We let others express the negatives for us—television shows are filled with violence and aggression; children act like criminals, and adults glamorize criminal behaviors. We vote to pay large sums of money to build more jails to contain the rage. It doesn't work, of course. Together, we should learn and teach our children to do anger so that so that we and they don't do rage. This is one job we must not delegate.

"We played the games of Dead and Lost
And Shot, Winners and Rescuers and War,
Good guys against bad, but not
House, that unpredictable field
Of power where Susan's dad beat her brother
With a belt and Larry's mother
Never went out and Ria's mother drank
A fifth a day and mine cried
Herself to sleep and never said why.
Daily we got back in the saddle
And rode the range, killing Indians,
Rounding up strays—Lone Ranger,
Roy Rogers and friends. Oh, just like
The kids today we played,
Except that the heroes are plastic now,
And sometimes the guns are real."[22]

We're all daunted by today's reality, even more that we were scared by yesterday's. Skills in verbal conflict will protect us and our children from a lot of hardship and exposure to impossible choices. As a top parenting priority, please make use of this uncommon sense in handling anger and anxiety.

> ✂ If you become an expert user of words, you don't act out and become an "ab-user."

Let's make sure that all the children will face the world with the right tools to go into good verbal battle and reconciliation.

Think about this: LET ANGER IN. Can you establish the expression of anger as part of your definition not only of freedom and femininity, but also of intimacy? Do you see why anger is a tool for protecting and maintaining your self-esteem? Do you see getting angry and setting limits as safeguards against your falling back into doing too much?

Your Turn! ANGER "IN" THE SYSTEM

Topic: Exploration of anger in different facets of your life

Purpose: Mastering the Anger Model

A) Review the Three Step Anger Model in the previous chapter. Consider what the harder and easier parts of it are for you: 1) Expressing anger emotionally and getting it out with no guilt; 2) Self-reflecting in detail and mulling over the matter; being fair to both yourself and the other person; 3) returning to interaction for communicating and problem solving.

B) Now, look at a system you engage in—your home, job, team, church, temple, club, committee. Are there mechanics in place for expressing negative feelings safely? Using the Three Step Anger model as a criterion, which are the healthy systems to which you belong, if any? Workplace? Meditation center? With whom do you do anger well? Your mom? Your friend? Your grown-up child? Your pet?

C) Can you begin to imagine anger and limit-setting as positive steps towards empowerment and maintaining closeness? Be as specific as you can with examples from your own life. As you get generally stronger, your Alice-size will get bigger and more stable and you will gain confidence with your limit-setting/anger skills. Are you feeling ready to deal more vigorously with the Impossible People in your life (the ones who don't meet the Four Attributes standard)? You can find the inner resources to <u>unchoose</u> them if you must, like the Little Red Hen eventually does. Although this weeding out may be difficult and bittersweet, it will create space to fill with better people and experiences.

You will find that this makes the best insurance policy for everybody's safety. We can do this. We can become role models.

Review the contents of your uncommon tool kit so far:
—Anxiety
—Anger
—Label shields
—List of healthy personality attributes
—IP Brief Tests
—Trance Awareness

And there's more to come. Read on.

12
RAISING YELLOW AND RED FLAGS
Don't Doubt Your Sense of Doubt

At this point, you have amassed new ways to build self-esteem from the inside. In this chapter, revisiting the relationship landscape, you can fine-tune your ability to anticipate discordance early, before it becomes a huge, time-sucking problem. An ability to size up people quickly will help you to steer clear of adverse situations and to do "damage control" when there are compelling reasons to stay in a relationship. We recommend a warning system, and we'll use Red and Yellow Flags to evaluate levels of emotional peril. Raise an internal Red Flag to indicate extreme danger to your selfhood and well-being. Yellow Flags indicate "proceed with caution." Keep your eyes open before you make any commitments. A reliable evaluation system will help you determine which chances to take and which to forgo.

With sufficient ability to spot dubious personality types, you can avoid getting involved with them. Many situations that might otherwise consume you can be avoided.

We begin with interpersonal Red Flags—Impossible People. Among them we find Control Freaks, Drama Junkies, Guilt-Drama Junkies, Drowning Swans, and Put-Down Artists. These people quickly compromise your sense of self and clarity of thought. Around such people, you keep trying harder (overfunctioning) while feeling worse and worse (lowering self-esteem).

Control Freaks conduct relationships as if they were military battles. Power issues dominate at all times. In this type of relationship, each party must fight for everything because everything is seen in terms of victory or defeat. Control Freaks insist that the towels be stored on a certain shelf, and they never buy you flowers just because you said flowers are what you enjoy.

With Control Freaks, everything comes down to this: Someone must surrender. The act of giving flowers isn't joyful and pleasing to these people—it is instead perceived as surrendering to your dominance. From a healthy perspective, this seems skewed, of course. The end result? You can't build real mutuality, warmth, or teamwork in this relationship. You will end up lonely and tired because all interactions are absorbed in the endless control dynamic and require your eternal vigilance. Most importantly, it's not clear what you actually get if you do win some control in the ongoing "battle."

Drama Junkies feel most alive in the midst of melodramatic situations involving angst and volatility. We're back with Rhett and Scarlett. DJ's are addicted to tension, trauma, and tenuous glory.

Like all addicts, they will throw every goal away, including happiness, for the "high" that emotional turmoil brings them. This drive for drama usually reflects a past in which, as children, they were neither heard nor seen unless they created something big. Becoming hysterical, flunking school, winning the trophy, being the prom queen, or crashing the car was required to get some attention.

A variation of Drama Junkies are the **Guilt-Drama Junkies**. They always act like they feel guilty—they draw attention to themselves by being super-anxious and super-shaky. Obsessed with worry and concern for others, they constantly pull for support. But all of your reassurance falls into a bottomless pit. It is of no avail. Life becomes about the drama of their guilt. You may reassuringly say, "Of course, it's okay if you come over." The Guilt-Drama Junkie will respond, "Are you sure? I feel so guilty about intruding." You reply, "Not at all. I think you're a *great* person. We're so glad you're here." The Guilt-Drama Junkie asks again, "Are you sure you want me to stay?" "Of course, we want you to stay." And so on and on and on. Their meekness and concern about not taking up space provides a thin veneer to cover up self-centeredness and grandiosity. It is a disguised form of "It's all about me!" Notice how much space and energy they do take up.

The world also has its share of **Drowning Swans** (a variation of the Guilt-Drama Junkie theme). Drowning Swans always need your help and require you to save them. They're chronically involved in some disaster and going under. Nothing ever stabilizes for long with these people. You need to grasp that something about their angst, horrible as it seems to you, feels really good to them.

Mixed in with their gratitude is pressure for you to keep on delivering your services.

Get it? It's all about them.

Don't overlook the **Put-Down Artists**. Throw that Red Flag up high with these guys and gals! Put-Down Artists are another variation of Narcissist. They perpetually insult you, though subtly. They exude the attitude that they are simply much better than you. Or, worse, they discount you altogether. You're not "there" enough to be argued with, competed with, or even actively rejected. You don't even represent a blip on their radar screens. No doubt, you know some of these people!

Yellow Flag items are less critical than Red, but nonetheless involve things that are likely to compromise the growth of a relationship over time. The following deficits call for immediate tossing up of a Yellow Flag: anger or anxiety avoidance, high competitiveness in significant areas, difficulty in accepting a share of responsibility in an unsuccessful interaction, an inability to state wants or needs, and discouragement that you state your wants or needs. All of these situations need Yellow Flags of caution and self-warning!

How to proceed? Keep a close watch on the depth and breadth of the problem, and set lower expectations for relationships with these individuals. For instance, go for coffee once a month; don't make a major or intimate commitment (like naming him or her a new best friend or future lover). If you are already seriously involved, if this is your mother or spouse, for example, you will still need to face the difficulties straight on. Try talking it through calmly. Some people really can change if you approach them wisely. If you realize that their limits are permanent, adjust your expectations downward and your protective firewall upwards. For example: What if you decide that Mom will never be able to see that she dominates the airways and can't listen well to others? In a situation like this, work on *not setting yourself up* for defeat over and over again. You may just need to stick to small talk and no talk (go to the movies, concerts, and the like). Stop presenting your treasured perceptions. It's a waste of your breath and it hurts too much.

Clara, whom you are about to meet, got hooked by a Put-Down

Artist. It took several rounds before she was able to see the dynamic. Making various excuses, she repeatedly brushed off the mini-barbs flung at her by Harriet. Clara didn't see how mean-spirited and damaging the interactions were, for herself or their long professional association. Harriet was adept at asking Clara penetrating questions. This was the hook—"See, she really is interested in me," thought Clara. Once Harriet had gotten Clara's full attention, she would sling some underhanded remark followed by:

I Really Want to Support You —Clara

"We met in a writer's group. Harriet repeated over and over how much more talented she thought we were compared with the others in the group. I didn't see it that way but didn't think that much about it. I certainly didn't sense any need to toss up any warning flags on account of her flattery. She would call and insist, 'I really want to support you as a writer, Clara. We really have to do lunch! I want to know what's going on with you, Clara.' I was struggling financially and lunches were not in my budget. 'How about breakfast?' I countered, thinking I could afford—both financially and with the time—a side-order egg and a cup of coffee. 'That works!' she'd reply cheerily (or was it eerily?). Then she'd insist on picking up the tab—my $3.50 + tip. (Still, no flag.) It didn't seem like a big thing; I've treated others to meals from time to time. She then noted that it was too bad my husband didn't make enough money 'so you can do this more often, Clara.' He actually makes a good living, but we have a child with a chronic illness, and there is always some unexpected expense. (At this point, I should have, at least, fingered a flag in my pocket, felt the fabric, and considered peeking at it.)

"Once, I had to bring my child with me to one of the group's meetings. Harriet commented, within earshot of my daughter, 'Oh God, Clara! How can you stand it?' (This was definitely Red Flag territory.) My reaction? I was put off, but again dismissed it because some people simply get uncomfortable around, shall we say, delicate children.

"Harriet asked if I would read her work and offer some sugges- tions. I pored over it, spending many hours. Next, she offered to hire me to do some dialogue polish for her novel. Since she was a friend,

I gave her a very friendly rate, only $100 for six hours of work. At the same time, our mutual editor asked her to do a read of my manuscript 'as a professional courtesy.' Harriet agreed. When I delivered Harriet's work to her, she blithely remarked, 'Let's consider this a trade since Toni had me read your piece.' Well, that was a Red Flag! Again, I decided to let it pass. I ignored the fact that, in the past, I'd read a lot of her material without ever mentioning money.

"Many more minor 'incidents' occurred. She'd remark that her house was better than my house. I really ought to go to the gym and lose some weight. My co-author was a bitch; my husband clueless. I didn't agree with her, and these uninvited assessments made me feel mildly uncomfortable. Still, her remarks seemed rather trivial to me, so I brushed them off. And she always presented things as if she were on my side, looking out for me, as it were. In retrospect, every one of those comments was deserving of a Yellow Flag. Put altogether, they added up to Red for sure.

"Finally, she invited me to attend a brunch for literary friends at her house. In order to show that I was not annoyed (or was it angered?) by the last incident, I accepted her invitation. 'I want to support you, Clara, by introducing you to all these important literary people,' she chimed merrily. By now, my guard was up. My husband advised me not to go. I went anyway. 'I don't know why you keep subjecting yourself to her,' he said as I waltzed out the door. I was wondering this myself, but said, 'Look, Honey, I have to stay friendly. We're in the same business. She's not <u>that</u> bad.'

"Well, she was that bad, and I finally got it. At dinner that evening, Harriet launched into reporting some intimate details of my life to this group who knew nothing about me except that I was a guest at the party. With the dinner party watching, she built me up and then knocked me down in one fell swoop. I was stunned. I tried to act like it wasn't bothering me, but left as soon as I could. Finally, I saw Red."

Clara took repeated abuse from a Put-Down Artist. Eventually, she recognized the pattern, woke up, and dumped the association. Amazingly, she managed to keep her Alice-size intact despite Harriet's repeated efforts to treat her with the same dismissive manner with which the Red Queen treated Alice. Clara, however, has a lot to think about. What trance of bad intuition did Harriet stimulate in Clara to keep her flying back into that flame over and over again?

> ✂ Failing to unchoose highly toxic people and situations is a reckless decision.

Another tool for evaluating psychological hazards is the Ant (A's) to Elephant (E's) scale. We've talked a lot about Elephant types. These IPs should be possible to spot by now. They are formidable, make you feel invisible and unheard, or throw you back into total accommodation, into an experience of impotence and servitude. Grandpa Joe, Colindy, and Harriet are examples.

Moving up the animal alphabet—but down in size—there are the D-people. Let's call them Dromedaries. D-people demand your attention and absorb lots of time and energy. However, a positive outcome may be possible. Regardless, relationships with these people still require Red Flags. For example, an issue may involve serious disagreement about an important ethical matter, like cheating on taxes or on a big exam; or it may be a major bump in a significant relationship, like infidelity or heavy drinking. It's necessary to face these issues directly and promptly because they are large enough to get in the way and stimulate overfunctioning. They may become major, insurmountable problems.

On the A (Ant) end of the scale, you might find: partner cleans the kitchen after dinner but fails to wipe off the countertops; person uses the last of the toilet paper without replacing the roll; toothpaste tube is squeezed from the middle. These might drive you mildly crazy, but there is no need for any flag waving on this front.

We could call C's and B's Cougars and Bulldogs. Your response to them will be personal and idiosyncratic, based on what you've lived through in your life combined with your unique style of coping. Everyone's sensitivity chart is different in this middle zone. The key is to know where you need to draw your lines and to not be afraid or ashamed to do it. For example, Mary and John are always twenty minutes late. This might be a C for one of their friends, but only a B for another. These sorts of actions do not necessarily call for raising any warning flags at all. However, speaking up, without blaming, about how something makes you feel might be advisable. The way in which people respond to your frankness will vary and give you valuable insight about the potential of different relationships.

Often you can turn B's into good humor if you've cleared the air about them. Armando and Enriqué are brothers and close friends. One is super-punctual, the other super-tardy. Their typical dialogue goes like this: "I'll arrive at ten," says always-late Armando. "Shall I add thirty or forty-five minutes to that estimate?" quips Enriqué. "Thirty would be just fine!" Armando laughs. And the day goes on without resentment.

If you find yourself reacting to an Ant situation as if it were a Dromedary or Elephant, then you most definitely have a Dromedary or Elephant lurking somewhere in your own history. Nailing poor, unsuspecting Frank for something when it's your father (from childhood memories) who has gotten you upset isn't fair. Likewise, nailing poor, unsuspecting Frank for something his mother did or said to you (in very recent times) isn't fair either. It's very important to become aware of your most common patterns of misfiring. Share this information candidly with significant others. Ask for theirs while you're at it. There are many variables on this theme. We all have displacement tendencies. Transparency goes a long way to sorting these things out quickly when they occur. And you can be sure that they will occur.

Your strongest issue may be that you have *bad intuition* as a result of your personal history. This may lead you to be actively drawn to dangerous and disappointing people (IPs). Pause to think about your reluctance to assess your selections carefully; consider how you might begin to overcome this. Remember that without an internal warning system in place, you will repeatedly put yourself at high risk—*avoidable*, unnecessary risk.

You can become alert to your tendency to be drawn to certain types (even when you know from experience that they are not good for you). Some Yellow Flag people (Bulldogs or Cougars) may be okay in certain contained roles. But not all. Clara tried to associate with Harriet in one specific setting (writing-related gatherings), and it did not work. Harriet, however, proved to be a Red Flag/Elephant regardless of the containment tactic. When Clara was considering a long-term connection with Harriet, with the hope of deepening trust and potential, she would have fared better had she proceeded with caution. So will you. Take more time to get to know the Yellow Flag person in question. Take it slow.

Now consider the Green Flag people. They offer you the welcoming space to build emotional safety and satisfying relationships. These people are able to express their feelings honestly and provide empathy, and they seek self-reflection. They are Red and Yellow Flag people IN REVERSE!

Do you detect any anxiety that may lead you to step back, to avoid these fine people with excellent potential? Though it indeed seems strange, this phenomenon plagues many of us, and bad intuition often rules the day. Try to remember your major fears, usually stemming from past events and people in your life. See if these patterns are currently operating. Most commonly, fears are rooted in the following erroneous thinking: Intimacy is dangerous because it will inevitably turn into something very negative, like domination, victimization, surrender, and loss of oneself. Does this resonate with you? Perhaps, you saw this happen to someone you love.

Guilt, too, may play a role in eclipsing a potentially gratifying relationship. You believe you do not deserve this good person. What are you so guilty of? Face this answer and whatever insidious elements automatically appear to be blocking you from engaging with this person. Surely, some of these beliefs about yourself are now outdated or false.

Understand your own strengths, weaknesses, needs, and preferences. Several important factors lead to successful, healthy relationships. Be willing to communicate. You know, it's not so hard to say, "Could you please scratch that itch on my back two inches to the left of my right shoulder. Ahhh! Thanks!" But many overfunctioners can find it quite difficult to say, "Jeffrey, when you open a package, would you please throw out the wrapping instead of leaving it on the counter?" The key is to dare to speak up. This is not always easy when you typically avoid confrontation. Try to remember that ducking conflict takes up time and leaves you frustrated! And, it saps your energy, even though you may not be aware of it.

As you become adept at using the Flag and Animal Systems, don't doubt your sense of doubt. The combination of good intuition and rational observation will produce sound judgment and wiser choices. None of this is mysterious or random. It's uncommon sense at work.

When you begin to select people and situations with greater discrimination and foresight, you may find yourself being "de-selected" more often. This can feel like rejection. However, instead of an indication that you're slipping, this is a sign that you are protecting yourself from emotional predators. You are now more fit to navigate through challenging relationship waters, avoiding relationship icebergs you can see plainly and those that are below the surface. Keep the Flag and Animal Systems in mind. As you learn to use them, you will grow more confident in deciding which risks are worth taking, and you will get better results. Reliable selection and de-selection are your best bets for keeping good company.

> ✂ If you select people poorly and can't de-select them, the results will be poor, no matter how well you perform.

Your Turn! FLAG WAVING!

Topic: Mastery of the Flag Waving "Warning System"

Purpose: Developing good selecting and de-selecting skills

A) Think of RED FLAG people—IPs, extremely dangerous to your emotional health—from your present and past. List them. They share all or most of the following characteristics:

Self-serving
Rewrite Reality
Demanding
Driven by power and domination
Lack empathy for others

To which of the subtypes described in the chapter are you most susceptible? Is there an historical link (mom, dad, sibling, etc.) involved in your super-vulnerability?

Consider the YELLOW FLAG people—emotionally limited, potentially disappointing, and possibly dangerous to your emotional health. Make your list from present and past. Members of this group share all or most of the following:

Avoid emotional depth
Frequently blame others
Avoid conflict
Avoid self-reflection
Offer empathy inconsistently

These people will not be able to meet your needs and goals for sustained intimacy and emotional safety. Train yourself (practice) so that you can swiftly heed the warning signs that require you to set strong limits with these people. For example, keep things casual and maintain low expectations. Recall the Little Red Hen and review your attitude and feelings about limit-setting.

B) What leads you to hesitate raising those Red and Yellow Flags, like Clara in the story? What leads you to ignore the flags once they are raised, as Clara did? Frequent stumbling blocks include fear of not being liked (even by the neighbor's dog, never mind an actual person), guilt (asserting your own will in any way may feel like a hostile act to you), and the entrancing spell of bad intuition, as a result of your personal history.

✄ "I can't believe at twenty-five years old, these women are turning themselves into pretzels just to get a guy!" ~Elana, 24

C) Now, think about GREEN FLAG people—capable of intimacy and of building emotional safety. List those in your life.

What helps you use your good intuition to choose these people? Who in your past do you link with as a good intuition choice? For instance, "Hey, my dad has the same great qualities that I am noticing in this person." Take a brief inventory of your past and list the "ones who got away" (like Pan with Echo) before you developed enough good intuition to choose them. This may prove to be bittersweet, but also quite revealing.

Only by accepting yourself can you wave the Green Flags and follow the Green Flag people. Think about a relationship in your life that was well chosen and has developed well—one with a friend, perhaps.

They all count. You count.

✄ It is necessary to take risks in order to pursue and achieve rich relationship goals. Selection will determine whether you are risking foolishly and recklessly or wisely and carefully. This is why selection is the most important variable in determining outcomes.

13
MAPPING A COUNTERPATH
Assess Risk to Make Cherished Choices

Fable: The Fire Story

Once upon a time, deep within a forest, there lived a witch who liked to capture sweet children and keep them under her spell. "Maybe even roast them for dinner!" some said. To keep the children from escaping, she would take sap from trees and rub it onto their faces until their eyes were stuck shut.

One day, she snatched a particularly appealing little girl who was playing by the edge of the town. The child sparkled with cleverness and curiosity. The witch put the sap onto her eyes and led her away to a cottage in the woods. There, in the clearing, the witch had built a huge fire. All around, the little girl could hear the voices of other children the witch had already captured. They were afraid. Blinded by the sap, they sat and waited; they couldn't run away. The new little girl shuddered in terror.

The fire was roaring hot, and as it grew even hotter, the children intuitively leaned back from it. But this particularly resourceful little girl was different. She too was scared, but she was especially observant and imaginative. These qualities spoke out in a confident private voice just for her. She listened to her own ideas even when they seemed far-fetched or risky. At that moment, she boldly leaned towards the flames, though the fire was very hot.

What happened next was interesting indeed. The heat melted the sap from her eyes. She was able to see! Quickly and quietly, she gathered the other children to her. She led them out of the thick, dark woods to where they were safe from harm. And they found their way home.[23]

Are you a risk-taker? If so, what kind of risk-taker are you? Do you see yourself as courageous or bold? Taking risks to make changes in your life and staying on track with them is, well...risky. Whether you feel comfortable taking risks or not, it is useful to examine how to assess which ones are worth taking.

We already know that we need to turn down the volume of the incessant <u>external</u> voices telling us what to do and the programmed <u>internal</u> voices of negative intuition and trance. When we build up the inner voice of good intuition and learn to trust its reliability, we journey away from the TT and into the land of uncommon sense.

There's more. *The Fire Story* speaks to the necessity of daring to take risks in order to protect yourself. The dictionary defines "dare" as "exhibiting adventurous courage,"[24] "risk" as "acting while accepting the chance or possibility of danger, loss, injury, etc.; to venture on."[25] We know that risk-taking is not confined to physical activities. It can also involve *consciously pursuing what matters most while facing up to the challenges that this may bring.* Daring does not mean dealing solely with overt threats to our lives or safety (as in *The Fire Story*). It's just as valid when we're confronted with threats to our time, priorities, and dreams or with subtle pressures such as lack of support from our general environment or flat-out self-sabotage.

If the particularly appealing/resourceful little girl had played it safe, she'd still be sitting by the fire with her eyes stuck shut. Or, by now, she might have been eaten by the witch. Which anxiety is worse, doing nothing and changing nothing, or doing something and changing something? Leaning towards the fire may have seemed foolish, but the voice of the girl's good intuition, strong and confident within, gave her the courage to do it. She broke with what was expected of her and trusted herself. Because of this, she was able to take a bold, innovative, life-saving step.

ON TRACK

Lauren had to face big choices suddenly. She was ready to lean towards the fire...

Lauren, Lauren, Please Come Back! You'd Better Come Back!

She is in the middle of her allowable maternity leave when an unanticipated problem arises. A partner in the firm, in charge of a major account, resigns. Lauren is the person who has the next best rapport with the client. Her boss asks her to shorten her time off and return to work at once. The client must not be lost! Lauren is a very efficient and responsible employee. Eager to rise in the ranks quickly, she's in a quandary. Complicating her decision is the fact that her husband is dissatisfied with his job and wants to quit. They've just bought a house, and three weeks before the "comeback call," Lauren received a generous raise, making her the more beholden to her bosses. What is this ambitious, conscientious, "good" career woman and enchanted, loving new mother to do?

Initially, of course, Lauren is depressed, overwhelmed with anxiety and self-pity. She first calms herself down sufficiently to reach a good "motivational" level. There's still some anxiety left, of course. But instead of letting it stop her, she uses it as motivation to explore her options assertively and find solutions for the problem. This takes several days.

Next, she addresses the problem systematically with a series of questions:

Question #1: What do I want most?

Question #2: What do I want the most in my <u>heart</u>?

Question #3: What are the worst-case scenarios I can <u>think</u> of if I act according to my <u>heart's</u> priority ranking?

Question #4: Will these worst-case scenarios lead to a <u>catastrophe</u> and/or to an <u>irreversible sense of regret</u> over time? (Are they tragic and eternal consequences?)

Question #5: How can I handle my anxiety so it doesn't poison the happiness of my choice?

Question #6: Is my decision nourishing to me?

Follow her along...

Question #1: What do I want most? Answer: To be with my baby and complete my maternity leave as planned...to be well-liked and admired by the firm, and make every advancement 'on time.'

Question #2: What do I want the most in my <u>heart</u>? Answer: Not to cut short my maternity leave...

Question #3: What are the worst-case scenarios I can <u>think</u> of if I act according to my <u>heart's</u> priority ranking? Answer: Well, I probably won't get promoted as rapidly as I would like. Some of my colleagues will never understand my decision and will think I'm throwing away my big chance. Some might even tell me to my face that I'm being foolish. Many will question my attitude and commitment to my career. I will definitely lose my impeccable status, which I've been working on my entire career. I could become so totally freaked out about all this that I'll start to feel torn apart inside.

With regard to my husband's concerns and the new house mortgage...we'll have to budget more tightly and he may not have the total flexibility he desires right now. This could disappoint him so much that he'll be quite annoyed at me. He might decide I'm being very selfish and say so, not getting it about the enormous passion I have about the issue of taking time to be with the baby. And I can understand his point, certainly, but I'm not letting go of mine on this one. What's the worst that will happen? Vijay may get majorly pissed off, but it will be temporary. I know he won't divorce me or stop loving me over this. However, I wouldn't be surprised if he did hurt my feelings in the process. We probably will need to have a number of discussions to work it out. I also might get angry at him for making this so damned hard, for being insensitive, and for not instantly understanding. But this won't make me stop loving him or divorce him either. Even though I'm dreading it, I'll hang in there and work it out, and, I know, so will he.

Question #4: Will these worst-case scenarios lead to a <u>catastrophe</u> and/or to an <u>irreversible sense of regret</u> over time? Answer: (Pause.) (Pause.) (Pause.) That's a hard one. Let me really hone in on the basics. (Pause.) I won't be fired. This time with my baby is absolutely unique. (Pause.) My answer is "No. It's bad, but it's not tragic or eternal."

Reflect: If the answer to Question #4 is "no," take the risk that supports your strongest preference. The answer to #4 will likely be "no" a high percentage of the time. So, most likely, you've just made a decision. Now, go on.

Question #5: How can I handle my anxiety so it doesn't poison the happiness of my choice? Answer: I must deal with the "torn apart" factor. I will strategize as thoroughly as possible to stave off all the worst-case scenarios. I have to accept that there are no guarantees and that I can't be perfect in my strategies. No matter how hard I try, I won't be able to think of every single contingency. Accept that skepticism, criticism, and lack of understanding are inevitable from the outside world, and possibly from my nearest and dearest. I will commit to working it out with my loved ones.

Prepare for this by taking control of how I will define those loaded evaluative terms like "fool," "attitude," "commitment," "success," "love," "loyalty," and "responsibility." They may trigger me, but I know that I am not being irresponsible. I expect some sadness, pain, and nervousness because I'm giving up some big things I have wanted and for which I have worked hard for a long time.

Question #6: Is my decision nourishing to <u>me</u>? Answer: Yes. Is it hard? Yes. Absolutely.

After making her choice and creating her "damage control" plan, Lauren goes into action. She volunteers to talk from home to the important client and meet with him once or twice to solidify the transition. But she sets a limit to the amount of time she is willing to put in overall. She also speaks to the partner who is leaving and gets his advice. Whether Lauren will receive her promotion right away, "as planned," she does not know. She does know she is going to remain firm in her decision. She is prepared for and willing to deal with the consequences of her choice—mourn the loss of the perfect game plan, that life long plan that she had designed and cherished. She has voluntarily given up a treasured course for something she has decided she wants more. She also initiates those heavy conversations with her husband. Will she have moments of doubt? Of course. She continues to reduce her anxiousness and strengthen her resolve by frequently reminding herself of her highest goal—to be at peace and to enjoy her baby to the max.

TO THE POINT

You are now permanently replacing overfunctioning with something better. This is risky. In preparation for this daring move, it's useful to nurture the kind of confident inner voice that the "particularly appealing resourceful little girl" has—it is both mindful and imaginative. This will prove indispensable for helping you to find another way, and to get on that track (your track) and stay there. As you awaken from a trance, the advice of your inner voice will grow more and more reliable. You will learn to trust it, even when it recommends something that seems counter-intuitive. And, like Lauren, you'll also be able to discriminate accurately between the kind of anxiety that <u>always</u> accompanies going towards challenging endeavors and the anxiety that provides a healthy warning sign to back away.

By employing a six-question structure as a problem-solving tool, Lauren was using a combination of her intellect and her feelings in a systematic fashion to reach a sound, integrated choice. Bringing the decision forward required taking some risks. Keeping it going will likely require additional ones. However, the alternative is staying stuck and often sacrificing something precious.

> ✂ "If you keep doing what you're doin', you'll keep gettin'' what you're getting." ~ Gramma

The six-question structure can be useful to help determine many choices, and is adaptable to a large number of situations. All the questions are significant, as is their order. Questions #3 and #4 are, perhaps, particularly noteworthy. They may, at first pass, seem over-amped and ridiculously dramatic. Keep in mind that unconsciously, if not consciously, we all slide towards a level of desperation or panic in times of uncertainty, especially when confronted with big decisions. Asking these questions about worst-case scenarios will bring out the unexpressed, unarticulated fears that may be silently hounding you. Once they are out in the open, it is easier to recognize how you may be exaggerating them when the pressure is on.

Question #1 will often bring up several mutually exclusive wishes and options, as they did with Lauren. This is alarming, but normal and inevitable. Let all the answers stand and push on to Question #2. These six questions used together are invaluable to restoring perspective and carrying the decision-making process forward to a trustworthy resolution.

PRESCRIPTION:

The Six-Question Structure is meant to guide you in developing the ability to stay conscious (awake, alert) and make wise decisions. It is a process that respects both the mind and the emotions in balance with one another. This is the soundest combination. Your final conclusions will reflect this. Rather than being driven by automatic pilot and bad intuition, you will use the healthiest parts of your self to access not distortions and impulses, but your personal sensibilities. This is freedom.

TO THE POINT

What characteristics do the resourceful little girl in *The Fire Story* and the resourceful big girl, Lauren, share? Foremost, they possess a willingness to jump off the standard path, even if it means dealing with consequences that may, at first, prove to be uncomfortable. They each conjure up a unique vision to follow. They hold personal convictions of their purposes. They stay open to change, but they refuse to remain trapped by short-term demands, setbacks, and convention. They feel good about themselves without looking for outside approval, and they don't follow the pack. They do not report a lack of anxiety. Rather, they expect it and field it as part of the process. They even feel satisfaction on most days.

With the endless options, societal trends, and trances that challenge our self-esteem, many of us are still susceptible to giving up our goals without realizing it.

Years ago, Ellen Goodman, the syndicated columnist, wrote a thought-provoking piece on the absorption of the venerable woman's college Radcliffe into Harvard. She called it "The Morphing of Radcliffe." Founded in 1894, Radcliffe, after more than 100 years, officially merged with it's male counterpart, Harvard, in 1999. The event perfectly captured the situation of being subtly co-opted, and why it is so important to be alert (un-entranced) and to take the time to examine what matters most to you to be doing.

Morphing—an animation term wherein one object is manipulated to look as if it seamlessly blends into (becomes) another—implies cutting-edge change, change that must be good. And, yet, we wonder, as Goodman says, "…when we have been welcomed on our own terms

[or] been taken over... that to get equality with men, women have given up separate spaces, different values."[26] She points out that "in the lopsidedness of this social change, women have changed more than men.... We know what will happen to the Harvard women, to all women, when they hit the barriers, when they try to balance work and family and real life."[27]

Sadly, we do know about having given up our separate spaces, physical and psychological, and our different values. Every day, we walk the dangerous and confusing line between merger and submerger—whether we think about it or not. The story of Radcliffe's merger with Harvard invites us to stay conscious of the cost of becoming or maintaining ourselves as overfunctioning women, to face the truth about the "lopsidedness" of these changes. We all do know what will happen when we hit the barriers and "try to balance," and what will happen when our daughters do. Is this the legacy we want to pass down?

There is no perfect or easy path out of the forest of overfunctioning. But we have been examining methods to grant ourselves what we need to be welcomed into the clearing on our own terms. There will always be pressures, standing like trees obscuring the view, eclipsing our sense of direction.

Following the new track, we constantly bear in mind the question: Where does the essential meaning lie for us? Listening to our self, while relating with empathy to others, is where the essential meaning lies. Personal growth along with responsibility is where the essential meaning lies.

The race continues on with many people grabbing for the spotlight—pushing, always pushing. Seeking to fill ourselves, we experiment with products, with photos of ourselves in triumph. Motivated to take risks not to accomplish well thought-out or noble deeds but rather to escape from internal distress, the pursuit can become compulsive, overfunctioning wherein we ignore even life-threatening dangers as we drive ourselves onward. (Remember Rita!)

OFF TRACK/ON TRACK
On Top of the World—"In May 1996, when the scene at the

summit looked like a rugby scrum, climbers documented their deeds with photos...and radio dispatches filed on the World Wide Web. Soon after...a storm killed eight climbers [who were both women and men] as the world tuned in from a safe distance."[28]

What did all the people crowding to the top in the 1996 expedition get? Neal Beidleman, climber, filmmaker, and a participant in the rescue operations, remarked, "...in a deeper sense, did the mountain make me a better person? No. Yet, climbers keep coming...because it is the path... that leads, they hope, to self-discovery. Everest rarely delivers such big personal change. 'It's like they say 'wherever you go, there you are.'"[29]

> ✂ Many of life's most important things aren't things.

Circle back to the relevant issue: What does deeply gratify people? What does deeply gratify *me*?

Julia Child, walking her own "counterpath," achieved both pleasure and a position of influence. She seemed to be doing this just because she wanted to. As most women were bursting out of the kitchen or wondering if they should, Julia (in her late 40s when she started) stepped into the kitchen and started to cook. And, without being consciously political, her demonstration of declaring her independent preferences started a whole movement. She elevated the status of cooking for American women to a fine art, not to mention that she infiltrated the Old Boys Network of Great Chefs. She lived to be quite old and pursued her delights to the last.

We often stop ourselves from following a counterpath. The familiar, habitual fears include: I'll commit costly errors and there will be big unknown payments for those errors. I'll suffer too much pain when I let go of "this" in order to make room for "that." Someone will be disappointed with me if I don't do X or Y. I'll make a fool of myself blazing this particular trail. *We worry about what people will say and try to please everyone or some special one. That's a sure sign to check in with yourself and make sure that a specific trance (or the Overfunctioning Trace itself) is not at work.*

In T. S. Eliot's famous poem "The Love Song of J. Alfred Prufrock," the protagonist gets so tied up second-guessing and worrying about what others will think of him that his anxiety becomes overwhelming and distorts his perspective completely. The grand and the trivial merge in his muddled mind: *"Do I dare disturb the universe? Do I dare to eat a peach?"* Ultimately, Prufrock is unable to act at all: *"And, when I am pinned and wriggling on the wall, then how should I begin?"* Finally, weary and having given up all hope, he laments: *"I have heard the mermaids singing each to each. I do not think that they will sing to me."*[30] Prufrock's problem was that he listened to everybody but himself.

> ✂ We can stop morphing. We can start listening to ourselves and to the others we select.

At last, indeed! At last, Barbie wakes up as her own person...

Barbie Talks Back (excerpt)

> *...If she'd programmed the computer chip*
> *What would she choose to say?*
>
> *"Give me back my rib bones, childhood,*
> *Something to eat, decent shoes,*
>
> *Pliable joints, ground under my feet,*
> *A good-enough family, a huggable body.*
>
> *Sometimes I'm afraid.*
> *Promise that you'll love me*
> *Anyway."*[31]

Think about this: ESSENTIAL RISKS: What risks do you feel you want to take now?

Your Turn! THE SIX-QUESTION STRUCTURE

Topic: Practicing a process that strengthens good intuition and good judgment

Purpose: Developing freedom of choice

A) Take a situation in which you must make an important choice. It could be about your job, family planning, or work. Now, apply the six-question paradigm to it. If you are having difficulty with this, ask a friend or someone you trust to do this exercise with you in a dialogue. Write down your answers or talk into a tape recorder.

B) In a few days, reread or re-listen to your answers. Is there anything to change? Has something been left out that needs to be included? If so, do that now.

C) If you haven't achieved clarity yet, ask yourself these additional questions: Is there something that you really want to do that you are not doing now? If you were to do it and fail, could you handle looking stupid or feeling foolish? What would be worse: to try and fail or to not try at all? Will pursuing your goals lead to tragedy or eternal ill effects? Are you willing to make yourself vulnerable in order to achieve a treasured dream?

If you feel very stuck, consider these new points:
1) If you do not have a special goal or dream, what is the fear that blocks you from finding it?
2) In your life, where's the judge? ...outside yourself or within?
3) Remember: Inevitably, if you keep doin' what your doin', you'll keep gettin' what you're gettin'. If you do something different, you'll get something different.

LIVING IN THE POSSIBLE

14
CHOOSING GOOD PEOPLE AND GOOD JOBS
Walk Your Talk

Fable: Atalanta

Atalanta is the great female athlete, the daughter of the king. She doesn't want or feel the need to get married. Responding to political necessities, however, she has reluctantly agreed to wed the man who is able to defeat her in a race. The penalty for failure is death to the contender. Atalanta runs because she likes to. Though she is confident in her abilities to win any contest, with her independence at stake, she willingly accepts help. The gods who protect her advise Atalanta to throw a golden apple out onto the track when anyone gets close to overtaking her. The contender will go after it and get diverted; she will keep going and easily cross the finish line in triumph. This scheme works well, time after time, until one day a suitor appears who isn't tempted by the golden apple. He ignores the first, the second, and the third apple, and he wins the race. Because of his physical prowess, his wise judgment, and restraint, he also wins her heart. They choose one another as equals, strong matched to strong.

The wonderful Atalanta tale celebrates a powerful, balanced woman. She possesses intelligence, self-discipline, and healthy self-esteem. She is wise. She thinks about things carefully and is comfortable requesting help. In contrast, the suitors are impulsive and foolish. All but one are drawn to the immediate allure of the moment (golden apples). They considered neither the most important prize, nor the enduring merits (Atalanta's hand in marriage and domestic happiness, plus political power). The results of this lack of foresight, skewed focus, and unwillingness to delay gratification are dire. One after another, the suitors lose their lives. The man who wins the race and Atalanta's heart does so because he unchooses the false prizes. This act of unchoosing enhances the probability that he may gain something substantive and lasting.

✂ Beware of instant gratifications.

The twenty-first century has seen exponential increase in the illusion that it is possible to have it all. But, in fact, the fundamental situation now is no different from the one which the suitors faced in the ancient fable. The question is: <u>Which</u> gold is of highest value in <u>this</u> moment?

It takes wisdom and courage to deliberately decline something. This is not passivity. It is an act, a purposeful act.

In the old tale, the victor consciously resists the lure of the apple. In the following modern tale, choosing <u>not</u> to do something eludes Sung Su, a young woman who owns a popular nail salon. Quintessential overfunctioner that she is, Sung Su can't extricate herself from the grip of her To Do List. She can't see how to change anything except to compulsively rework and manage…:

The List

"I find a frustration that myself and all my clients confirm: As women, we drive ourselves for perfection in all avenues—work, home, even play. The day is comprised of lists and lists, and I find myself resenting my husband because he doesn't seem to have a list, at least, nothing like my list. My common sense says he's not being a jerk; he just doesn't rely on a list.

"A classic example is this: I take out the garbage because I'm the one who remembers and he's already gone. A common occurrence. I roll it down to the street only to have it spill onto some bushes, and I throw my back out picking up the can. This takes extra time and I'm frustrated and mad. Then, I'm mad at him, also, for not doing this one job since I'm doing all the other jobs. But is it his fault? No. Because… did I ask him for help? No! Not that I should have had to remind him, but that's another story, right? So, I just keep telling myself, 'Sung Su, it's just an occurrence.'

"On his days off, he's great to himself (goes golfing, gets a massage). Me? I cross items off my To Do List, then fall into bed exhausted at the end of the one day I'm supposed to be relaxing. Lists are always a problem. So now I show him my list, which is always long and detailed. I'm not sure if this will help. I know I bring it on myself. Have I thought about having a baby? Oh, yes! It's my heart's desire, but, really, how could I fit it in? I want to put that on the list, but I haven't. I know that sounds foolish and superficial, but I'm already on the edge, you know?"

Sung Su is suffering because she works all the time, uses her day off to do everything else, and doesn't effectively enroll her husband in sharing what else needs to be done. Nor does she ask for his perspective on things.

The only course of action she can see is to get her husband to understand her To Do List better. She's aware that her so-called solutions aren't working, but continues both to overfunction and to put off into an indefinite future what she says matters most to her to be doing—having a baby! She stays locked into a system that she $\triangle$ knows doesn't work. She keeps repeating it, and it keeps not working. A whiz at business, she would never address a problematic issue in the salon in this bizarre fashion.

Sung Su is so revved up on automatic pilot (in a *To Do List Trance*) that she makes dubious unchoosing decisions. She won't drop anything from the list on her day to relax. She doesn't take the time to talk to her husband about her dreams—or his dreams. Instead, she dumps her list on him, a myopic approach to her long-term goals.

How is she going to get the cherished prize (the baby) by approaching things this way? At this point, if she would unchoose a few things (I will not take the garbage out. I will not work on Sundays even if it means I will lose X amount of money.), she could free up some time to genuinely connect with her husband and figure out what she wants out of life.

CHOOSING "I WILL NOT"

Unchoosing can be defined as exercising one's I Will Not with awareness. It can consist of *abstaining* from taking on new things, giving up something (or someone) that takes up time and space. This is the first step of a three-part process that includes 1) unchoosing, 2) letting go, and 3) then choosing. Some people call it prioritizing, but "prioritizing" is one of those trance trigger words that has the potential to throw us back into the TT. It skips the first two steps and jumps right to the third—choosing. If you do not follow the steps in order, <u>informed</u> prioritizing will not happen.

You frequently must give up something in order to <u>make room</u> for something else. The winning suitor realized that he had to unchoose the golden apples if he wanted to get the princess. It is significant that, in the myth, the apples are not fake, making the dilemma complex and true to life. The suitors believed they could quickly grab an apple or two and still get the girl. It didn't work then; it doesn't work now.

> ✂ By asserting as high-priority our Right to Unchoose, we can open up space in our life, both emotional and physical.

More things don't have to be done than one might think. Maybe we don't have to label the giveaway clothes, read the latest novel, clean out the garage, check email every two hours, or redo our resumes. Maybe we don't need to buy a state-of-the-art cell phone or the most glamorous designer dress, take the bigger job now, or use the newest, cleverest, ergonomically-designed can opener.

How do we prepare the ground for unchoosing? A key prerequisite is periodic *sorting*. Sorting is not merely deciding to discard or keep things, though that may be refreshing in its own right. Sorting is not just one more thing to do. Sorting involves going through one's *thoughts and feelings*—an internal inventory—to get familiar with what is important to do and what is not necessary. It's like weeding a garden so the flowers can thrive. To sort successfully, you need to accept the principle that shedding something represents progress, not defeat.

> ✂ Taking action is often thought of as taking something on. Unchoosing is a respectable, sometimes profound, form of action—taking something off.

Catherine says: "I left my job because I wasn't being a wife to my husband or a mother to my child. I had two days per week to get everything done. I couldn't say, 'Let's let the dirt collect in the house until we can't walk.' I just couldn't. That's just not me."

But Carolynn says: "Well, I just ignore the grunge under the table. I've decided that I can live with it and that it's not important to me."

You might have stayed at the job because you love it or have basic financial obligations to meet. You might have pulled out the broom because letting the dust collect was too high up on your scale of what's intolerable. Or you might find sweeping relaxing. Or you might have kept the job and thrown out the broom. ...or left the job and still thrown out the broom. There are no external standards to follow. It's all individual. So get to know yourself better.

> ✂ Consult your sensibilities so that you can prioritize in a conscious state.
> ✂ Only your vote counts in this (s)election.

Always lurking in the background is the relentless pressure to do things because they're trendy or familiar, whether they suit you or not. After Alma Mae faced up to the fact that she'd chosen a career entirely based on her placating-mother trance, she could consider...:

What Else She Might Want to Do
"I finally was able to admit to my mother that I hated being an accountant and I wanted to change professions. She, of course, replied, 'What are you going to do, Alma Mae? All that education! You're so successful! I'm sure you *don't really want to* give all that up!' I didn't really have an answer for her because I didn't have a clue what I might want to do. To make matters worse, I realized that she had nailed something big: I resisted changing careers because I feared that others would view it as a regressive misstep, a big mistake. Yet I knew I had to move on.

"For a time, I worked as a reporter at the local newspaper. I didn't make much money, so I kept a few of my long-term accounting clients. This kept me afloat while I continued to try to figure out my direction. In time, I went back to school and got my masters degree in journalism. It was a financial sacrifice to do this, both on a day-to-day basis and in terms of my long-range savings plan. In the eyes of some people, it was also a comedown in status. But I'm glad I persevered. Now when I get up in the morning, I really look forward to what I will be doing each day. That's a small miracle in itself. Have I landed my dream job? No. But, I can see that, in time, I may be getting more of the kinds of assignments I would like. And, I might add, making this change was excruciating, but, in the end, it has been good."

Taking responsibility for one's actions triggers anxiety and self-doubt. In any choice, we could be criticized, mocked, or proven wrong. Deciding <u>not</u> to take action is particularly daring. It bucks the "do more/do everything" trends (trances). The odds of our being harshly judged increases. We're still somewhat susceptible to the familiar "feminine" model of passivity that we've been taught— the "don't make waves" stance, "don't be controversial" stance.

> ✂ Unchoosing, which is an active and deliberate choice to <u>not</u>, contrasts sharply with not choosing.

In the following story, three sincere people search for a balance in caring about themselves and those they love, and discover the complexity and profundity associated with unchoosing.

The Road Not Taken

Once upon a time, a nice man named Bob was married to a nice woman named Ann. They were very happy together. But, in the kingdom where they lived, as in all kingdoms, things were not simple. Bob was a gay man, but he fell in love with Ann. They had worked out the sex part satisfactorily because they loved each other. Yet Bob still yearned to combine, with one man, a deep sexual and emotional relationship, something he had not accomplished in his bachelor days.

This is what happened, according to Ann. "I loved and understood Bob well. After many conversations with him and lots of private thinking, I agreed to be open to his trying this thing. My reasoning was that it was not competing with 'us,' and, therefore, not threatening to me.

It was just a different kind of experience for Bob. After all, I had confidence in our love and trust and thought that our open communication style would make it all work okay. And, for awhile, it did.

"Of course, because Bob is a great guy, he did find a male lover, also a nice man, and they became involved. For some months, I was genuinely happy for Bob and we continued together relatively unchanged. But, as time went on, six months or so, the whole situation began to upset me. I could feel the split in his energy and the enormous effort he had to put into being devoted to both Greg and me. Our 'us' did not feel the same. I grew insecure, angry, and unhappy. At first, I felt terribly guilty about having these feelings at all. I kept quiet and buried myself in 'shoulds,' and tried harder to make it okay. And I threw myself into my career, working more and more overtime.

"But, I just couldn't stand things the way they were. It took months for me to muster up the courage to face Bob with my fears, my feelings, and my anxiety about my feelings. I was sure he'd be angry and disappointed. In addition, I knew the stakes. I could be forcing the end of the marriage I treasured. Still, I realized that this was not a situation I could live with indefinitely. Scared to death, practically choking on my words, I approached Bob. 'I've done my best. I've really tried, but I can't do this anymore. I know that Greg is a decent and fine person and so am I and so are you. The point is a person cannot have two marriages. At least, I can't. You are going to have to pick which marriage you want. I realize I'm putting it all on the line here. I know I'm giving you an ultimatum, but I don't know what else to do, so I have to take this chance. If I don't, I will just get weirder and weirder so our relationship won't work anyway.'

"Bob's first reaction was as I expected. He was very angry and hurt. He blamed me for going back on my word. He was right. I had. He felt that I was being unfair. My change of heart was causing him pain and putting him in a bind with his lover, whom he cared for deeply. I acknowledged all this but was adamant that I would not continue with things on their present course, even if it meant giving him up. I added, 'I am sure you will need time to sort out all this for yourself as well.' Though this limbo would be pure agony for me (and probably for him, too), I wanted to be as fair as I could. I needed to give him the time he needed.

"The entire time I was telling Bob that I could not be with him anymore under these circumstances and that I was asking either for a monogamous commitment or a divorce, I wept as if my heart would break. I was still turned on to him. I could feel the strong physical ache and yearning in my body the whole time, intense. But, even when Bob cried and asked me to reconsider my stand, that this was hurting us both and he loved me, I kept to my decision with that NO. I was miserable...and, yet, I held my line. I had to.

"After much soul-searching and inner turmoil, Bob chose to stay with me. This meant he had to unchoose Greg. Revealing this to his lover was one of the most traumatic and significant experiences of Bob's life, just as my stand had been for me. Although he was making his decision of his own free will, this did not lessen his suffering. But we came together to rebuild our 'us,' which has worked out over time."

TO THE POINT

There are several assumptions about unchoosing:
One says: "When it's time to unchoose something—when it is right and wise—you will feel you really don't want or like the thing anymore. It will feel good to unchoose it." *No such luck! Most often, as in the story of Ann and Bob, unchoosing does not mean that you don't want the thing (or relationship) anymore. Unchoosing is giving up something (or someone) while still wanting it in order to be able to fully choose something (or someone) else. This is laced with sadness and loss, sometimes anguish. It's important to let yourself feel all these emotions. Having them does not mean you made the wrong decision. Some sense of bittersweetness may always remain with you.*

Both Ann and Bob went through a process that contained a number of challenging facets. Ann did not reach clarity about her feelings immediately. Even after she did, she had to reflect further about whether she was willing to unchoose her husband. This also took time and soul-searching. Eventually, she sorted out her priorities. The marriage was not working for her under those circumstances. Finally, she declared what she needed directly. She did not lay a guilt-trip on Bob or judge him. Nor did she take a higher moral position.

She openly acknowledged the fact that it was quite inconvenient that she'd had a change of heart. Then, she gave Bob a chance to examine his feelings and make his choice, although waiting for his decision caused her anguish to go on even longer.

It took many months of sorting, taking stock, and experiencing a roller-coaster of emotions for Bob to come to know which relationship he wanted more. Then, he was able to take a stand, unchoose, and mourn the loss of his lover. Through the years, both Ann and Bob have celebrated their successful marriage, not perfect, but always deeply honest.

> ✂ Living happily ever after is never without tears.

The experience of unchoosing can be quite uncomfortable. But individuality depends upon unchoosing. The value in sorting out your preferences and accepting the consequences forms the moral of countless fables and myths. The road is tough—thorny bushes cover the castles, deep forests must be traversed, temptations lurk everywhere and must be rejected, false paths abound, spells need to be broken, dragons must be slain, identities are often confused and must be clarified, princesses and princes suffer dearly to learn lessons, and then they get redeemed—just like life. Illusions must be stripped away so insight and transformation can be gained. Just like life.

Another familiar assumption says: "Unchoosing is defeat." We've equated setting limits and drawing lines in the sand with "I can't" or "I'm afraid to try." Saying "no" seems dangerous; it might reveal you're not a successfully overfunctioning superwoman after all. After all, we are what we do, right? Maybe you will be perceived as hard to get along with, not a good team player, unfit. Labels and more labels... *Actually, unchoosing is a brave and gutsy act: It means you have the courage to give up something that matters to you. Furthermore, saying "no" is not generally a popular stance—except, of course, to those anathemas currently in vogue, whatever they are. These days, we say no to drugs, unprotected sex, butter, and gas-guzzling vehicles. Last year, who can remember? Next year, who knows?*

Unchoosing brings us in touch with the demise of the pervasive belief that: "If you work very hard and are very good, you can get it all. You can have your cake and eat it too." Because the very act of unchoosing defies having your cake and eating it too, we vigorously avoid it. *Not even the good and hard-working can have it all. Even worse, unchoosing also involves admitting that you cannot do it all, or perfectly, or seamlessly. The elimination of this assumption, which the overfunctioner has been trained to accept, is unsettling and can only happen in stages.*

✄ Triumph lies in feeling good despite not having it all.

Finally, unchosing also disproves the idea that if you plan hard and think enough, you can almost totally control things: In reality, uncertainty is mixed into every situation, whether or not we choose to acknowledge it. Rather than being frightened by this, we might consider the exciting side:

We observe some common characteristics in women who successfully navigate a counterpath. 1) They defy the pragmatic, safe, politically correct course when necessary in order to honor their internal sensibilities. 2) They accept that they cannot control all variables. 3) They endure criticism, labels, and other external noise. 4) They know they will frequently be misunderstood. 5) They stay flexible, not rigid. 6) They are creative and willing to take risks. These women think on a different track.

ON TRACK

Carrie, who moved from running a high-powered sportswear company in Los Angeles to opening a tiny shop in Santa Monica where she sells one-of-a-kind jackets, says, "I'm working harder than ever and have less money, but my life is wonderful. Every piece of clothing is an expression of my imagination, of who I really am. I am finally being an artist now and love owning my small business instead of working for a large, corporate enterprise."

Lawyer's Brief "—Pam"

"'What a pity!' 'So talented.' 'So bright!' 'So well-trained!' 'So headed for the top!' 'Wasting all that money that her parents spent to educate her.' These phrases crashed through my head like cymbals. Everyone warned me that I was committing suicide career-wise. I felt horrible because, for as long as I can remember, I have wanted to be a lawyer. But after my twins were born, I realized I no longer wanted to work lawyers' hours. Though I've never been a controversial type, suddenly everyone in the firm was talking about me. It was even in the air that the firm was going to let me go altogether. But I stuck with my decision to work part-time or not at all. I told them I would give one hundred percent in the office, but when I left the building, I was off duty. Oddly enough, though skeptical and grumpy at first and serving me up only second-string assignments, my bosses kept me on.

"I worked hard and well, doing everything possible to become as good a lawyer as I could. The main thing was that I was making myself happy by spending a lot of great time with my kids, not dragging my work along for the ride. And then, strange to tell, I made partner. In fact, I made it quickly even by male standards. They came to admire me for being not only competent but true to myself."

✂ Following the unorthodox path requires Unchoosing and Choosing. This means the guiltless exercising of what you will and will not have in your day.

Unchoosing takes courage. But what do you risk when you're either unaware of your highest desires or you are ignoring them?

Reporter's Report —Cokie Roberts

"… people are trying to make choices about home versus work… I went happily to Greece when my husband got a job there. You can take some time that's not a direct path in terms of your career… do something interesting… come back and succeed professionally, if that's what you want…. *We are going to be in this work force…a long time, most women…fifty years. There's plenty of time to succeed.*"[32]

As Cokie Roberts discussed in her KQED radio interview on Michael Krasney's *Forum* show, she let her job in America go. Though it took her a while to find work in Greece, a special career opportunity did come along. She could never have known that ahead of time or orchestrated it. Pam, too, followed her heart's priority and unchose the conventional, "sure-thing-total-dedication" professional track. Carrie gave up a hot job in LA for something more, well, funky. Everyone thought these women had lost their minds. However, the catastrophes predicted by others did not occur. Good things happened that they could not have anticipated or planned.

Cokie continues, after many decades, to enjoy a wonderful career. Pam is not only a respected attorney, but she has become a role model, with great influence on a number of other women. She's still following her own example and works part-time so she can be with her kids without feeling exhausted or multi-tasking. One of Carrie's jacket designs has been picked up and is being carried by a larger store.

Carrie, Pam, and Cokie defined "Success" as: acting on their personal convictions and passions, putting out their best effort, and accepting the outcomes. How do you define it?

> ✂ Just because everyone else is running around doing X... that's just everyone running around doing X. It doesn't give you any information about yourself. Knowing what's most important to you makes it easier to accept anxiety and act boldly in your own behalf.

It should be noted that choosing the tried and true path isn't a bad thing if it suits you and if what's being offered is genuinely what you want to do. This is called "agreement."

In order to become well-informed about your own priorities, to hone in on them and to experience things in the here and now with delicious intensity, you must get rid of internal clutter. When you pare down to your basics, not only will the big things stand out, but you will also notice and delight in the little things that have previously passed you by. The process of sorting leads to knowing when to smell the flowers and when to throw them out. This produces an abiding fulfillment.

PRESCRIPTION:

Sorting through and getting to one's personal priorities are, in themselves, entirely personal matters.

We have discussed some methods and strategies for keeping ON TRACK in your life: 1) Trance awareness; 2) Accepting the anxiety of periodic self-doubt and isolation from the throng; 3) Making sorting a part of on-going problem-solving; 4) Accepting the unexpected and expecting serendipity to play its part; 5) Creating your own definitions of Satisfaction, and Achievement, which ultimately underscore your sense of self-worth.

Cokie, Carrie, and Pam thought carefully about their goals and took the time and energy to do self-reviews regularly. Cokie chose her partner (nurturing a relationship), personal curiosity, and love of adventure over linear, efficient, traditional career advancement. Pam chose kids and the hearth (nurturing relationships) and gave up the glory and fast-track in her career. Carrie chose a more creative life in a less glamorous setting with less money and less prestige. They all rejected the goals of pleasing the crowd and avoiding disapproval. Though they remained committed to their careers, they took the high-risk option.

THE WORKPLACE STUFF IS TOUGH

Navigating at the job can be rough-going. It takes skill and perseverance. If you accept everything in the workplace without question or reflection, you give up all your power and set yourself up to be dominated. So, speak out.

Remaining on the bosses' good side while challenging the so-called, proper career-track will require:
1) clarity of vision
2) tolerance of anxiety
3) self-respect
4) determination
5) patience.

Of course, you will NOT always get your way. Often, progress is slow; you may prevail gradually or experience forward motion mixed with setbacks, rather than have immediate triumph. This is the nature of changing a system thorough individual action. Some systems (organizations) are so dysfunctional that they remain rigid. Once aware of this, you may decide to leave altogether, if you have that option. Never-the-less, trying in itself is both self-affirming and groundbreaking. Even if you have to back down, your ideas will be noticed and remembered; your footprints will remain.

> ✄ When you choose NOT TO DO, instead of being everywhere in pieces, you get to be somewhere in one piece.
> ✄ The path to independence is paved with Sorting, Unchoosing, and then Choosing.
> ✄ Mono-tasking is a fine choice—often the best one.

Think about this: "I WILL NOT." Do you find it difficult to unchoose the seductive golden apples in your life? How much time does chasing them take up? If they were not there, can you imagine what you would seek?

Your Turn! UNCHOOSING AND SORTING

Topic: Clearing off the To Do List by Unchoosing

Purpose: To find which gold is of highest value to you in this moment

A) Sorting and unchoosing can help you leave the TT behind permanently. Taking routine internal inventories is a good habit to have. It's as valuable as daily flossing and can be done as quickly and more discreetly. When you first start to sort, try to recognize whose voice is speaking, whose opinion is being expressed. How often is it really yours? Identify the many things about which you don't yet know your own opinion.

B) Where is it written that you must do this and not do that? By now, you recognize that you have been indoctrinated with the ideas of the family kingdoms in which you were raised. The texts from which the Automatic Pilot gets programmed is filled with rules and regulations which were established there long ago.

Not found in any library, The Book of Sally, The Book of Rosalyn, The Book of "You" sits on an internal shelf. Pick it up. Dust it off.

Open it. Since you may not have time to read the entire book all at once (certainly not if you're still overfunctioning), flip immediately to the "Commandments" section. Here you will find the imperatives that are supposed to drive you forever. How you measure up to them largely determines your actions, self-esteem, and sense of well-being. Discover some rules that you can laugh about even as you continue to obey them. Identify any that you can break or discard—soon or now.

Here are examples from the books of some fine upstanding women we know:
• Feel guilty for any break in the seamless flow of daily schedules.
• Apologize profusely and frequently for misdemeanors (large, medium, and small), including forgetting where something is, not sorting the laundry, asking for help ("I'm sorry to ask, but could you possibly..."), and general underperformance of "wifely" duties (whether you are married or not!).
• Don't get into a bad mood. Feel guilty for not being in a good mood.
• Work very hard. Don't complain.
• Feel guilty about feeling exhausted or mentioning it.
• Complete all work assignments on time even if there are an unrealistic number of them. (Always be willing to work overtime anytime.)
• Feel guilty for not calling back right away.
• Apologize to your partners/roommates for insisting they take out the garbage.
• Keep the house tidy. At the least, do a "quick pick-up" every night.
• Do not leave any cobwebs and dust balls (and their like) in the house.
• Color-coordinate. Carry the right purse for each occasion.

(contnued on next page)

- Feel guilty for making cake from a package.
- Don't be thin-skinned or "too" emotional.
- Don't be aggressive and/or intellectually visible in mixed-gender groups or in the family or at work unless directed to be so.
- Perform many parts as needed, ranging from dazzling (on demand), to intellectual, to demure, to....
- Satisfy the needs of loved ones and bosses while remaining low-maintenance yourself.
- Pay careful attention to your appearance and grooming while seeming not to be paying careful attention to your appearance and grooming.
- Rarely, if ever, get angry.
- Above all, never do nothing.

As you clear out the voices, your own silent voice may sound something like this: I do not need to do this now. I do not need to do this tomorrow. I might do this sometime. Just 'cause my mom or my friend does this, doesn't mean I have to. Perhaps, I never need to do this. Just because I <u>could</u> do X doesn't mean I <u>must</u> in order to feel good. I will not do this. I will do that. I will not relate to Tom. I will not relate to Dick. I will relate to Harry. Wow!

C) Think about mourning—when you give up something you want for something you want more. What is the hardest thing you have voluntarily given up in your life so far? What made it so hard? Did giving it up feel like a failure? Did you disappoint your mother, father, teacher, supervisor, lover? Is there something in your current life that you now recognize you need to give up—even though it will be painful—in order to make room for something or someone else?

✂ You can build one's body by exercising it. The same goes for one's courage.

15
MAKING CHERISHED CHOICES
Reclaim Time; Create Well-Being

"This house feels like a kitchen without a kettle and it bothers me."
~ Dehlia, writer, artist, mother, daughter, sister, wife, toast-maker

Diary Entry: Rockin' Revolution!

I love this place! Lots of rooms just for sitting quietly—parlors. Then, we discovered the long front porch and its Adirondack rocking chairs. Those rockers were so seductive…so inviting! We just sat there comfortably for the longest time and thought about things. We talked with each other, didn't feel the usual compulsion to pull out our laptops to work, didn't get up and run to the next thing. There was certainly plenty more to explore about the old hotel. But that front porch held us. It possessed a special magic. My mom grew up in a town like this with porches in the front. Neighbors would sit out in the evenings and talk. How sad for that custom to have disappeared! Maybe, I ought to start a Rocking Chair Revolution—stop people from jumping up, running around so much. But then, thinking and talking might get us in touch with our discontents and our real needs. We might want to take action to change things. Now, that *would be* a revolution![33]

Many women don't have the option of not working, of course. The bread-winners don't have time to make bread. And we're strung out. Many women with no financial imperative choose to work. And they're strung out. Yet, no matter where we are on this spectrum of options, we have to believe that we can find restorative moments, time to make things special, to create tangible magic for ourselves and those we love. Otherwise, emptiness haunts us. So think about how and where you can start rocking, a little bit at a time.

You don't have to be baking bread to make sure that those simple moments exist. A shared meal as part of your family life, for example, can go a long way towards creating the feeling of being wrapped in a cozy cocoon of caring. These times matter. They matter a lot.

> ✄ Just because it doesn't advance family achievement along the grading scale—like doing homework or practicing the violin—that doesn't mean it's trivial.

⌂   Countless things, not reflected on the Dow, do matter. Mandy, for instance, doesn't have grand expectations for high achievement all the time. She simply wants to enjoy having the family together in the evening.

Because It's Important to Me!

"When I was growing up, my mother was working full-time. Evening meals were always a *Swanson's*™ TV dinner in front of the TV. I liked the little compartments because it made me feel like there was some structure to dinner, but, the truth was, there was no pleasing structure to it at all. When the meals came out of the oven, we set up the TV trays and mindlessly watched whatever was on that evening. It was haphazard. It didn't offer any emotional nourishment.

"I know my son would *loooooove* doing that, just sitting in front of the TV for dinner! Actually, my husband feels okay about it too. It doesn't seem important to them to sit around just talking together or whatever. But it's important to me! And I think that's a good enough reason. I like to cook; it's fun for me. I want dinner to be sweet. If I can get them to join me, sometimes it's perfectly delightful. Other times, it's a real struggle. You know, the 'Do I have to, Mom?' stuff. I say, 'Yup.' And we do it and he's a little grumpy. I'm okay with knowing that some of the time they are just doing it for me. I do lots of things just for them, after all."

We particularly applaud this parental wisdom. Sometimes you as a parent do know best/can see the big picture better than your five-ten-fifteen year old. On this subject, Rosalyn's friend Monisha tells one on herself. She is fond of holding up a photo of herself and her two sisters and children in England wearing their school uniforms and crying. "We hated being there," she muses and bitterly resented our parents for two whole years. "Now, all three of us look back on this as the childhood experience that had the most profound positive effect in shaping our entire future lives. I have since thanked my mom and dad for insisting." There is a parenting message in here!

Rosalyn remembers nine-year-old Sofia running into her room, slamming the door, screaming, "I won't go. You can't make me." We had just announced to our children that we'd been selected to go on Semester-at-Sea for one hundred days. We thought she'd be thrilled. Little did we know. Sofia did go because we made her go. On the college application essay, she wrote how this and a month doing volunteer work in Nepal (I forced her to go with me on that one, too!), changed her life in amazing ways. She has expressed her gratitude countless times.

This is not just about exotic travel or community service. It can be about not answering the phone(s) during Sunday breakfast or going on a family hike or (fill in your own). This is also not about dominating children and controlling their every move. Life is full of opportunities to give them lots of independence.

> ✄ Parenting well is a matter of balance.

Mandy's family members do not share her enthusiasm for this ritual. Having dinner together as a family without distraction has tremendous value to her and brings her great joy. And it makes sense to her as something that will have a lasting emotional impact for her son even if he is not aware of this now. Mandy has confidence in her conviction.

Think about what is meaningful for you and your children. What are your highest aspirations for them, and how will you achieve them? If you're chronically tired and rushed (overfunctioning) or are scared to displease family members, the easy way out often seems like the only way out. Sedate the kids, sedate yourself, and just go along with what the others say they want. You may cower even though sometimes you suspect (trust your good intuition) that their preferences are coming from deep within their overfunctioning/exhaustion trances or from the normal myopic vision of childhood. Only by mustering enough courage to de-select items, events, things, and opportunities, can you gain the time and energy to find what is vital to you and valuable for them. Certainly you will need more vigor to stand up for these priorities.

All this just for "dinner"? Yes!

P.S.: Mandy has observed that even when Tony and Paul come to the dinner table listless and grumpy, by the conclusion of the meal, they have perked up and seem refreshed. Even the ploy of "I want to sit at my desk and finish my homework" does not seduce her. She's determined to train her child to not overfunction and to take a pause even for something worthwhile.

Maybe that's why "they" didn't want people sitting like that, rocking, talking, thinking.... It's subversive. We have accepted, without a fight, "their" running off with the porches because no "self-respecting" overfunctioning woman could tolerate being seen rocking instead of working. Recall Bev's treasured marmalade tradition and how it fell apart because she didn't give herself the necessary time to protect it. She could protect that time and reap the rewards. When we ask her what she thinks of this, she remarks, "It's a great idea! But, you're kidding, right? I don't even have time to read STOP signs!" Then, laughing, she quips, "And it's not funny... Gotta' go! See ya." Bev's stance is unequivocal. Though nothing jells very well in her life, she sees no other options available to her. But we do.

> ✂ Reclaiming time is an act of strength because it's a basic step towards building personal preferences and power.

△   We have had an off-balance relationship with time for a long time. When we actually manage to get some, generally we fill it back up with tackling more things from the To Do List—with more and more mechanical precision. This is what so many prescriptive books and articles for women's lives have advised us to do: overfunction more efficiently so that you can get even more done! We don't pause to ask fundamental, obvious questions. We act as if there is intrinsic merit in "getting more done." What is *more*? What is *done*? We now have the sense to know it's a one-way street leading to burn-out, low self-esteem, and emptiness.

THE PAUSE THAT REFRESHES

If we could just sit back down on that old porch for a while… talking with our friends…smelling the breeze in the air…

Rita: I had this aunt who used to just drop by. I really loved it. (It's something I'd like to do, but I wonder, "Should I call first?") She was also the only adult who ever got down on my level physically when she talked to me. That made a lasting impression.

Sally: I love the small daily rituals. For instance, it's vital for me to have an unhurried cup of tea in the afternoon.

Dehlia: You know, I believe kids are more attached to these little rituals than we think, like having a piece of toast together after school. They're in such a rush trance themselves, so pressured. But they can be tempted by friendly persuasion. You are doing them a favor by making them slow down. It snaps them out of it for a while. Stick with your convictions about this. So what if you get labeled old-fashioned!

Carolynn: Oh, yeah, I liked riding my bike after school. It was a way for the neighborhood kids to get together. It wasn't about the fastest and the best. Biking hadn't been co-opted into the major competitive, consumer-driven sport it is now.

Jaclyn: Some friends moved to a small town, and I wondered why. It's so remote. Didn't they miss all the stuff an urban center offers? I went up to visit and had a good time. Everybody knows everybody. All the storekeepers greet you by name. They take the time to talk to you. No one worries about conflict of interest or a hard sell. It was far from boring up there.

Rosalyn: Just exactly when did "personal" come to mean a trainer, your computer, or something you only tell your lawyer, clergy, or therapist?

Jaclyn: Yeah, absolutely. And what's more, in that small town, I noticed that getting somewhere wasn't so complicated. Moving more slowly became an option. My friend says that even on his work days, time feels different.

Rita: My mom tells the story of the milkman who came to her house every Friday morning. He would walk into the kitchen without knocking, open the fridge, check out what was there, decide what she needed, restock, and take the empty bottles away. He never cheated her, and she trusted him not to. I would trade in a lot of modern conveniences for that one!

Tracy: (sighing) Yeah. My life has truly become a drive-through experience. Highways, parking lots, fast-food service, and malls. Sometimes, I see someone I know passing by. Sometimes, somebody waves. I'm always taken by surprise when that happens!

TO THE POINT

There was an experiment done with cats. The cats were brought up in an environment consisting of only vertical lines. Eventually, the scientists replaced the vertical lines with horizontal lines and the cats could not see them. The experiment was then reversed and the cats were placed in an environment with only horizontal lines. When these lines were shifted to a vertical direction, the cats could not see the verticals. Look at the powerful part conditioning plays in what we can literally see! If trained horizontal, you see only horizontal. If trained vertical, you only see vertical. If trained to overfunction, we have a difficult time seeing any other possibilities.

A letter regarding an earlier version of our book bemoaned:

"[Your book is] a good book—well conceived and nicely executed...

"Even despite that fact, my main problem...is that...women have to (or want to) work, and women have to (or want to) be the primary child caregivers. It's the way of the new world, and it's too bad that the women's movement ended up putting more women in chains than it took out, but it's a reality.... The women's movement assumed, wrongly, that women could do it all. My generation was the first to be taught this from babyhood, and I can tell you how disillusioning it has been for members of my generation to realize that something has to give. But we have structured our lives in such a way that nothing can, so what gives is really our selfhood, which is what the women's movement was supposed to provide in the first place."[34]

An eloquent statement of despair from a twenty-something young woman.

Is changing overfunctioning impossible? We don't think so. Still, it takes thought, imagination, and persistence as to how you are going to design your own exit strategy. To change yourself, you need time. To provide your kids a rich childhood, you need time. And so do they. So, we have to figure out how to get it and how to stop filling it up with overfunctioning when we do.

A woman, featured on a radio talk show, had written a book on the history of air conditioning. The program posed the question: How has air conditioning shaped your lifestyle? Someone who called in recounted that one summer there had been an electricity blackout. The children normally sat inside watching TV, but the sweltering rooms (with no air conditioning) drove them outside, complaining, of course. Yet, this event utterly transformed their play. From passive couch potatoes, they became physically active, from minimally interactive and listless, they became imaginative and connected with each other. All this happened even though it was almost unbearably hot outside. The long, hot, lazy days of summer that the caller remembered so vividly from her childhood were, suddenly, restored in present day, if only for a short while. External circumstances forced the children to recover a lost treasure.

In this and the following story, the children get an opportunity to stimulate themselves in exciting (non-passive) ways, but they can't sustain it. Can you see a link between these events and the overfunctioning life?

Go Out and Play! —Sally

"The next door neighbor has two little nephews my son's age. They come over to play. One sunny day, the adults wanted to have some tea. I told the boys, 'Look how beautiful it is outside. Go into the yard and find something to do.' I found myself locking them out, something my mother used to do to us when we were kids (with the parting words, 'Come in when the sun goes down'). The boys tolerated the lovely day for about ten minutes and then they were banging on the door, 'Let us in! We're bored.' I was like, 'No way! You guys stay out there and figure something out. There's a swing, fort, climbing structure, yard, trees. Figure it out.' Very soon, they just stood at the back door chanting, 'Let us in! Let us in!' We just caved. I never got to finish my tea. The kids never got to deal creatively with their 'boredom' out there."

Do we need to break the ACs, TVs, CDs, DVDs, PDAs, computers, and cell phones or have energy blackouts, to support the physical and emotional health of ourselves and our kids? We don't think so. But we all have to make active efforts to get time back and keep it on hand to do something of emotional value. We can try exerting ourselves to set some limits on passivity and to assert some personal convictions about what we and our children need and don't need. We know from Mandy's story that it's not simple. It's reasonable. It's desirable. But it's not simple.

> ✂ So, what treasured legacies does spending time together sew? How can you sow the seeds?

We know something's been wrong, something's missing. Although at the pace with which we live, it's hard to notice what—fantasy, imagination, unstructured play, ability to tolerate quiet and temporary frustration, reading, talking, actually spending time together in a shared activity without lots of props.

We think that one way of achieving satisfaction is to turn to rituals, consistently a cherished activity in human culture. They draw attention to things in a specific, focused way. They mark the rhythm of time— and distill that rhythm in a dance. *Interestingly, though rituals take time to enact, they have the effect of expanding our sense of time.* Rituals offer structure, and they create connection, as opposed to more disconnection.

These days, we pass over rituals. But we also mourn their loss and yearn for them. We find ourselves seeking them out once more because they matter, and we know that they provide meaning to us; something that is lacking in our lives. Olivia wonders:

⌂ **Who Cares?**

"I'm bringing up my two boys alone. With their wild straw hair and gold earrings, they strut about the house, already taller than me. This past Christmas, we were planning to be away. I wanted to put up a tree anyway but didn't wish to appear overly sentimental and un-cool. So, I ran it by the guys. I said, 'Since we're going to be away, I guess we'll just dispense with the tree at home.' I took their collective nod to mean, 'okay, we agree, no tree.'

"One morning, as I was bringing clean clothes to my fifteen year old's room, I noticed that, on his desk, he had constructed a tiny Christmas tree out of assorted greens. Underneath were some little cards and tiny presents with names on them. Finding this was a sweet shock. I realized then that the ritual of the tree was important to him after all. I had wrongly assumed that the boys were indifferent.

"That night, I told them that I'd had a change of heart. I wanted a tree after all. Neither groaned nor hesitated about going out together to buy one. When we brought it home, we stayed up late decorating it with all the trimmings! They even ignored their phones."

Olivia didn't have the conviction to enact a tradition that she valued. But when she discovered the little tree on her younger son's desk, she stopped overriding herself. She found a way to make the ritual happen, and everyone came together to enact it, and they reaped the reward of being wrapped together in the joy of decorating the tree.

Marika stumbled upon a realization about our culture. The event she describes dramatically increased her awareness of her own version of poverty.

Life Is but a Dream

"In India, on a Semester-at-Sea, dozens of us students (ages eighteen to twenty-two) spent a night with Dalits, you know, the Untouchables—those below even the lowest caste. The village consisted of thatched huts, no electricity or indoor plumbing, little furniture. Clothing was old and worn. But everyone was so clean—hair gleaming, white teeth flashing smiles, and they were excited to see us. They sat together companionably, and sang, danced, played instruments. They laughed easily. They shared themselves with open hearts.

"Then they asked us to do something for them. Several students started to hand out things—candy, clothes; a few even reached for their money. 'No,' the villagers motioned. It was singing they wanted or a dance, something from our culture...something personal that showed our spirit.

"We talked nervously among ourselves and had an almost impossible time coming up with anything that had meaning to us. Finally, we all settled on singing 'Take Me Out to the Ball Game' and 'Row, Row, Row Your Boat.' Not exactly spiritually deep! But there wasn't much intense emotion that we could connect with our culture. That really bothered me. I felt bad. I thought of my little niece and nephew back in Philadelphia and how impatient I usually am, with little time to play with them. We usually do something with no thought or substance, like watching endless hours of TV while I'm usually texting a friend. I made a promise to myself that I'd be different when I got home. I needed to give them time and do something emotionally valuable. Where's the 'juice' in our culture anyway? Those Dalit kids gave themselves. We brought things to give, but they were asking for us!"

GIVING OF OURSELVES TAKES TIME

Rituals involve giving of ourselves, but they are different from "overfunctioning" giving. They act as a hedge against the speed of life; they buffer us against periods of personal and cultural drought. Establishing or re-establishing rituals starts with giving ourselves permission to have them. They change the ordinary into something special. They delight. They bring solace. Their magical essence reverberates through the years. They interrupt overfunctioning trances and help us stay out of them.

The versatility of rituals is remarkable. Rituals can develop into legacies, a gift we give to others. They increase self-esteem and ward off the TT.

What's in a Score Card?—about Doris Kearns Goodwin, historian and writer

When Doris was a little girl, her father, a great baseball fan, told her that he wouldn't know the weekday ball game results or details unless she listened to the radio for him while he was at work. Doris diligently attended to the play-by-plays, and when her dad came home, she would give him a full account. He sat down and listened carefully to every word. Performing this task made little Doris feel extremely important. Of course, as a child, she didn't know that all the information he wanted was in the newspaper. She believed that she was the sole carrier of the precious data.

This simple routine, belonging to Doris and her father, had vast, unpredictable implications for Doris's life. First, it fed the closeness of their relationship. It made her feel great about herself. She alone was the bearer of the important news, and he gave her 100% of his attention. Without pre-planning or masterminding, the ritual also contributed to her choice of career. After all, she had been Dad's historian. And baseball has remained her personal passion.

Rituals can serve as tools for problem-solving. In the overfunctioning whirl in which we live, when things go wrong, it's tempting to look outside ourselves to fix the problem. But finding the right expert or remedy is daunting in itself—slogging through yet another endless swamp! And it may not be enough. Sometimes what we pick could be too limiting—or the wrong answer altogether.

In another account from Doris Kearns Goodwin's life, she tells of a time when her mother had become ill, and a childhood ritual applied in present time surprisingly became a device for healing.

Ritual to the Rescue—about Ms. Goodwin and her mother

When Doris was very young, her mother read to her. And when she grew old enough to read, they read in tandem. This forged a strong, special link between the two. Many years later, Doris's mother became so ill that she couldn't talk. It caused her to become withdrawn and depressed. Doris was unsure what to do. Then she recalled that childhood tradition they had both cherished. Only this time, she was the one who did the reading. She made this little ritual into a daily practice. It provided solace for them both. Little by little, her mother began to recover her voice. Eventually, they were able to read in tandem again.

✂ Working on a Ritual Portfolio is as significant as working on a stock portfolio.

All is not lost if you don't have any rituals on hand. You can begin at any time to create them or borrow one from someone you know.

- Rituals are rehabilitating. They quiet anxiety temporarily. They provide comfort.
  - Simple routines can take away emptiness and fill us a little.
  - Rituals connect people together.
  - Rituals can be created easily and cheaply.

Jetta and Elizabeth, roommates, had hit lows. After Jetta opened her mind to the idea that rituals weren't just stupid and a waste of time, she let Elizabeth introduce her to a small something:

The Treat Treatment

"We were both bereft. Jetta had just lost her mother and left her husband all in the same month, and I had just lost a boyfriend, my hopes, and my sanity. So neither of us had much of anything left. We felt beaten down. Money was tight. I was clinging onto a bunch of small rituals. I acted as if my life depended on them; at that point, I think it did...making sure every day to have one fresh flower on my bedside table, taking a walk at sunset, reading the paper in bed every Sunday morning, buying a long pretzel stick almost every day and dipping it in ice cream like I did in the first grade. I encouraged Jetta to think of something from a happier time that might give her some solace. At first, she couldn't think of anything. Then she remembered a nighttime treat from her childhood: warm milk with vanilla. This turned into an evening event for us—just the thing for two insomniacs! And it brought back sweet memories of her mom.

"There were other little things we ended up doing together—making sure to build a fire on a chilly night so that, though we were ice-cold and empty inside, we were enveloped in warmth, at least temporarily. We lit candles at dinnertime and set the table nicely even if the dinner itself was meager. I insisted on having one set of colorful sheets that made my bed feel cozy, fresh, and inviting. Jetta liked the idea and did the same."

When you are sad or in an anxiety-ridden state, if you don't throw yourself into overfunctioning to try to avoid your pain (which ultimately doesn't work anyway), a ritual can help. It can give you a little time to experience <u>real</u> rest—soothing and nurturing before you have to face the continued onslaught.

> ✂ Instead of overfunctioning relief, which is exhaustion, numbness, and frenzy masquerading as respite, rituals provide a sustaining bit of restoration.

Carolina, the woman who dared to speak up to her boyfriend after he dumped her but then regretted it and apologized, was still not dating six months later. She started jogging to keep in shape. She recalls, "A couple of guys from my apartment building and I made a trio. We would run two miles to the local coffee shop, pitch in together to buy one croissant, cut it into thirds, and eat it. One morning, the guys couldn't make it, so I was on my own. I realized that enacting this little croissant ritual had come to have meaning for me. Silly as it sounds, when I got to the coffee shop, I couldn't resist the urge buy the croissant and cut it into three pieces. I brought their pieces back in a little bag. Having grown up in an affluent but emotionally bleak family, all hard edges and no cozy curves, I hadn't learned how to find or create warmth. This experience was a kind of revelation to me. When they weren't there that day and I missed them, the ritual of cutting the croissant brought up warm feelings inside me."

> ✂ You have a right to have a rite.

Rituals have restorative power in relationships. They touch people deeply.

Ritual to the Rescue—about Elana, then age fifteen, and Rosalyn, ⌂ her mother

"We had just had a bad fight—you know, over autonomy, hers and mine—typical teenage daughter and mother stuff. She had yelled, said mean things to me, cried, slammed her door, and locked it. I was shaken, angry, and discouraged for the umpteenth time. Then it came, 'Mom, will you read it to me?' She unlocked her door and appeared, red-eyed, carrying her teddy bear from childhood in one hand, her high-school assigned novel in the other. So, we sat down on the couch on opposite sides, and I began to read <u>Oliver Twist</u>. It sounded so wonderful spoken out loud. Gradually, my daughter inched towards me, and, as I heard the sound of my own voice saying the words, I realized that I had read to her aloud almost every day for the entire fifteen years of her life. This was like comfort food for her, a still point in a swirling adolescent world, a place that will never vanish for us, where we can always go together. By this time, I noticed, she had put her head in my lap."

Rituals can connect the past with the present.

Found: The Biscotti Recipe

Two gentlemen, very excited about something they were carrying, were overheard at a local cafe. From an ordinary brown bag, one took out a biscotti and said, "This is it!" The other looked with intense interest. The first continued, "My great-great grandmother's recipe, which she brought over from Italy. It's in an ancient cookbook, which has now come to me. It's a little different from the current gourmet kind, an authentic Italian peasant woman's version." Both became silent, relaxed, companionable. An early spring sun dappled its light on the courtyard. They ordered their coffee. When it arrived, they slowly picked up one biscotti each. What followed: examining, dipping, comparing notes, talking about other family traditions.

Found: Tante's Rolling Pin—Rosalyn talks about her great-aunt

"Tante was, for her time, a classic old maid, with her dowdy clothes so tidily groomed, her tight grey bun, the firm set of her jaw, and precise bustling walk. She taught school to four generations of third, fourth, and fifth graders, telling tall tales, explaining principles of grammar, and reading aloud. Many years later, I met dozens of former students who acknowledged her as a lifelong inspiration to them.

"She read to me always (and I see how this became a natural part of my mothering with Elana and Sofia). Also, every Friday afternoon after school, before the Sabbath began, Tante would bake cookies and I would help. She had her own personal rolling pin, never used my grandmother's. It was all wood, without separate handles. With utter concentration and a grin, Tante rolled it into the dough.

"When Tante died, she had no accumulated material wealth, only several old pickling crocks, some well-worn storybooks, and the rolling pin. As the oldest grandchild, these were passed on to me. I've always used Tante's rolling pin for baking. And now my daughters do too.

"When we moved several years ago, we couldn't find the rolling pin for six months. I was worried that we might have lost it. When it was finally discovered deep in a carton, Sofia, my younger daughter, kissed it. I cried a little. Elana, ever-practical, said, 'Well, the cookies will finally return to normal.'"

Rituals can help establish and nourish a reasonable pace that is sometimes performance-directed, sometimes not.

"I'll do *it* myself!" should mean not only our goals, our paths, and our priorities, but also our pleasures. We must be willing to devote our time to pursue those choices, to persevere on our own when necessary, and to take risks when we have to. Just as important, we need to take time to reflect at the end of the day. Like Mandy, we can insist on the simple daily practice of a cozy evening meal, *sans* interruptions, *sans* the telephone ringing, *sans* the TV blaring in the background (or foreground).

> ✂ It's revolutionary to push Module Living aside.
> ✂ Without time to reflect, think clearly, and feel deeply, choosing wisely is not possible.
> ✂ Time is power.

Pacing yourself can get you to that reflective place. If you refuse to be distracted by the giant ads, the big-screen-TV-music-blaring-constant-action scoreboard, or your ticket stub number to claim the prize giveaway—all that ersatz reality—you can really be where you are, perhaps at the ball game...like Doris and her dad...or somewhere else of your choosing. You can have a full experience. Like this...

the warring caps red vs. green
percolate across the stadium

the pulsating throbbing crowd
anticipating an expert flick of the wrist
the crack of the bat

the fly ball
the catch, the drop
the collective breath

safe!
a gasping rousing release of emotion

then nothing to do
but await the next play
such sweet heresy [35]

These days, in this kingdom, daring, personal vision, and conviction are required to put a simple concept such as *taking time* and *pacing* into operation. Embracing a slower rhythm will help wrest you from the vestiges of the automatic pilot and numbness typical of the Overfunctioning Trance.

PRESCRIPTION:

When trying to pace yourself, carefully consider these expressions: "Find time." "Make time." "Bide your time." "Take time." "Pass time." "Spend time." "Buy time." You must be willing to do all of these, in order to "have time."

> ✂ Overfunctioning "kills time."

Do you really want to kill time? Wouldn't you rather fill it in a deliberate fashion? In other words, if you were Sung Su and a client would pay $60 for a manicure and pedicure on Sunday, are you willing to buy that hour back for yourself at the cost of $60 in order to not have your Sunday interrupted—to spend time doing something special for yourself? Special can be something as simple and cheap as doing nothing. More heresy!

Imagine sitting in the rocking chair as you think freely, turning things over...doing nothing...talking...comfortable... before you have to get up and run around again. This is pacing rather than racing! Give yourself time to FEEL the difference. Remember your rituals or make some up for yourself. Stop for a moment. Savor the legacies you've collected throughout your life. They belong to you.

✂ Slowing time down gives you time to think straight.

✂ Slowing time down gives you time to see the little gratifications all around you.

✂ Slowing time down grounds you in the moment, elevating many mundane little things into gleaming experiences.

✂ Modules don't gleam.

✂ You may have to buy time to spend time in accordance with your desires.

✂ Take time to cultivate a spirit of delightful uselessness (like at the ballgame). Glimpse the sweet heresy!

✂ "I want the door left open. It is important to me. And that is a good enough reason!" ~Sofia, age four

✄ "I want to eat dinner with my family because it is important to me. And that is a good enough reason!" ~Mandy, fifty

Think about this: THE TIME FACTOR. Do you yet feel entitled to take time and have it? Do you dare have moments of uselessness?

Your Turn! TIME AND MEANING

Topic: Getting time back without guilt

Purpose: Learning to pace yourself and create meaning

A) What rituals could you build into your life to safeguard your time and create tangible magic? Remember some things from your own childhood. It may help. What special thing or practice would you lobby for (as Mandy does with dinner) if you had the time and energy and willingness to annoy somebody? Who stands as a barrier, blocking you? Include yourself as one of the potential suspects. What are the messages this person is giving you? Examine the merits of the messages carefully, studying each word, not swallowing the phrase whole. Do you agree that they make sense? If not, cast them aside.

B) Since you cannot count on the air conditioning cutting out (or some other technical glitch), you are going to have to create that interruption that makes you aware. Examine the following loop:

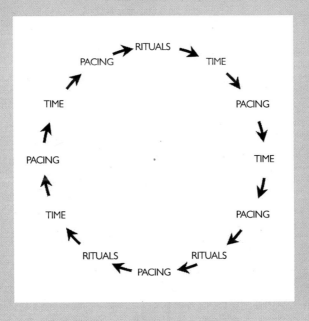

You can start anywhere in the circle. Any one of the three can help you create the other two. What is your current vicious circle? Can you draw that? Compare it to this circle above.

C) Think about some special goals you hold dear for yourself and your loved ones (especially the children). Can you see how mastering the pacing-time-ritual circle will help you make these dreams come true?

16
BECOMING YOUR OWN HERO
Redefine Success, Freedom, and Creativity

Finding What's Lost
by Dorianne Laux

In the middle of the poem my daughter reminds me
that I promised to drive her to the bus stop.
She waits a few beats then calls out the time.
Repeats that I've promised.
I keep the line in my head, repeat it under my breath
as I look for my keys, rummage through my purse,
my jacket pockets. When we're in the car, I search
the floor for a jack-in-the-box bag, a ticket stub,
a bridge toll dollar, anything to write on.
I'm still repeating my line when she points
out the window and says, "Look, there's the poppy
I told you about," and as I turn the corner I see it,
grown through a crack between the sidewalk and the curb.
We talk about it while I scan driveways for kids
on skateboards and bikes, while the old man who runs
the Rexall locks up for the night and a mangy dog
lifts a frail leg and sprays the side of a tree.
Then we talk about her history essay and her boyfriend,
and she asks again about summer vacation, if we're
going somewhere or just staying home. I say
I don't know and ask what she'd rather do, but by now
we're at the bus stop and she leans over
and, this is so unlike her, brushes her lips
quickly against my cheek. Then, without looking back,
she's out the door, and the line, the poem,
is gone, lost somewhere near 8th and G, hovering
like an orange flower over the gravel street.[36]

This poem recounts a moment in a typical day. Tactical logistics interrupt the poet-mother. She exerts great effort to hang onto her creative momentum against what she initially experiences as the petty, but inevitable, intrusions of reality. They relentlessly take over. But something surprising and profound occurs. The poet-mother discovers that small bits of reality present their own unexpected, precious rewards: "'Look,' says her daughter, 'there's the poppy I told you about,' and as I turn the corner I see it, grown through a crack between the sidewalk and the curb." After that comes "the brush of her lips quickly against my cheek, so unlike her." The poet-mother savors this contact even as she loses the original line for her poem. She's content with the exchange—a poem for an intimate interaction with her daughter. Then, just as she's convinced her muse has vanished, she notices herself plucking magic fragments from the ordinariness at hand, "hovering like an orange flower over the gravel street." Her poem coalesces where reality is, and her muse sings to her again.

ASCERTAINING REALITY

Taking stock of things as they really are, without adding a story to it, negative or positive, editing it, or distorting it in any way, can be called the Discipline of Ascertaining Reality. It takes an unflinching frame of mind and courage to observe what is there and what isn't. This enables one to penetrate to the essence of the moment and the essence of the matter. Sometimes, as Sung Su said, "It's just an occurrence." Sometimes, it's something else entirely.

The great blues singer, Ruth Brown, ended up, mid-career, falling on hard times. Both her professional and personal life had gone sour. She was left with a family to support alone. So, Ms. Brown did something that she and countless generations of women knew how to do. She cleaned houses. Because she possessed an internal sense of worthiness, this job did not devastate or humiliate her.

One day, when Ms. Brown was working as a maid, she heard one of her own recordings on the radio. As she listened, she became angry. Her record company had cheated her out of royalties. This had, in part, created her financial difficulties. In that moment, she resolved to regain the money that was rightfully hers. It became her vision and her goal. First, she focused on finding legal help, even though, initially, she didn't know how she was going to pay for it. She kept to her efforts, unflinching. Slowly, she surmounted barriers. A way opened. In time, she also restarted her career.

When asked by Terry Gross, on a "Fresh Air" interview (National Public Radio), how she felt about her misfortunes, Ruth Brown emphasized that she had neither bitterness about that part of her life nor any sense of shame. She described her ability to focus on scrubbing the toilets and polishing the furniture as well as she possibly could, taking as much pride in this work as she ever did in her more glamorous role as a star singer. As Terry Gross probed to uncover what it took, it became clear that Ms. Brown drew from the depths of her being, which was rooted in her childhood experience. She had been lucky enough to be loved and consistently valued by her mother and father. This had provided her with inner resources that no negative outer circumstances could alter. The old treasure chest had, when she needed it, produced the ample gold that she had always carried there.

This does not mean that you are doomed if you've had a childhood bereft of love and positive regard. You must look somewhere else for materials with which to build those resources. Were they from a teacher or relative, someone else's mother or father? It's important to re-collect these and store them inside.

> ✄ It's never too late to begin harvesting from both past and present experiences.

Strengthening your self-esteem and sense of entitlement to measure full Alice-size will enable you to take the journey along the counterpath of your own design. You will deal with adversity as it comes and with mistakes as they are made (your own/and those of others) without losing your way. You will not need to give reality a spin or overfunction in order to feel better temporarily; instead, you'll hold the course and discipline of ascertaining reality and the pacing of time. You will handle what comes as it comes with innovation and self-knowledge.

Once you're not too anxious to stay anxious, you will stop kidding yourself about the realities of your Impossible Jobs.

This moment, though unnerving, is freeing. You can make new choices now. Note: Others will surely accuse you of making foolhardy, illogical unchoosing decisions. For instance, in order to take an interesting, forty-hour-a-week position in a nonprofit organization, Anna Jen announced her intention to reject the corporate job that would require sixty-hour work weeks and many business trips but guarantee her several million dollars within five years. Her headhunter lost all professional decorum and yelled angrily into the phone at Anna, "Are you crazy? Do you know what you're throwing away?" A.J. did know what she was throwing away. She also knew what she was getting and why.

"I actually surprised myself," she said, "by deciding not to take the grand-prize job. But, when I returned home, I couldn't sleep. I paced in my bedroom and cried for a while. In the morning, I was a bit of a wreck. But I had discovered something of value about reality. Sometimes, the initial reward for getting wise is to feel lousy. It's like that TV show with the three doors, and the healthy choice is Door Number Three. Door One probably has that fantastic position with the high-end firm. Door Two has connections, glamour, stock options, and other gold.... When you open Door Three, there's pain. That's what you get for opening the right door. Seems to make no sense. But it's there that something remarkable can happen, something lasting.

"The truth is that you have to pick that damned third door, take the pain in order to shake out of your trances, and reach the mind-set to make decisions that integrate both head and heart. After you've waded through the prizes, Doors One and Two lead only to brick walls. Door Number Three? Well, you look further and you'll find another *inner* door, and that one leads to somewhere." The job that Anna took has proved fulfilling, both in terms of the kind of work she is doing and in giving her more time to be with her young children.

That hidden inner portal behind Door Number Three is where treasures await. Though it's a strenuous process to reach that secret inner door, it opens to the opportunity for independence and balance. And it will lead to improvements so dramatic that they may aptly be called Transformation.

Anna Jen's little Three-Door Parable has wide applications indeed. While she thought of it in terms of jobs, you can plug it in to wrestle with any demon or decision.

For example, as we know, many women, young and old, use other people (men and women) as a life-support system—to draw from them self-esteem and affirmation. This is a common trance, an addiction actually, and it explains why so many of us stay entrapped by IPs. The only way out is to seek the Third Door. Abstain from the drug (man or woman) and endure the high anxiety that will accompany this. At first, the effort will inevitably cause self-esteem to plunge and insecurity to rise.

In order to detox from an addiction, you may struggle for a long while and be unhappy, but you will recover. No longer desperate, you'll be able to make better choices as Anna Jen did. It takes going through Door Number Three to leave Impossible Jobs and Impossible People behind for good.

> ✄ The only instrument you need for transformation is yourself.

THE VICTORIOUS CYCLE

PRESCRIPTION:

Here's the Victorious Cycle. The more you practice it, the stronger you get. [The symbol "→" means "this leads to."]

Start: looking without editing (spin/hype) at "what is" and
    "what is not"
→ facing that reality, however painful
→ a capacity to listen more accurately to yourself and others
    (you are less motivated to distort things!)
→ gaining insights worth keeping
→ making satisfying and compassionate connections with people
    (intimacy) and to objects and places (fun and gratification)
→ giving up people/situations that are trouble
→ focusing and choosing more confidently and wisely
→ being genuinely present both for yourself and for selected others
    in ways that lend true value and meaning
(back to 'Start'…)

△ Coming this far out of the TT and getting on track, you no longer have an investment in shoring up your own rationalizations and illusions. You now have at hand the basic psychological skills and strengths necessary to get off the overfunctioning treadmill and onto a transformational track. The process of seeing reality unadorned and responding to it *as is* creates a strong foundation of grounding for nurturing your dreams and imagination.

Women like Ruth Brown, Anna Jen, and Lauren possess vision and purpose. They also possess the courage to follow these through regardless of what the world does or does not say. Instead of living in the TT, they create their own kingdoms to inhabit. They don't see the need to justify themselves.

⌂ Ella, for example, appears at fist glance, to be rather uninteresting. However, she proves to be very interesting indeed. All her kids are turning out to be especially generous, happy, and responsible. Those scary serious problems of adolescence bounce off them. Meanwhile, a lot of teens in her respectable middle-class extended family and neighborhood are going down for the count. Ella must be doing something right. Ella is Mari's:

Schlumpy Sister-in-Law

"Forever, my sister-in-law, Ella, has been judged by our family and others as scattered, disorganized, and, frankly, sort of boring. She sometimes appears depressed and lazy. We have always criticized her because her house is messy even though she doesn't work outside the home. She has no taste. She can never get it together. But since her children became teenagers and are doing so terrifically, my mother (her mother-in-law), who has disapproved of Ella and virtually ignored her all these years, suddenly has gotten curious and begun to speak more to her. We've discovered that Ella has spent a lot of time (and still does) sitting on the couch talking with her children. I'm embarrassed to say that I, too, automatically assumed that Ella had no game plan. Quite the reverse proves to be true. We're trying to make up for devaluing Ella for so long."

✂ By whose priorities and visions shall we be driven?

This is a small story with a big message. In the midst of chaos, Linda sizes up a situation and, without hesitation, acts boldly. Most people would have considered her nuts for doing what she did. Linda…:

Parts the "Red Sea"

"It was rush hour in New York City. My boyfriend and I were on our way to a concert. I wasn't going to miss the beginning because some friends of mine were in the opening band. But we were trying to go across traffic at the mouth of the Lincoln Tunnel—a big mistake. Suddenly, I just saw the path through. Although I was wearing my black dress, pearls, and stiletto heels, I jumped out of the car. To my boyfriend's amazement, I stopped the traffic with my hands and motioned him to go. Everyone followed my directions. We sailed on through and made it on time."

Why did they listen to Linda? She seized the moment and concentrated her whole self on one particular goal—getting to the concert. She saw what was happening (ascertained the reality of the traffic jam), and attached her own creative spin (envisioned the path through), and signaled for help. The world, for a sweet moment, moved at her command!

✂ Reverence for a zesty life requires a strong component of irreverence for a lot of what's out there.

✂ A great recipe: Take ascertaining reality (groundedness), add personal imagination plus resourcefulness. That's good magic!

In the following story, during a visit to his child's classroom, Bruce, an ordinary person like you and me, gets keenly in touch with the reactions the children experience in a magical moment. As Santa Claus, Bruce allows himself the enjoyment of enacting the fantasy of the mythical character while simultaneously engaging in philo-sophical musing on a complex question: *What is real?* He becomes:

⌂ **A Christmas Gift**

"Not so very long ago, I found myself donning a bright red costume stuffed with pillows, my face masked by a white beard and makeup such that my own son could no more recognize me than his classmates could. With a bag full of presents, I burst into the schoolroom, ho-ho-ho-ing my way into the heart of a myth. Twenty-nine little faces gaped, aston-ished at the big jolly giant they had just been singing about. And Santa can tell you that this is an experience that everyone should have at least once. The wonder and innocence on their faces, of course, would make any day, but there proved to be more than that. Each face had a unique mix of shyness, affection and incredulity. But, on a few faces—only a few—was the beginning of skepticism and the concomitant fear, 'Is it okay to doubt Santa Claus?' It might prompt us, in the same way as we peer at our big red world with its fakey white beard and pretty presents to wonder: *Is this for real?*"[37]

On the one hand, Bruce immerses himself in the Santa Claus spell. On the other, he watches the struggle within those children who are uncertain. He doesn't feel compelled to judge the skeptical chil-dren in their timid doubts or the innocent children in their wonder. He observes both groups and allows himself to contemplate: *Is it okay to question commonly held beliefs? When do fantasy and the joy of imagina-tion cross over into dangerous gullibility and delusion?*

> ✂ It's good to generate difficult, fascinating questions. Abide with them over time. It's an anti-quick-fix!

Observing tangible realities with care is where the mother-poet started to gather her power. The process began with a state of mind. Lingering there, she observed the moment's simple beauty. The moment became full. She had been in a rush, distracted, and bothered. But she was able to override the external influences pulling at her. She was able to be flexible and didn't get stuck because of her original plan. Instead, even though she was reluctant to change what she was doing, she grasped the opportunities that presented themselves. We see her as a hero who is able to draw from an internal source of power to extrapolate wisdom, amusement, intimacy, and delight. By shifting gears, she allowed herself to receive a life-affirming surprise—a connection with her daughter. She also got the poem.

PRESCRIPTION:

As you shed the trappings of overfunctioning, look around and find those who are doing a counterpace instead of the main race.

There are individuals out there, able to listen to and hear a different voice even if it's whispering. They ascertain reality and add their own imagination to that base. It's a discipline, like meditation. In order to hear the whispering, they practice quieting both the mind and their environments. Within this frame, they experience—as the twentieth century poet, Wallace Stevens, so aptly expressed in his poem, *The Snowman*—"One must have a mind of winter…For the listener, who listens in the snow…beholds Nothing that is not there and the nothing that is."[38] From that place, the possible is free to arise.

These people have the fortitude to go for alternative doors and prizes and seek peace of mind. Their revolutionary acts are taking place noiselessly somewhere nearby. They may not be dressed fashionably or sitting in a mansion, but they are living grandly.

Can you access your capacity to envision life differently? Is respecting your personal inspiration on your To Do List?

"We have been as usual asking the wrong question. It does not matter a hoot what the mocking bird on the chimney is singing. The real and proper question is: Why is it beautiful?" ~Annie Dillard

And, maybe, a different question occurs to you or no question at all! There are all kinds of minds, all kinds of sensibilities, and all kinds of ways to observe beauty—the eternal.

Think about this: LASTING WISDOM. Who are the real heroes in your life? Are you ever your own hero?

Your Turn! HEROISM

Topic: Reviewing helpful tools

Purpose: Practicing uncommon sense

A) Select several (not all; the others will wait) of the graphs, charts, and structures in this book and look them over. Unchoose and choose which ones beckon you now. Do you feel you have made some of these teachings your own? Have you tried any of them out yet to see if they really work?

B) Go at your own pace. Be irreverent and question what you're reading and how it applies to your life. Stop whenever you feel like it.

C) Bring to mind the combination of thinking and feeling in tandem. Experiment—for a little while only—with finding your own version of this combination in relation to an issue which you are currently mulling over. Just notice what the experience brings. Don't judge or grade yourself. Thinking and feeling in tandem may or may not seem like a new experience to you. Likely, though, it will be a pleasant one that you sense will have many uses. Now, relax for a while.

D) When you are ready, sooner or later, consider this idea: Everyone has a signature tale—an old story, myth, fairy tale, or the "plot" of a book (like Alice in Wonderland or Kafka's The Trial, for example). Even if we have never thought about it before, most of us "know" our tale immediately. It seems to tell our life story or how we believe the world works or a combination of these things. A picture of whom we were supposed to become and how we were supposed to behave is often embedded in the narrative. In other words, our signature tale acts like both a script and a prophecy.

Signature tales have great power over us until we gain enough control and understanding to alter parts (or all) of them in order to "envision" and live life differently. Pause and reflect (perhaps this has become part of your good intuition by now): Can you identify your signature tale? You may surprise yourself by saying, "yes" and by feeling a rush of conflicting emotions when you do—particularly when you tell the story aloud.

Some of you may even feel repelled or frightened by your selection. Do not dismiss it for that reason; it contains important messages for you. Most signature tales provide a mix of affirming and distressing insights. Some of the information may be immediately obvious; other aspects may reveal themselves more gradually as you keep company with the story. You have probably already guessed that The Little Red Hen has been Rosalyn's choice since she was a small child, hearing it for the first time. For years, she had no idea why it drew her in so completely.

Holding your signature tale in mind will help you to stay conscious about various patterns you fall into and the automatic assumptions you make so quickly that pass beneath your notice. Placing the tale directly in front of you (instead of its lurking within) will heighten your awareness in positive ways. With compassion for what you have lived through in the past, can you now gently begin re-scripting your present and future?

E) Now, again, give yourself some time to relax. In fact, take a moment to wander through your senses: Notice all the colors around you; now, feel the air touching your skin, your clothes… your breathing… Whatever there is to feel, revel in the present moment.

17
FREEDOM
Cast Off Overfunctioning; Live the Possible Life

Fable: The Tale of Dame Ragnell
~ from the King Arthur legend

A long, long time ago, in the misty wildwood, King Arthur traversed his horse upon the pasture of a baleful black-hearted knight. The black knight threatened to kill the trespasser. But when he realized that it was the renowned King Arthur, he offered to spare his life if, in one year's time, Arthur would to return with the answer to a riddle: *"What is it that women want most?"* The king thought this to be a proper bargain, easily won, and agreed without hesitation.

He rode back to his castle, confident that the answer would be handily forthcoming. But, when he asked every woman in the land, no one could agree on the answer. "Women want beauty!" exclaimed one. "Of course!" twittered another. "But that's not all," she said, "some want children." "Oh, never mind her. We all want youth," insisted another. And another sighed, "We want to be left alone!" The king could not find a single answer to the question.

And so, one year later, King Arthur returned as agreed, but without hope of saving himself. As he approached the edge of the forest, an old crone blocked his path. She was gnarled and withered and so bereft of beauty that he could barely stand to look at her. She introduced herself, "Good King, I am Dame Ragnell. I know what you seek." "Speak up, Woman!" Arthur implored. "If my answer saves you, Sire, will you promise to fulfill my simple wish?" As the king was in a rather sticky spot, he readily agreed to her terms. With his promise secured, she whispered the magic answer into his ear. "How obvious!" he exclaimed. "I, too, would want the same."

With his heart finally at ease, he rode to the designated meeting place and waited for his opponent to appear. "How now, King Arthur!" sneered the black knight. "You have returned to meet your fate." "Not so, Sir. I have the answer to your riddle," Arthur countered with a cunning smile. And he thus spoke: *"What women want is the right to rule themselves—to do with their own lives as they wish."*

The king's answer was as a sword that hit the black knight with such force that he blew into a dark cloud of dust, never to be seen again. Relieved, Arthur turned towards home.

The old hag woman was waiting for him. "And now, Good King," said she, "We had a bargain. It is time for me to collect." A man of honor, the king lifted the old dame onto his horse and they rode together towards the castle.

It was the wish of the dame to marry the knight of her choice. When she and King Arthur arrived, the knights were called to assemble at the Round Table. The dame dismounted the king's horse and walked with great deliberation around them. Finally, she selected the handsomest and most youthful—Sir Gawain.

Gawain bowed gracefully to his destiny. But, the stunned silence of his fellow knights soundly echoed throughout the castle walls. "Well, then," the king broke the pall, "shall we get on with the wedding?"

A feast was immediately prepared. The affair was somber. Everyone except the dame arrived in a dour mood. After the celebration—if anyone but the dame could call it that—Sir Gawain and his bride retired to a special bed chamber prepared for them by the king's attendants. Dame Ragnell awaited Gawain's invitation to join him in their marriage bed. He did not stir, nor would he look directly at her.

"So, Husband," said she, "You will not take your wife into your bed?" He was silent. She snarled, "So, I am not of high enough birth for you?" He was about to speak when the dame barked, "Nor do I come with a dowry..." Finally, he uttered, "And you are not young." His words lacked the propriety of his noble position.

Then, taking pity on him, she took his youthful hands in her old, knotted ones. She kneeled before him, imploring, "Sir Gawain, look deeply into me. Nobility is not a right of birth. It is measured truly by the good one does in one's life. It is true that the beauty of my youth has faded, but I am possessed of the beauty and wisdom of my age."

Gawain felt ashamed. Her words moved him so that he kissed her. And, as he did, the ancient lines in her face and hands gave way to the most soft and beautiful woman he had ever beheld.

He was puzzled, but she explained, "I have been held by a spell that could only be broken if the finest of knights were to marry me of his own free will." He was captive. "But," she said, "only half the spell has been broken. Now, you must choose. Will you have me as a fair maiden for all the world to see or in the privacy of our bed chamber? Gawain, choose!"

The young knight paused to reflect. She waited. Finally, he said, "This is not a decision for me to make. I see the true beauty within you. I bow to *your* choice, Dame Ragnell." "So, Husband,' she asked, "I have the right to rule myself?" "Yes," he replied with complete assurance. "And I may do with my life as I wish?" "Yes," he confirmed without hesitation. With that, the spell on Dame Ragnell was entirely broken.

This ancient legend, told and retold through many centuries, celebrates women's sovereignty as our deepest desire and goal. At its foundation, sovereignty is freedom from external control. It implies that you have the right and ability to make independent choices and take charge of your life and that others have that same right and ability. Self-governance does not call for an hierarchical structure of control. Rather, one has a horizontal relationship of mutuality and equality with others. It is "power with." Sovereignty connotes neither tyranny, self-absorption, nor selfishness. Tyranny is about taking away the freedom of others, whether on a personal, national, or global level. It has a vertical structure and constitutes "power over."

Like the ancient dame, we want the right to rule ourselves. The dilemma for the modern woman is to sort out what her deepest desires and goals really are and then to find a way to protect the time to achieve them. Overfunctioning as a solution simply does not work because we're always left with a shortfall—things like incomplete experiences, feelings of frustration and discouragement, or no feelings at all. Overfunctioning does not produce the satisfaction for which we yearn.

In the following quote, journalist Marcia Carlson, lists the aspirations women of her generation have for themselves and have succeeded in achieving. She describes the race that this requires and the terrible cost. Where's the victory? As the young editor so aptly put it in her letter to us, "how disillusioning it has been…:"

> "...we looked back and saw our moms as chumps
> ... We'd run banks, law firms, and corporations while
> raising picture-perfect children who would like us
> as well as love us ...As we race from boardroom to
> courtroom, soccer practice to PTA, with hardly a
> moment to savor any of it, the thought occurs to us
> that she (mom) may have been right."[39]

Going out into the world, participating more extensively, becoming solvent, these were Feminism's ideals for liberation, to women in the twentieth century. But we too readily adopted a narrow, problematic view of independence. We must amend this in the twenty-first century. As we have seen, this can be done by questioning the assumptions embedded in evaluative words and altering them for ourselves—words like productive, successful, beautiful, worthy, contented, free, meaningful. We shall shift our ideal from Barbie™ (poor dear girl) and Superwoman (who now looks frighteningly like Barbie™) to a woman with a uniquely feminine blend of what we take from within and from without. Thinking things through with our individual and collective sensibilities and complete spectrum of feelings, we'll seek more communication among the generations. As we take command of ourselves and unchoose impossible people and impossible jobs, we can approach men in more gratifying ways.

Because sovereignty is based on discovering our authenticity and living it, we will look for a balance between commitment to ourselves and to others. We can now identify that we want to savor what matters most to us, whether at work, at home, or both. We will take responsibility for those things. And we want the right to work at a pace that doesn't make us resentful, exhausted, or sick. We will choose cooperation. The store, office, gym, and kitchen do not need to be open 24/7. We understand that neither you, nor I, nor we can do it all. We will seek to discover and wake up from our trances—both personal and societal.

Is freedom too big a responsibility? Perhaps we shouldn't take it on.

Freedom is a complex phenomenon. Historically, most people who have managed to get free have run back into enslavement. How could that be? In his book Escape From Freedom, published in 1941, psychologist Erich Fromm made incisive observations that seem haunting and even prophetic when read today. He noted that, even in a democracy, individuality underscores our aloneness in relation to the world around us. Fromm asserts that freedom produces "an unbearable anxiety" that can drive people to willingly give up their freedom in order to overcome this unwelcome sense of being separate and alone. As a result, they abandon their spontaneity and creativity, eclipse the authentic expression of their thoughts and emotions, and move towards a compulsive version of automatic conforming.

The price paid for not being able to live with this anxiety is high. Sadly, we can see this syndrome all around us today. As overfunctioning women, we too easily accommodate to assuage the anxiety we feel; we attempt to micro-manage the anxiety of those around us. Our dreams are thus on-goingly recalibrated and, as a result, co-opted bit by bit. When we overfunction and call that freedom, we are actually habituating to loss of freedom. So, it matters deeply and personally that we seek to protect our individuality. How we go about doing that is a highly individual matter. We will pass on by example to our children, both female and male, what we chose to become and *how* we chose to get there. Will we show them how to maintain themselves as sovereign individuals?

We're no longer interested in controlling others with "I'll do it myself!" or self-absorption or selfishness or bullying. As self-governing individuals, we seek to build relationships—at home, at work, and in our communities—that are characterized by mutuality and equality: "power with" or "alongside." This is positive power, not domination.

Our goal is to move towards a balanced mix through the discipline of choosing and unchoosing. We apply simple criteria:

1) Do I want/need to do this at all?

2) What do I actually need/want to do?

3) Do I want/need to do this now?

4) What is the worst-case scenario if I choose my preferred activity in this situation?

5) Am I willing to take the consequences of my choice?

Dorothy, in *The Wizard of Oz*, discovered something invaluable through the traumatic events that she had to face so far from her home in Kansas. But, she carried within her the inner resources (the emotional links with loved ones) to create home wherever she was. We have strayed far from that essence and would now like to restore it without sacrificing what we've gained. With some effort, we can reclaim and rekindle the connectedness we have lost in our homes, in our communities, and as individuals.

The answer to the dilemma lies not in abandoning the work force and running headlong back to the house, nor in overfunctioning more efficiently. *We will no longer do that.* We'll work with individual and unique designs, and we'll support and advise each other without judgment. The potential rewards produce attainable magic.

When you make your choices, don't expect the world to agree with you. Katie finds no support from her external environment to mother in a way that suits her. She is:

Another Kind of Woman —Katie

"I'm an American woman living in Switzerland, and I've just had a baby. The societal norms here and my European husband's beliefs run counter to my picture of motherhood. For instance, breast-feeding my child is important to me. And not one person has anything to say except... 'neurotic, unnecessary, passé, unmodern, perhaps unhealthy.' I have always been timid and soft-spoken, reluctant to call attention to myself. I'm pretty shaken and upset by all the disapproval. But I am not unnerved. I am breast-feeding my child, enduring all the talk, and being misunderstood. I find support in my e-mail connection to my friend, Lara, back in the States."

We may definitely make some people uncomfortable when we decide to do things differently. Those to whom we are close may feel angry and disappointed because we are disturbing the status quo. They may be attached to it *on a survival level* and fear to let go. They take their pride in "my daughter the lawyer," "my glamorous wife," "my friend the mountain-climber," "my partner who makes $200K a year."

The illusion that life can be manipulated simply and easily with pop-in modules is gone. We may be concerned that we don't possess the complete "right" map, but we know a lot more than we used to. Anxiety is our fellow traveler in any change process. As Katie said, "I just set my sights on what I cared about most in the big picture, withstood the criticism I was receiving, and took it forward, one day, one step at a time. I sincerely believed that nursing my baby would be best for both of us. So that was my choice for this precious time."

Who can forget Rita, who was on automatic pilot? For quite some while after her accident, she continued to drive herself in the same old ways over the mountain. Gradually, however, she began mulling over her experience of going off that cliff. It dawned on her how lucky she was to be alive. When Sally read her the "Comin' 'Round the Mountain" story, an account in Rita's own words just weeks after the accident, Rita was fascinated, "I couldn't see it at the time because I was too blinded by my sense of obligation. I lived by a lifetime accumulation of 'shoulds.' In the end, though, the accident showed me I was already taking huge unnecessary risks. I was shocked to see how crazy and dangerous it was to live like that. Finally, it wasn't about the 'question of not doing it' or 'losing ground.' My fear of disturbing that paradigm no longer held power over me. In fact, I started questioning everything. So, I took different kinds of risks and shifted many things. The result: After twenty years, I kissed that job good-bye. And you know what? My company did not want to lose me. They worked it out for me to work from home. Now, that's a switch! But one that I am quite enjoying."

Though the situations (or people) you are dealing with may not change, you can broaden your options.

Bianca's Show

"I'm a makeup artist. I said no to 9 to 5. I decided I needed an unconventional schedule. I told myself I wanted to make the most money in the least number of hours so that I could spend as much time as possible with my daughter, who was going into adolescence. I didn't know how I was going to make it happen. While I was trying to figure this out, I substituted on the Sunday night show for someone who was out on a medical leave. Normally, I would have just moved over when she was ready to come back. I didn't have any idea that I would have the guts to say that I didn't want to give up that show when she was ready to come back. By then I'd made my reputation, and the words just came out of my mouth, 'This showtime really works for me. I don't want to cut Terry out, but I don't want to give this up either.' I surprised myself. I continued, 'What can we figure out together?' To my amazement, the network agreed to keep me on that show and added one more that worked out for Terry. So not only did Terry get to come back with her expected number of hours, but I now have a schedule that allows me to make the amount of money I need and to spend the time I crave with my daughter. Next time, I won't be so afraid to ask for what I want."

The conversation about overfunctioning has been going on for a long time with only incomplete resolution so far. Together we can continue searching and moving ahead—imperfectly.

All heroes, fictional or real, have lapses and commit errors along the way. Snow White takes the poison apple from the old woman and eats it, although the dwarfs have warned her not to deal with strangers. The Little Red Hen keeps repeatedly approaching the same animals in the same old manner before she "gets it." Anna Jen keeps working diligently, precisely, efficiently, and without complaint for many years until the day she was able to see that she was not deriving satisfaction on any front. Her sense of herself as a good mother and an efficient worker was crumbling. She had to figure out a new way to combine both work and home. Even when she clearly understood her new goals, it still took some time to reach her better mix.

> ✂ Heroism is a process.

"I'll do it myself!" is the overfunctioning woman's mantra. Now, it takes on a different meaning and tone. You now know that you are going to have to: 1) see things just as they are—no editing, no story, no trance; 2) unchoose something (or some things), suffer the loss and experience the mourning; 3) unchoose impossible people and impossible jobs promptly; 4) choose time for figuring out what matters most and then choose those things and people; 5) take courage to apply your own creative touches, personalizing your own life story.

To support this, we will use some of the other tools we have gathered to move us out of the TT and the overfunctioning way of living:

1. *Listening Without Fear* helps us to not be used up by time-wasting or reality-twisting people.

2. *Expressing Anger* can help us to set limits, be honest about what we think and feel, and be heard.

3. *Modulating Anxiety* helps us to utilize feelings of discomfort as a signal for change and motivator for risk, rather than as something from which to run.

4. *Drawing Lines* sets parameters that allow you to focus your time and energy.

> ✂ Anxiety is fuel necessary for traveling towards your dreams. It will help you to not sell yourself short.
> ✂ Take a counterpath to personal sovereignty.

We recently read Jaclyn's story aloud to her. Remember her Baby Schedule (Chapter One)? She gasped and said, laughing, "Oh, gosh! Was that me? That <u>was</u> me! Well, I've got two kids now. I'm still working very hard, but I've found my limits. You know, I'm just not the man I used to be! And thank God for that."

More Balls than Most —Sally

"I was at lunch with my Dad's business partner, Clancy. We were catching up on things and people who share our lives... how his grand-children were growing, how so-and-so was doing. The topic turned to Angela. Angela, slightly younger than I, is a beautiful, intelligent, highly paid woman who runs a small, profitable manufacturing company. 'I always knew Angela would make it,' Clancy glowed. 'She's got more balls than any man I know.' When he said this, a shot of adrenaline rushed through me. I bristled at this 'ultimate compliment.' I also recalled that when we last talked, Clancy complained the entire time that lunch with Angela was taken up with her on the cell phone, frantic because the nanny had failed to retrieve the children at the appointed hour. The rest of the day's activities needed to be re-coordinated, and Angela was the one who had to do it.

"'How old are her kids now?' I asked, keeping my voice calm but still feeling a bit of rancor coming on. 'Seven and ten,' he replied, then added, 'She has it all—great husband, family, successful business, money.' I thought about what he meant by successful and asked myself, 'Am I not successful?' For a lingering moment, I felt less than Angela, then competitive with her. Finally, I took a deep breath and privately congratulated myself for some of the things I've accomplished, both big and small. I'm a serious artist. I'm dealing with the complexities and challenges of having a special needs child. I make a great garden. I make time for my friends. In that moment, I began to feel better and did not compare myself with Angela's version of success."

How far and wide afield we will cast our influence is, of course, up to each of us. Some will live out personal sovereignty in our own backyards, homes, and workplaces. Others will seek a broader societal platform. Never mind that we might, at first, be taken for curiosities. People will begin to take notice. Over time, we will be seen as inspirations and heroes, as Anna Jen the banker and mother of three, Lauren the businesswoman/mother, Julia the cook, Ella the stay-at-home mom, Cokie the mother and journalist, Dorianne the mother-poet, Ruth the singer, and others are. There is room for us all to educate and seed our homes and communities with alternative responses to overfunctioning. We can create lives that will set a different example for our children.

Living an aware, free life can be daunting, but it is also rich with possibility. It puts into practice sound psychological principles and enduring values that get you beyond the TT, nurture the heart, kindle the hearth and build a true foundation for whatever you define as "Success."

Think about this: FREEDOM AND INDEPENDENCE. You're on track now, awake and free. How does it feel? Who would you like to be?

Last Turn! USING ANXIETY WELL—ADVANCED TECHNIQUES

Topic: Anxiety is a key change-agent

Purpose: Using anxiety to achieve a flexible range of responses for increasing satisfaction and staying free

A) Try to actually create anxiety—discomfort, tension, stress, fear, worry, upset, even panic. Typically, this can be done just by reviewing your day past or day future. Or conjure up some repetitive notion that haunts you: "I will end up as a bag lady." "My children will abandon me as soon as they can." "I make a fool of myself at work." "I got too angry at William." Stay with this discomfort for exactly two minutes. Notice once more that you do not die. Try this several times over a week or two. When the clock runs out, stop yourself. See if you have developed strong enough self-control to really stop obsessing.

B) If you have previously identified yourself as a person who tends to experience too little anxiety, go back, once or twice a week, to the *Minutes Game* from the exercise in Chapter 6. Keep increasing your time of creating anxiety and staying with it by one minute until you've gotten up to fifteen or twenty minutes. Stick with that. You can learn to consistently see and admit what really makes you anxious—you know, those things that you have previously insisted on sidestepping. Staying unaware of what is disturbing you is what the overused phrase "in denial" really means. Pause frequently to proclaim victory for yourself. Catching and holding anxiety when you've made a habit of avoiding it in the past is an extraordinary step forward and will open up a world of positive opportunity.

C) Think if there is anyone who can *help* you bring your anxiety down constructively or who can *help* you bring it up constructively. This should be a person who relates to you with kindness and understanding and yet is capable of confrontation from the heart.

My Life Catches Hold

I, with monotonous tread, plodded through
until my life seized the reigns.
Then, of its own accord,
A mysterious force began to move me.
Quietly, at first, my life took furtive tones
to warn or advise.
But, I, so distracted, could not deduce meaning
or decipher clues.
Then in reply, the fires within
flared up to cleanse the field of
Mind and Soul,
preparing for a future season.
No hindrances nor obstructions
did those happy flames encounter.
Pacing, pacing to their goal,
the fires eventually subsided.
Seedlings of Hope grew,
Yielding an exceptional harvest
of Joy.

~ **Sofia Haas**

AFTERWORD
Going Down The Right Road Well

You already know too well the operating instructions for the Over-functioning Woman. Here is a summary of the operating instructions for the woman of uncommon sense.

1) Just because something feels natural doesn't mean it is good. It may be **bad intuition** and mean only that one has been induced into that particular trance for a long time.

2) Change is frightening and always involves dealing with internal **anxiety** and those external forces that press to keep the status quo going. Anxiety, in the correct dosage, is the spur to change. It delivers one to the edge of one's learning curve. That's what happened to Sir Gawain in *The Tale of Dame Ragnell.*

3) **Anger** is a by-product arising from getting disappointed with others and from maintaining individuality. It should be accepted as normal and inevitable. Its healthy expression can contribute to resolutions, growth, and a reduction of frustration. Anger helps to protect sovereignty.

4) One must **unchoose** many things/people in the course of a life because this is the only way to really have and sustain what one chooses and to experience it fully. The pain involved in the process cannot be avoided.

5) One must **be selective among paths and people**. The emperor's designer clothes may seem to glitter, but he is naked. Pass on by.

6) One has to **mourn** what one gives up. There is no escape or shortcut available.

7) One must take courage to **pace** life slowly enough to **find time**.

Within this time found, people, imagination, and creativity can be nourished and savored. Only through these means can beauty, one's inner voice and spirit, peace of mind, and meaning emerge and endure.

8) Material things are only material things. They may provide convenience and temporary pleasure, but they do not, in themselves, provide **sustenance**.

9) **Sovereignty and freedom** are daunting states because they spotlight that one is alone. Yet, because sovereignty offers the richest and most enduring rewards, it is worth getting there and holding on. No other options produce anything but fleeting satisfaction.

10) **Wisdom in decision-making** is possible. Perfection in decision-making, like in everything else, is impossible.

11) The success of any outer journeys—jobs, marriage, climbing mountains—depends on the success of the **inner journey**.

12) The art of taking time to **consider things** promotes good decision-making. It helps one to take action suitable with one's goals. It is always useful to consider the worst case scenario. If it's not tragic, one is certain to be able to handle any consequences that do occur.

13) **Ascertaining reality** unflinchingly and blending it with **one's uniqueness** produces personal vision. This often generates spontaneity, happiness, productivity, and hope. It also builds capacity to solve problems creatively. This is the source of real-life magic. It also ensures that one won't be thrown when, inevitably, a difficulty arises, be it a disappointment, bad luck, or even a tragedy.

14) We all deserve the opportunity to rule ourselves and the right to have our individual sensibilities. From this base, we can write our own life stories. We are capable of mastering skills that guarantee a **personal bill of rights** and a new perspective for ourselves and others.

15) We are all **entitled equally**.

Each one of us will share what she knows and partake of what our heroes know, handing down wisdom through the generations and to the world at large. The Overfunctioning Woman is not the best we can do. What follows her? What shall she be called?

"The way will open." ~ Quaker saying

AUTHOR BIOGRAPHIES

ROSALYN RIVKIN, MSW

Rosalyn earned a BA in Literature and History from Swarthmore College and her Master's Degree in clinical social work from the University of Michigan where she was a National Mental Health Association Fellow.

She has long been a pioneer in presenting key concepts in psychology and family systems theory in a vivid and accessible way to individuals, families, and organizations.

During a forty year career as a psychotherapist, consultant, speaker, and educator, Rosalyn has worked in the private and public sectors: in graduate programs, university teaching and training clinics at the University of Michigan, The California Graduate School for Couple and Family Therapy, and The Sonoma Institute. She's worked at child guidance centers such as The Irving Schwartz Institute at the Philadelphia Psychiatric Center and The Families with Dependent Children Program (a division of the Contra Costa County, California Child Welfare Department), the Michigan Public Education system and the Traveler's Aid Society. She has also maintained her own private practice and consults with various businesses in Northern California and on the East Coast.

She has carried her messages to several continents and onto the high seas as ship's mental health counselor with the University of Virginia/Institute for Shipboard Education's Semester-at-Sea™ program.

Women in the workplace and child-rearing (She prefers to call it "child-raising.") have always been two of Rosalyn's most cherished priorities. She particularly enjoys working with teenagers, young adults, and their parents. Over the years, Rosalyn has seen firsthand the increasing unhappiness caused by being caught in overfunctioning and the Treacherous Triangle. In a world ever more complex, she has encouraged and helped women of all ages (18 to 80s) to gain uncommon sense. She has been inspired by the remarkable resilience and courage they show as they move forward.

Married and the mother of two daughters now off on their own,

Rosalyn is a walker and stargazer, amateur stage manager, lover of stories, ships, and porches, watercolors, and weavings. She is a passionate world traveler.

SALLY PARK RUBIN

Sally trained as a fine artist at Boston University's School of Fine Arts and San Jose State University, where she graduated with a BA in sculpture. She also studied linguistics and cognitive biology with Logonet, Inc., an educational corporation; she worked under the tutelage of Dr. Fernando Flores and the staff of the *Ontological Design Course*. Sally has worked as a writer and an artist in various mediums. In the past twenty-five years, she has been a sculptor, monoprint artist, art teacher, animator, and art director and producer of animation in her own boutique 3D animation company. Sally has written screenplays, ghost-wrote *Living Aikido* (North Atlantic Books), and has polished dialogue for novels, documentaries (*Tibet's Stolen Child*—a Garthwait & Griffin film), and an upcoming major motion picture, *Ollie the Otter* (Critterpix, Inc.). She is currently producing an independent feature film. She is a passionate activist for children's health issues and is an essay contributor to KQED's *Forum* and *The Autism Perspective*, a quarterly magazine. Sally has taught Aikido at the Aikido Institute, Pacific Boychoir Academy, and to private clients. She holds a second degree black belt and has practiced yoga/meditation for over 35 years. She lives in Oakland, California with her husband and son.

ACKNOWLEDGMENTS

ROSALYN'S ACKNOWLEDGMENTS

I admit, "I did not do it myself." Many people have lent their hands and voices of encouragement over the long and varied history of putting together this book.

Without my clients, students, mentors (from World Literature, Art History, and Psychology), and their stories of struggle and triumph, I wouldn't have had rich material to develop, nor much insight to share. Thank you all.

My women soulmates have always given me a sense of emotional safety and joy. They provide me ballast (Wallace's wonderful word) every day. I cannot imagine life without them: Barbi, Susan, Wallace, Myumi, Kaethe, Barb, Elizabeth, Jane, Naomi, Toya, Sharon, Sabriga, Robin, Miriam, Esther, Linda, Archer, Kathy, Laura, Ronda, Sandy, and Jill.

I am grateful to my good friends who are men—for being facts of life, not just fantasies: David, Tony, Bob (1 and 2), Bernie, Sandy, Steve (1 and 2), Andrew (1 and 2), Al, James, Jon, Len, Peter (1 and 2), Walter, and Michael M.

My mother and father, Zelda and Ellis Rivkin, helped make me brave and resourceful, and they still inspire. My father-in-law, Chuck Haas, has been adding to my garden of poetry and prose for many years now, an enchanting experience.

My mother-in-law Emilie Haas, no longer here in person, I carry in my heart always. Alongside is Uncle Ned who, I feel, is still singing to me. I remember my special Uncle Z.C. Every time I hold a book in my hands. I think of my remarkable friend, Peter Dorman, who treated me to many a lovely turn of phrase and a peony on a postage stamp.

Many thanks to Sally's husband Ed, in whom artistic and techincal gifts morph, in a special way, with a kind heart. His resourcefulness and patience have been invaluable. My deepest gratitude to Sally, rarest of rare birds, forever steadfast and funny.

My husband, Michael, is unique. He teaches me a lot about uncommon sense and how to pace my days, shares the weaving of a colorful parenting tapestry, and paves the way with warmth and laughter.

I dedicate this book to my dear daughters, Elana and Sofia, who have made the magic possible. Finally, I acknowledge the Little Red Hen, my constant reminder of imperfect beauty and heroism.

Rosalyn Rivkin

SALLY'S ACKNOWLEDGMENTS

I would like to particularly thank the following people from the bottom of my heart:

Gurumayi Chidvilasananda and Siddha Foundation for the innumerable and rich experiences of the heart and for instilling in me what it takes to steer a steady, joyous course even when fire is burning down the house.

My husband, Ed *Murari* Rubin, for his constant love and consistent belief in me and this project. My son, Sam Rubin, for his quirky humor, his clarity, and for being exactly who he is.

My father, the late Dr. Colin Park, for the many patient hours he spent teaching me how to write. My mother, the late Mildred Anne Fraser Park, for her Scottish sense of humor, without which I never would have made it through this project or, for that matter, life.

My mother-in-law, Phyllis Kanter Rubin, for her friendship and for offering useful suggestions along the way, both for the book and for my life. Uncle Herschel and Aunt Ruth for being the great, wonderful people that you are and for your generous support towards the completion of this project.

Nancy Kicherer...for all the help, moral support. You rock, Nance!

Uncle Ridley Enslow, Cousins Ridley and Brian, and my father-in-law, Manning Rubin...thank you one and all for taking an interest and offering advice; Aunt Flossie for always being there to talk to; Linda Enslow and my brother-in-law, Jim Rubin, for keeping me sane with many good-humored discussions.

My brilliant teacher of *Ontological Design*, Dr. Fernando Flores, for teaching me how to, as he would say, "navigate in language."

Jane Copass for setting me on a healthy path of self-inquiry so many decades ago.

Kirsten Vaughan and Kitty Ross for their expert editorial direction.

Dorianne Laux and Robin Chapman for their amazing and inspiring poetry. THX&HUGS2 Bruce King. Sofia Haas for sharing her soul.

Lisa Kindblad for her friendship and moral support and for Hannah. And Joan Diamond—educator extrodinaire—for making my life infinitely easier.

Thank you and bless you...Marge, Carol Z., Jocelyne, Elaine, Osnat, Rita, Catherin, Alex, Mindy, Heidi, Renee, Shelley, Marnie, Liz F., Kathleen Caldwell, Marcy, Cathy Sultan, Naim, Shakti Butler, Monnie, Dania, Lisa's C & E., Maurean, Maria A. Julie R., Angelique, —Andy Park and Debbie Eichlen no longer with us—and Sister Elizabeth Hague.... Rhamba, Gay Ducey, Joe, Chris, and Alexander.

Thank you to Sandy Boucher and to Tory Pryor and Barbara Neighbors Deal for shepherding the project at various points.

Fred Hertz and Brad Bunnin for gentle counsel.

Elana and Sofia Haas for their good humor and patience while their mom and I wrote this book. Michael Haas for his intellect, for reading many versions, and for his expert commentary along the way.

And, of course, to Rosalyn Rivkin for her partnership and offbeat humor while we persisted through many changes, challenges, and life events in the writing of this book. You showed me how to be crystal clear. I dedicate this book to you...

...and to the many wonderful women I have met along the path and those I have yet to meet.

And to The Hen...*Keep on Cluckin'!*
Sally Park Rubin

REFERENCES

Ch. 1: Overfunctioning
1. Thanks to J. Meinert for sharing her baby's schedule.

Ch. 2: The Self-Esteem Factor
2. http://www.menshealth.co.uk/index.php/v2/anorexia_in_men; except from Gary A. Grahl's Skinny Boy: A Young Man's Battle and Triumph Over Anorexia (American Regency Media)
3. Matteucci, Jeannie, "Santa's Helpers / No time for Christmas chores? Hire someone to decorate, wrap gifts or plan a holiday party," *San Francisco Chronicle*, 3 December 1997. HOME p.1/Z1.
4. Fields, Denise and Alan, *Baby Bargains Secrets* (Boulder, CO: Windsor Peak Press, 2003), back matter.

Ch. 4: We Keep Buyin' What They're Sellin'
5. Shellenbarger, Sue, "More Managers Find A Happy Staff Leads To Happy Customers," *The Wall Street Journal*, 23 December 1998: B1(E).
6. Ibid.
7. Healy, Melissa, "Female Candidates Lambasted for Juggling Kids, Career," *San Francisco Chronicle*, 11 July 1998, p. A4
8. Ryan, Joan, "Bosses Not Babies At Issue," *San Francisco Chronicle*, 16 April 2002, A-17.
9. Olson, Elizabeth. "Nursing Mother Goes to Court for Exam Time," *New York Times*, Monday, September 10, 2007. VOL. CLVI....No. 54, 063, p. A18.
10. FreshPatents.com, http://www.freshpatents.com/Electric-breast-pump-dt20060921ptan20060211335.php

Ch. 5: The Invisible Driver
11. Carroll, Lewis, *Living in Wonderland*, New American Library, Inc., 1960, 114.

Ch. 6: Taking the Wheel
12. Pipher, Mary, *Reviving Ophelia* (New York: Penguin Group, 1994), 22.
13. Ibid., 25.

Ch. 7: Welcoming Anxiety
14. "The Sleepy Family" is from a story told on a children's record (early 1950's). Origin unknown.
15. Merriam-Webster, *New Collegiate Dictionary,* 7th ed. (Springfield, MA: G.&C. Merriam Company, 1967), 40.

Ch. 9: Drawing Your Own Lines
16. Charming Hostess, *Eat*, Vaccination Records, 1999. Compact disc.

Ch. 10: Demystifying Anger
17. Flexner, Stuart B. and Leonore C. Hauck, eds., *Random House Dictionary of the English Language, Unabridged*, 2nd ed. (New York: Random House, 1987), 79.
18. Ibid., 1594-1595.
19. Lerner, Harriet Goldhor, *The Dance of Anger* (New York: Harper & Row, 1985).
20. Ibid.
21. Forster, E.M., *Howard's End* (London: Edward Arnold, 1910).

Ch. 11: Operating the Rules for Anger
22. Chapman, Robin, *The Way In* (Huntington Beach, CA: Tebot Bach, 1999), 7.* Ms. Chapman is a Posner Poetry Award winner. Visit Robin's illuminating blog: http://robinchapmanspoemaday.blogspot.com

Ch. 13: Mapping a Counterpath
23. The Fire Story: recounted from a friend; source unknown.
24. Flexner, Stuart B. and Leonore C. Hauck, eds., *Random House Dictionary of the English Language, Unabridged*, 2nd ed. (New York: Random House, 1987).
25. Flexner, Stuart B. and Leonore C. Hauck, eds., *Random House Dictionary of the English Language, Unabridged*, 2nd ed. (New York: Random House, 1987).

26. Goodman, Ellen. "The Morphing of Radcliffe," *San Francisco Chronicle*, 27 April 1999.
27. Ibid.
28. Breashears, David F., "The Siren Sounds of Everest" *National Geographic*, September 1997, 133–135.
29. Ibid.
30. Eliot, Thomas Stearns, "The Love Song of J. Alfred Prufrock," *Prufrock and Other Observations*. London: The Egoist, Ltd., 1917.
31. Chapman, Robin, *The Way In* (Huntington Beach, CA: Tebot Bach, 1999), 76.

Ch. 14: Choosing Good People and Good Jobs
32. Cokie Roberts, interview by Michael Krasny, KQED, Public Broadcasting for Northern California, 1998.

Ch. 15: Making Cherished Choices
33. Rubin, Sally Park, Diary Entry: Late Autumn, 1994, Mohonk, N.Y.
34. Holly's letter: Thank you, Holly, for sharing this with us.
35. Rubin, Sally Park, *A Day at the Game*; unpublished poem.

Ch. 16: Becoming Your Own Hero
36. Laux, Dorianne, *What We Carry* (Rochester, NY: Boa Editions, Ltd, 1994), 35. Ms. Laux has been awarded with a Pushcart Prize, two fellowships from the National Endowment for the Arts and a Guggenheim Fellowship. She is a professor in the University of Oregon's creative writing program and the MFA in Writing Program at Pacific University.
37. King, Bruce, "A Christmas Gift." Our thanks to Bruce for sharing his beautiful short story with us. You can find Bruce saving the environment, one building project at a time. Visit the Ecological Building Network website at www.ecobuildnetwork.org.
    The current (and primary) project of EBNet is the development of modernized earthen building standards to promote and develop the most environmentally and culturally friendly building system of all. Bruce is the author of "Design of Straw Bale Buildings," "Making Better Concrete," and "Buildings of Earth and Straw"

(Bruce King cont.) (Green Building Press, www.greenbuildingpress.com).

38. Stevens, Wallace, "The Snowman," *The Collected Poems*, New York: Vintage Books, 1959, 9.

Ch. 17: Freedom

39. Carlson, Margaret, "Mom's Way and My Way," *Time*, 20 October 1997, 42.

INDEX